I Danced on Broadway

I Danced on Broadway

Memoir of a Career on Stage

LEE WILSON

McFarland & Company, Inc., Publishers
Jefferson, North Carolina

Unless otherwise noted, all illustrations are from the author's collection.

Library of Congress Cataloging-in-Publication Data

Names: Wilson, Lee, 1946– author.
Title: I danced on Broadway : memoir of a career on stage / Lee Wilson.
Description: Jefferson, North Carolina : McFarland & Company, Inc, Publishers, 2024. | Includes bibliographical references and index.
Identifiers: LCCN 2024028551 | ISBN 9781476696362 (paperback : acid free paper) ♾
ISBN 9781476654232 (ebook)
Subjects: LCSH: Wilson, Lee, 1946– | Musical theater—United States—History—20th century. | Ballerinas—United States—Biography. | Women dancers—United States—Biography.
Classification: LCC GV1785.W55 A3 2024 | DDC 792.802/092 [B]—dc23/eng/20240729
LC record available at https://lccn.loc.gov/2024028551

British Library cataloguing data are available

ISBN (print) 978-1-4766-9636-2
ISBN (ebook) 978-1-4766-5423-2

Front cover image: I'm well into my 70s, but I'm still kicking!
Photograph by Lesley Bohm.

Printed in the United States of America

McFarland & Company, Inc., Publishers
Box 611, Jefferson, North Carolina 28640
www.mcfarlandpub.com

This book is dedicated to the many people who contribute
to the magic of musical theater, including, but not limited to:
dancers, singers, actors, producers, directors, choreographers,
writers, composers, lyricists, production designers,
set designers, lighting designers, costume designers,
hair and wig designers,
casting directors, musical directors,
orchestrators, conductors, musicians, stagehands,
wardrobe supervisors, dressers, company managers,
house managers, box office personnel, reviewers, publicists,
ushers, angels, and audiences.
You make the world a better place.

Acknowledgments

I would like to thank
the New York Public Library,
Cindy Lubke Romero/San Diego Union Tribune/Zuma Press Wire,
Suzanne Regan at Camera 5,
and
the entire team at McFarland & Company.

I would also like to thank
Meredith Babb,
Lesley Bohm,
Claudia Cagan,
Kevin Lane Dearinger,
Sheldon Epps,
Dick Hamilton,
Owen Imholte,
Baayork Lee,
Melissa Manchester,
David Newey,
Barry Pearl,
David Henry Sterry,
and
Robert Woods.

Table of Contents

Prologue

I still remember the first time I heard these lyrics from *South Pacific*—and they hit me like thunderbolts: "You've got to be taught to be afraid / Of people whose eyes are oddly made, / And people whose skin is a different shade—" *Taught*?! It had never occurred to me that prejudice was taught, and as I listened to the lyrics that followed, I realized that indoctrination began at birth. No lecture or book could have hit me with the power of that song. Never again could I hear a generalization about race or gender without questioning its purpose and its accuracy.

At its best, musical theater is dazzling entertainment that gives insight into the human condition and creates empathy. Musicals introduce audiences to new worlds and give them new perspectives on the ones they know. I had the good fortune to spend most of my working life in musical theater and to work with some of the great performers and choreographers of the late 20th century, including Agnes de Mille, Alvin Ailey, Michael Bennett, Bernadette Peters, and Donna McKechnie. I participated in the legendary rehearsals of *A Chorus Line* at City Center in 1976, the triumphant opening on the West Coast later that year, and the brilliant performance that made *A Chorus Line* the longest running show in Broadway history in 1983. I performed in hits like *Hello, Dolly!* and flops that closed out of town—like Alan Jay Lerner's *Lolita, My Love*. I danced in shows that opened and closed on the same night, and I danced on Broadway in four successive decades.

The story of Broadway is a story told by men. The creators of the shows and the critics who write about them were and are predominantly male, but when I read their points of view, I sometimes wonder: *Did we see the same show? How can you state that a plot is trivial when a young woman's life is at stake? Don't you hear the women's voices?*

I listen to the women, and I hope to amplify some of the voices that have touched my heart—and to sing out with my own.

1

Hello, Dolly! (1967)

I fell in love with Broadway musicals before I ever saw a musical on stage. When I was a little girl, my father sang show tunes while he worked in his garden and pulled bright yellow dandelions out of the lawn. On warm Saturday mornings, as the blades of his lawnmower cut through the sweet-smelling grass, Dad sang loud and clear: "Oh, What a Beautiful Mornin'"—a song filled with images of nature and the joy of seeing them. I understood even then that a song could make a chore become play. A song could change my perspective.

"Oh, What a Beautiful Mornin'" is the opening song from Rodgers and Hammerstein's hit musical *Oklahoma!*, and the premiere of that show in 1943 marked the beginning of the Golden Age of Broadway. During the late 1940s and 1950s, while my three younger brothers and I were growing up in the suburbs of Wilmington, Delaware, Rodgers and Hammerstein wrote one hit show after another: *Oklahoma!, Carousel, South Pacific, The King and I,* and *The Sound of Music.* Lerner and Loewe wrote *Brigadoon, Paint Your Wagon, My Fair Lady,* and *Camelot.* Golden Age musicals included *Kiss Me, Kate, Guys and Dolls, Annie Get Your Gun, Gypsy, West Side Story,* and *The Music Man.* Throughout the 1950s, songs from Broadway musicals topped the charts, and every Christmas, when my parents gave me new cast albums, I memorized every song.

Just after my 15th birthday, my ballet teacher, James Jamieson, gave me a dance solo in an amateur production of *Annie Get Your Gun*, a musical about Annie Oakley that he was directing and choreographing. This was the most exciting experience of my life to date. I loved the fact that Annie—the woman—could out shoot and out sing the male sharpshooter Frank Butler, and I loved singing the Irving Berlin music that included "There's No Business Like Show Business." However, at the age of 15, I was already committed to a career in classical ballet. A year earlier Mr. Jamieson had taken me to company class with Ballet Russe, and the ballet mistress had told him that if I had been 16, she would have taken me into the company on the spot. This confirmed what my mother had told me—that my future was in classical ballet. A few months after my performances in *Annie Get Your Gun*, I moved to New York to study at the Ballet Theatre School and finish my senior year of high school at the Professional Children's School.

My move to New York gave me the opportunity to see my first musical on Broadway: *Bye Bye Birdie*. Sharon Lerit, one of the girls in my classes at the Ballet Theatre School, was playing a small role in this Tony Award–winning musical about an average teenage girl from Sweet Apple, Ohio, who is chosen to receive—on TV—the last kiss of rock star Conrad Birdie before he joins the U.S. Army. Sharon, with her dark hair and knitted brow, was perfectly cast as the Sad Girl to whom Dick Van Dyke sang "Put on a Happy Face" (a number the company performed on an episode of *The Ed Sullivan Show* that has been posted on YouTube).

As I watched the show, I could see myself performing Gower Champion's breezy choreography, and I knew I would love dancing in the show—but the dancers also sang—and even though I had sung with the junior choir at church, I didn't know if I could sing well enough for Broadway. Besides, I was a serious ballet dancer, an elite dancer, not a fun-loving Broadway gypsy. My mother had taught me to aim for the top, and the most respected dancers were classical ballet dancers. Nevertheless, later that year, when I went to see *The Sound of Music*, I found myself hoping that someday I might play 16-year-old Liesl. I couldn't imagine a role that suited me better—except maybe the role of Clara in *The Nutcracker*. I hoped that between tours with a ballet company I might be able to perform in Broadway shows.

Shortly before I graduated from high school, my dad was transferred to Geneva, Switzerland, where he became Product Supervisor for DuPont International. Mom gave me a choice: stay in New York and join a ballet company there, or sail to Europe first class on the S.S. *United States* and find a company there. I chose the free trip to Europe. I love to travel. I love adventure, and I figured that ballet is not dependent on language, so I could work anywhere in the world.

That fall, 1962, at the age of 16, I made my professional debut as a classical ballet dancer in a command performance for Prince Rainier and Princess Grace in Monte Carlo. I danced in Paris and Bordeaux and Vichy and Naples. I performed for gun-toting revolutionaries in Algeria, and worked with some of the great dancers of the late 20th century, including Rudolf Nureyev, Erik Bruhn, and Rosella Hightower. At 17, I became première danseuse of the Bordeaux Opera Ballet, the second largest ballet company in France, but as much as I enjoyed dancing roles like Clara in *The Nutcracker*, I disliked dancing on a raked stage and decided not to renew my contract. At 18, I returned to the U.S. and joined the Metropolitan Opera Ballet under the direction of Dame Alicia Markova. However, the more time I spent in New York, the more I wanted to perform on Broadway.

The musicals I saw during the mid–1960s were superb: *Hello, Dolly!*, *Fiddler on the Roof*, *Sweet Charity*, and *Mame*. These musicals made my heart sing, and they gave me new insights into the world around me. I was also attracted to musicals because dancers on Broadway perform eight shows a week—more than I was performing as a classical ballet dancer—and I loved everything about performing: the costumes, the makeup, the music, the camaraderie, and the opportunity to be someone other than me.

Moving from ballet to Broadway was a risk. I had a track record in ballet—and a mentor—Rosella Hightower, a star dancer who later became the first woman and the first American to direct the Paris Opera Ballet. Madame Rosella wrote to me periodically from Cannes and reminded me that she could always find me a job in Europe if I chose to come back. I also had friends at the Metropolitan Opera Ballet where John Gutman, an assistant general manager, told me that Dame Alicia wanted me to dance the role of the dead Juliet in next season's opera *Romeo and Juliet*—a plum role, but not to be confused with the role of Juliet in the full-length ballet. At the Met, I had paychecks and health insurance 52 weeks a year.

On Broadway, I had no track record and no mentor. I would probably have gaps in employment between shows and gaps in health coverage, but I decided to follow my heart.

I called my mother and told her that I was leaving the Metropolitan Opera Ballet at the end of the season. Mom didn't understand why I was leaving the security of the highest-paid ballet company in America for the uncertain, less prestigious, world of Broadway, but I was 21, and I knew what I wanted to do. The question was: Could I?

In the spring of 1967, Jack Gilford was starring as Herr Schultz in *Cabaret* on Broadway and was also playing Frosch (the jailer) in *Die Fledermaus* with the Metropolitan Opera. At a post-performance reception at the Met, I introduced myself to Mr. Gilford and asked him, "How do you get jobs on Broadway?" He told me that *he* got jobs through his agent—but he didn't think that most *dancers* had agents. (They didn't.) Mr. Gilford said I was probably too young and too small for *Cabaret*, but he had a little arrangement with the box office and could get me a complimentary ticket to see the show. After the performance, he would introduce me to the dance captain, Bruce Becker, who could tell me everything I needed to know.

On the appointed evening, I dressed in my most sophisticated dress and walked from my room in the Washington Jefferson Hotel on West 51st Street to the Imperial Theatre on West 45th Street. Mr. Gilford introduced me to the house manager, who escorted me down the aisle to a seat in the front center section of the orchestra. I was in a premium seat for one the hottest shows on Broadway.

Cabaret is dazzling entertainment and an indictment of complacency. In the opening number, "Willkommen," the Emcee welcomes us to the cabaret and tells us to forget our troubles, forget the outside world, because inside the cabaret, everything is beautiful. It is 1929, and we are in Berlin, where the Nazis are gaining power. Sally Bowles, the singer in the cabaret, can't be bothered with politics. She is trying to convince herself that she is leading a unique and glamorous life by painting her fingernails green and jumping from one man's bed to the next. Fräulein Schneider, Sally's landlady, recognizes the threat of the Nazis, but the Nazis are her friends and neighbors, and she needs a license to run her boarding house, so she breaks her engagement to a Jewish man and hopes that if she keeps a low profile, she will survive. Herr Schultz, the Jewish fruit shop owner who loves Fräulein Schneider, can't believe the Nazis would do anything to *him*—after all, he's *German*. Soon, the Emcee is marching in a goose-stepping chorus line with swastika armbands, and anti–Semitic jokes are part of the show. While we watch the entertainment and laugh at the jokes, the Nazis take over the country.

Joel Grey was superb in his Tony Award–winning performance as the sexually ambiguous Emcee, and Jack Gilford was unforgettable in his Tony-nominated performance as Herr Schultz.

Cabaret is set in a specific time and place, but the theme is timeless and universal: When the majority remains silent—whether out of ignorance, laziness, self-interest, or fear—a militant minority can seize power with disastrous results. This has happened before; it will happen again. Fräulein Schneider sings "What Would You Do?," and that is a question each of us must answer: What would *I* do? Would I have the vision and the guts to oppose the threat—or would I make excuses and bury my head in the sand?

After the show, Mr. Gilford introduced me to the dance captain, Bruce Becker, who confirmed that I was too young and too short for *Cabaret*—something I had known by the end of the opening number. However, he told me to read *Backstage* and *Show Business*, two trade papers that were published every Thursday and contained information about upcoming shows and auditions. I wasn't a member of Actors' Equity, the union that covers Broadway performers, so Bruce told me to look for the open auditions—open to everyone—union and non-union. (Ballet companies and opera companies are covered by the American Guild of Musical Artists.) Bruce also advised me to audition for *everything* until people got to know me.

Backstage had an audition notice for the Vietnam tour of *Hello, Dolly!* starring Martha Raye. As much as I love to travel, I wasn't eager to fly into a war zone, and I doubted that entertaining troops in the jungle was the ideal way to begin a Broadway career, but Bruce had told me to audition for *everything*, so I went to the audition.

The open call was scheduled immediately after the Equity call, and Joe Helms, the dance captain of the Broadway Company, appeared to be the sole decision-maker. The choreography was right up my alley, but at the end of the audition, Joe simply thanked us all for coming. I was disappointed and relieved at the same time.

As I picked up my dance bag, Joe asked me, "Why don't I know you?" I told him I had been dancing in ballet companies. "I really like the way you dance," he said. "I'll tell you the situation. For the Vietnam tour, we gave priority to girls who had already done the show on Broadway. I only needed a couple more girls, and I found them this morning at the Equity call. Would you be at all interested in the Broadway Company?"

Broadway?! You bet I was.

"One of the twins is leaving for another show, and we need to replace her. Are you willing to dye your hair blond?"

"Absolutely."

In quick succession, I joined Actors' Equity, signed my contract for the union minimum of $130 dollars a week ($20 a week more than the starting salary at the Met), and had my hair dyed golden blond at the expense of producer David Merrick. In the afternoons, I rehearsed with Joe Helms in a studio, and in the evenings, I watched performances of *Hello, Dolly!* at the St. James Theatre.

What a wonderful show it was! The book, suggested by Thornton Wilder's play *The Matchmaker*, is by Michael Stewart (*Bye Bye Birdie*; *Carnival!*); the music and lyrics are by Jerry Herman (*Milk and Honey*, *Mame*, and *La Cage aux Folles*), and the original direction and choreography were by Gower Champion, the man who had directed and choreographed *Carnival!* and *Bye Bye Birdie*.

Hello, Dolly! is jam-packed with song and dance; the costumes are beautiful, and the story celebrates the value of community and the fulfillment that comes from sharing one's talent and wealth. Dolly states at the beginning of the show that she is going to marry the curmudgeonly miser Horace Vandergelder to spread his money around because, "money ... pardon the expression ... is like manure. It's not worth a thing unless it's spread around encouraging young things to grow!" By the end of the show, Dolly is engaged to Horace

Vandergelder, and his money is not only encouraging the *young* people to grow, but also the middle-aged miser himself.

In Craig Zadan's book *Sondheim & Co.*, Stephen Sondheim is quoted as saying that *Hello, Dolly!* is a hit because audiences like the "fairy story" that "says that a loud, middle-aged lady can get the man she wants," but that is not my take-away from *Hello, Dolly!*. Dolly may be loud (although Betty Grable wasn't) and middle-aged (*horror of horrors*!), but she is a smart, hard-working jack-of-all-trades who is very popular in the community, and Horace is a selfish man who wants a wife who can perform a laundry list of chores, including "washing and blueing and shoeing the mare"—all things that Dolly, the jack-of-all-trades, presumably knows how to do—or can learn how to do. Dolly is not marrying a prince who will give her an easy life—and she knows it—but Dolly also knows that marriage to Horace will give her purpose in life, humanize Horace, and benefit the community. I think *Hello, Dolly!* is an uplifting show because it celebrates the value of community and the benefits that come from sharing talent and wealth—not because the show implies that a loud, middle-aged woman can get the man she wants.

In my experience, smart, popular, hard-working women have no trouble attracting men, but as the 21st century moves into its third decade, a growing number of single women are side-stepping marriage because, as several studies have shown—and as Bella DePaulo states in "The Social Lives of Single People," marriage weakens other social ties. Single women have more friends, closer ties to family, more interaction with neighbors, and are more likely to be politically active than married women. Many women today don't want to give up those social benefits for marriage.

In June 1964, the summer after *Hello, Dolly!* opened, the original cast album knocked the Beatles out of the number one position on the charts, and later, the original cast album of *Hello, Dolly!* was replaced by Louis Armstrong's new album, also titled *Hello, Dolly!*. By the time I joined the show in the summer of 1967, *Hello, Dolly!* was a smash hit destined for future productions in dinner theaters and summer stock. I couldn't have asked for a better show for my Broadway debut.

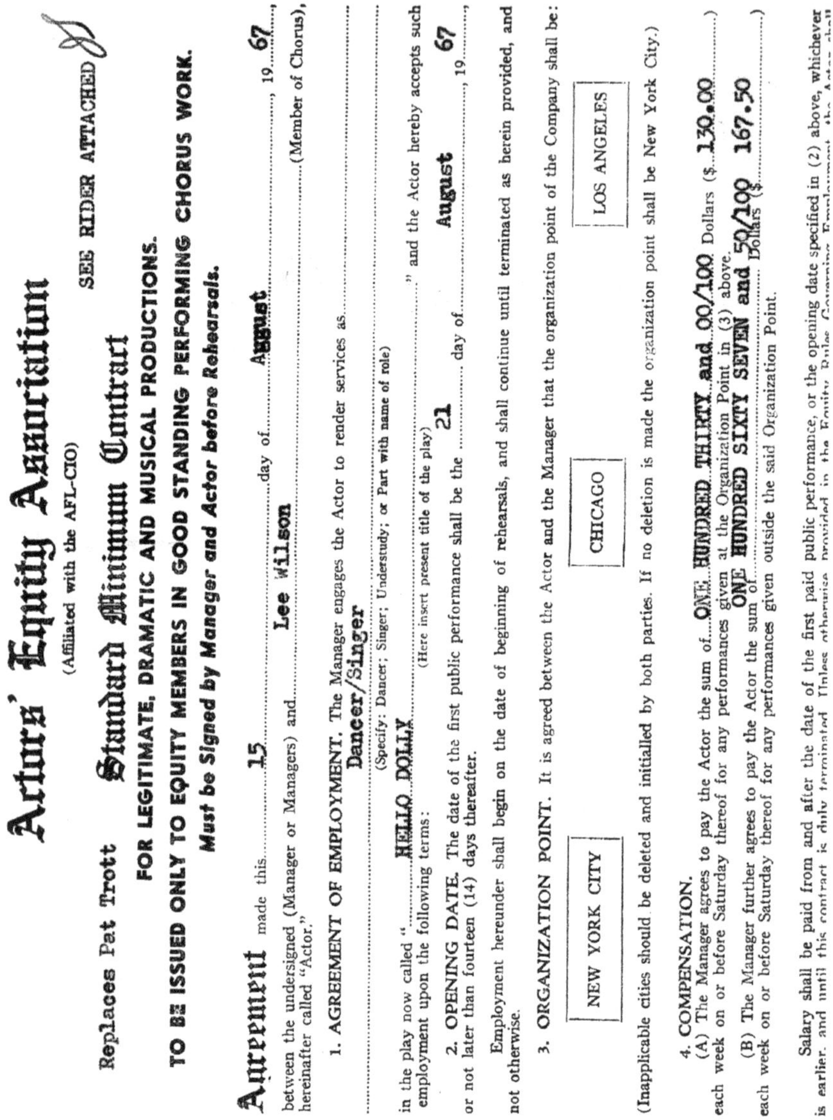

Actors' Equity Association

(Affiliated with the AFL-CIO)

SEE RIDER ATTACHED

Replaces Pat Trott

Standard Minimum Contract

FOR LEGITIMATE, DRAMATIC AND MUSICAL PRODUCTIONS.

TO BE ISSUED ONLY TO EQUITY MEMBERS IN GOOD STANDING PERFORMING CHORUS WORK.

Must be Signed by Manager and Actor before Rehearsals.

Agreement made this 15 day of August, 19 67, between the undersigned (Manager or Managers) and Lee Wilson (Member of Chorus), hereinafter called "Actor."

1. AGREEMENT OF EMPLOYMENT. The Manager engages the Actor to render services as Dancer/Singer

(Specify: Dancer; Singer; Understudy; or Part with name of role)

in the play now called "HELLO DOLLY" and the Actor hereby accepts such employment upon the following terms:

(Here insert present title of the play)

2. OPENING DATE. The date of the first public performance shall be the 21 day of August, 19 67, or not later than fourteen (14) days thereafter.

Employment hereunder shall begin on the date of beginning of rehearsals, and shall continue until terminated as herein provided, and not otherwise.

3. ORGANIZATION POINT. It is agreed between the Actor and the Manager that the organization point of the Company shall be:

NEW YORK CITY | CHICAGO | LOS ANGELES

(Inapplicable cities should be deleted and initialled by both parties. If no deletion is made the organization point shall be New York City.)

4. COMPENSATION.

(A) The Manager agrees to pay the Actor the sum of ONE HUNDRED THIRTY and 00/100 Dollars ($ 130.00) each week on or before Saturday thereof for any performances given at the Organization Point in (3) above.

(B) The Manager further agrees to pay the Actor the sum of ONE HUNDRED SIXTY SEVEN and 50/100 Dollars ($ 167.50) each week on or before Saturday thereof for any performances given outside the said Organization Point.

Salary shall be paid from and after the date of the first paid public performance, or the opening date specified in (2) above, whichever is earlier, and until this contract is duly terminated. Unless otherwise provided in the Equity Rules Governing Employment, the Actor shall

***Hello, Dolly!* gave me my first Equity contract. The rider referenced at the top right corner provided that producer David Merrick would cover the expense of transforming me into a blonde and maintaining the color throughout the run of the show. The initials are those of Jack Schlissel, the general manager. Since this is a chorus contract, it was printed on pink paper.**

The beautiful, dance-friendly costumes in *Hello, Dolly!* were designed by Freddy Wittop, who had designed the costumes for *Carnival!*. I am back-stage with my newly blonde hair, wearing my costume for the polka dance contest in the Harmonia Gardens Restaurant.

In the summer of 1967, Betty Grable, the 1940s movie star, was playing Dolly. (The original Dolly was Carol Channing, who was succeeded by Ginger Rogers and Martha Raye before Betty Grable took over and Martha Raye went to Vietnam.) Miss Grable was beautiful, charming, and energetic—although one of her choices astonished me the first time I saw it. The show is set in the 1890s, when women's dresses reached to the floor, but during the title song, Miss Grable lifted her skirt *above her knees*! My astonishment turned to understanding as she took the position of her most popular pin-up photo, and the audience roared its approval. Of course! In the late 1940s, 20th Century–Fox had insured Betty Grable's legs for one million dollars, and the audience wanted to see those million-dollar legs.

The entire cast of *Hello, Dolly!* gave me a warm welcome. During the overture for my first performance, I took my position on a cart offstage right. Betty Grable hopped onto the cart beside me and whispered, "What's your name?"

"Lee," I said.

"I'm Betty," she said. "Welcome to the company." Her unassuming manner belied the fact that during the 1940s, she was the number one box office draw in the world, and I later learned that she always considered herself to be—first and foremost—a dancer. Her boyfriend, Bob Remick, was a blond dancer in the ensemble who always had a smile on his face. He was much younger than she, but the couple seemed devoted to each other, and they were still together when Miss Grable died of lung cancer less than six years later.

I had met Linda Bonem, my "twin," in ballet class long before I was cast in *Hello, Dolly!*, and I couldn't have asked for a better, more supportive twin. Fun-loving Harvey Evans, our boyish Barnaby, introduced me to the brilliance of his latest Beatles album, *Sgt. Pepper's Lonely Hearts Club Band*, and two of the other principals—Dan Merriman, a big Texan in his late thirties who played Rudolph, and June Helmers, a pretty blonde in her mid-twenties who played Mrs. Molloy—invited me to join them for dinner between shows at Joe Allen, a show-biz restaurant on 46th Street. Joe Allen had thick, juicy hamburgers, spicy black bean soup, a bustling bar, and Broadway memorabilia on the walls. On matinee days, many of the diners were wearing stage makeup, and Dan and June seemed to know them all. Dan and June were longtime friends, and both were married to singers who were out of town with the new musical *How Now, Dow Jones*. They usually had dinner together on matinee days and traveled together on Sundays to visit their spouses and return with the latest gossip about *How Now, Dow Jones*.

During performances, I stood in the wings and enjoyed the pitch perfect performances of Will Mackenzie as Cornelius and Harvey Evans as Barnaby, but the performance I watched most closely was that of Leland Palmer as Minnie Fay. She was absolutely wonderful in a role I hoped to play in the future. (At the time, I would never have guessed that it would be 16 years before I got the chance.)

One day between shows, as Dan, June, and I entered Joe Allen, Dan pointed to a window card hanging on the wall—a 14" × 22" poster for *Kelly*, which at that time was the most expensive one-night flop in Broadway history. Dan said, "Remember how it feels to be in a hit show. It might not happen again for a long time." I was undaunted by his bleak prognosis because Dan was primarily interested in opera, and his only other Broadway credit was an opera more than ten years earlier. I was confident that I would dance in many Broadway shows and that many would be hits.

I savored every performance of *Hello, Dolly!*, but in the fall of 1967, *Hello, Dolly!* wasn't selling out, and I heard rumors that the show might close after the holidays—but David Merrick, the great showman, had other plans. He gave notice to everyone in the Broadway cast, terminating our contracts on November 9 after the Thursday night performance. He canceled the Friday and Saturday performances, and on Sunday, the all-Black touring company starring Pearl Bailey and Cab Calloway opened on Broadway. All-Black casts and inter-racial casts were not uncommon on Broadway, but no producer had ever opened a musical with an all-white cast, fired the white cast, and replaced it with an all-Black cast. *Hello, Dolly!* was back in the news with a firestorm of publicity, a new set of rave reviews, and new audiences. The following spring, the 1968 Tony Awards gave almost ten minutes to *Hello, Dolly!* (viewable on YouTube), and Pearl Bailey, not eligible for a regular Tony Award because she was a replacement, was given a special Tony Award. David Merrick's stunt gave his fading show three more years of life.

I had little time to mourn the loss of *Hello, Dolly!*. Only days after receiving my two weeks' notice, I landed my next Broadway show, *Here's Where I Belong,* a new musical based on John Steinbeck's *East of Eden.* The novel was a classic; a film based on the novel had made James Dean a star, and the choreographer was the legendary modern dancer and choreographer Hanya Holm. My Broadway career seemed to be humming along. At the time, I didn't know that the Golden Age of Broadway—the only age I had ever known—had come to an end, and within five years, nearly half of the Broadway audience would disappear.

2

Here's Where I Belong (1967–1968)

On December 3, 1967, producer Mitch Miller placed a full-page ad in *The New York Times* announcing the commencement of rehearsals for his new Broadway musical *Here's Where I Belong*. The ad stated that United Artists Records was producing the cast album. *Wow*! I hadn't even thought about the cast album. This would be a fascinating experience—and I knew the album would be in good hands.

Mitch Miller, a bearded man in his mid-fifties, was a classically trained musician who had been head of Artists and Repertoire at Columbia Records. In the early 1960s, his hit television show *Sing Along with Mitch* had made him a household name. On the first day of rehearsals, it was clear that he was in charge as he enthusiastically introduced the creative team:

Choreographer Hanya Holm, age 74, had a German accent, a striking profile, and hair pulled back into a low bun. She was one of the "Big Four" in modern dance. In 1952, her choreography for *Kiss Me, Kate* became the first choreography registered for copyright at the U.S. Copyright Office. (In the U.S., choreography didn't become copyrightable until 1976, so Hayna Holm registered her choreography as a drama—a groundbreaking move.) Hanya Holm's many Broadway credits included *My Fair Lady*—at that time the longest running musical in Broadway history.

The writer, composer, lyricist, and director were all young men around the age of 30. Writer Terrence McNally was a rising star with two Broadway credits in short-lived plays. (He later won Tony Awards for Best Book of a Musical for *Ragtime* and *Kiss of the Spider Woman*, and Best Play for *Love! Valor! Compassion* and *Master Class.*) Robert Waldman and Alfred Uhry, the composer and lyricist, were new to Broadway. (Uhry would later receive a Tony nomination for Best Book of a Musical for *The Robber Bridegroom* and would win in that category for *Parade.* He would also win Best Play for *The Last Night of Ballyhoo,* and the Pulitzer Prize for *Driving Miss Daisy.*) Director Michael Kahn had one Broadway credit—*The Freaking Out of Stephanie Blake,* a recent play that had closed after a few previews. (Kahn would later receive a Tony nomination for Best Direction of a Musical for a revival of *Showboat.*) However, in December 1967, the most reassuring thing about these four young men was the fact that Mitch Miller believed in their talent.

The cast was accomplished, but there were no star names—no names like Mary Martin or Julie Andrews that people in the Midwest would recognize from television appearances or previous cast albums. In fact, the cast for *Here's Where I Belong* had more credits in straight plays than in musicals. Paul Rogers, a British actor whose Broadway credits included the title role in *Macbeth,* was playing the lead role of Adam, the father of twin boys in their late teens. Paul had just won the Tony Award for Best Actor in a Leading Role in a Play for Pinter's *The Homecoming.* As critics would later note, he had a fine singing voice and an impeccable American accent.

Ken Kercheval was playing Adam's favorite son, the blond, outgoing Aron. Ken had Broadway credits in both plays and musicals and is probably best known today as Cliff Barnes on the TV series *Dallas.* Walter McGinn, whose sole Broadway credit was Timmy in *The Subject Was Roses,* played Aron's twin, the shy, darker son whom Adam belittles—the role played by James Dean in the film.

Heather MacRae, a fresh-looking blonde of 21, was making her Broadway debut as Abra, the teenager who becomes Aron's girlfriend, but later realizes that Cal is the better man. Heather was catnip to the press because she was the daughter of Gordon MacRae (star of the musical films of *Oklahoma!* and *Carousel*) and Sheila MacRae (the actress starring as Alice Kramden on the hit TV series, *The Jackie Gleason Show*).

The roles of the estranged mother, Kate, who runs a whorehouse, and the housekeeper, Lee, were played by Broadway veterans Nancy Wickwire and James Coco. The cast had impressive credits, but their names wouldn't fill seats. The show would sink or swim on word of mouth and reviews.

The first walk-through of the show introduced me to the story. The first principal onstage was roly-poly Italian-American Jimmy Coco—shuffling, bowing, and speaking pidgin English with a Chinese accent. *Very funny—but why is he pretending to be Chinese?* In the second scene, Lee explained that he was raised speaking the King's English, but speaks pidgin English in public because that's what people expect. *Wait! Is the character Chinese?* Yes, the character was Chinese. *Yikes!* Jimmy Coco was a terrific actor—Neil Simon would later write *Last of the Red Hot Lovers* for him—and I would soon discover that he was also a wonderful colleague, but he was *not* Chinese. In the following weeks, I learned that playwright Terrence McNally and Jimmy Coco were very good friends—but that didn't change the fact that Jimmy was miscast, and the comedy he played so well in the opening scene didn't set the right tone for the rest of the show.

The miscasting of the first principal onstage wasn't the biggest problem with *Here's Where I Belong*, but after one reading, I really didn't know what to make of the show. It was a musical, but not a comedy.

The biggest dance number was the "Lettuce Ballet": Adam decides he can make a fortune by shipping ice-cooled lettuce to the East. During the ballet, the dancers harvest and pack the lettuce into boxcars. Cal works tirelessly side by side with the Mexican workers while Aron enjoys picnic lunches with Abra. Hanya created some interesting visuals, including the "lettuce toss" in which the male dancers tossed the girls down a line spinning them around like heads of lettuce on a conveyer belt. She also created a human merry-go-round: The boys walked counter-clockwise in a circle with their left arms raised at a 135-degree angle toward the center of the circle to form the roof of the merry-go-round while the girls jumped up onto the boys' right hips, put their left arms around the boys' shoulders, and made circles with their legs, as if riding bicycles in the air.

I wasn't sure why there was a merry-go-round in the lettuce fields, and my upper arms ached from this lift and another more problematic lift: The girls sat on the floor to the left of the standing boys. We reached up, took the boys' hands, and jumped so that we landed with our right shins and right cheeks on the left shoulders of the boys. Our right kneecaps were in front of the boys' shoulders and our ankles behind, while our extended left legs pointed high into the air. Even in rehearsal skirts, without voluminous petticoats, this lift was tricky.

My partner and I were one of the first couples to execute the lift successfully, so Hanya asked us to demonstrate the lift for the other dancers. Again and again and again. Then she had us demonstrate for the individual couples that were having trouble. Again and again and again. Near the end of the eight-hour rehearsal day, my partner and I were exhausted. We reached for each other's hands, lost our grip, and I fell hard on my tailbone. As I winced in pain, Hanya cried out, "You've lost it! You've lost it! Do it again!" And we did it again and again until I was almost in tears.

Shortly thereafter, I read an interview with Hanya in *Dance Magazine* in which she said, "I drill them beyond endurance, until emotional value appears ... if you don't have the spark, lifting your leg isn't going to help." I agree that dancers must have a spark—that lifting their legs is not enough—but I don't believe that drilling dancers until they crumble creates "emotional value." A choreographer should be able to verbalize or demonstrate what she wants—or have an assistant who can communicate for her. Bullying a dancer doesn't help. In retrospect, I think Hanya knew she was not producing her best work and was frustrated with the show.

Three of the dancers were of particular interest to me: Gene Gavin, Graciela Daniele, and Michele Simmons.

Gene Gavin, tall, dark, and handsome, had the most impressive résumé of the dancers, but he was quiet and self-effacing. He had danced in the first ballet performance I had attended when I was seven years old—the Slavenska-Franklin Ballet—and he had spent several years with the New York City Ballet before performing in ten Broadway shows, including *West Side Story*. Gene was one of the strongest male dancers, but I guessed (correctly) that this might be his last dance in a Broadway show because he was in his late thirties and wore a toupee that was of great concern to the creative team. Would a man in Salinas in the early 20th century actually wear a toupee? Should Gene dispense with the toupee onstage? Gene was a constant reminder that the career of a dancer is short.

Graciela Daniele, an Argentine beauty, had trained as a classical ballet dancer in her native country and traveled to France to further her career. After seeing a production of *West Side Story*, she decided to dance in musicals, moved to New York, and performed in the original Broadway cast of *What Makes Sammy Run?* I admired Graciela's powerful stage presence, strong technique, and passion for life. She was the person I trusted to give me advice, and she later became an acclaimed Broadway director and choreographer whose credits include *Once on This Island*, *Ragtime*, and a Tony Award for Lifetime Achievement.

Michele Simmons, a serious Black girl, was one of the youngest dancers and had a modern dance background. I was in awe of her quiet confidence. She gave the impression that she knew exactly where she wanted to go and had no doubt that she would get there. Michele became a soloist with the companies of Alvin Ailey and Donald McKayle, and choreographed for television and film before getting a PhD in anthropology and becoming a doctor of chiropractic medicine specializing in dance and sports injuries.

I was the sunny, bubbly ball of energy who had dialogue as a schoolgirl in several scenes. My primary wig had curls that were designed to look like Mary Pickford, and I went back and forth between ruffled dresses with the Mary Pickford wig, and farm clothes, brown body paint, and a jet-black wig with two braids.

After six weeks of rehearsals in New York, with reporters and photographers popping into rehearsals on a regular basis, *Here's Where I Belong* traveled to Philadelphia for a three-week pre–Broadway run. As I walked from my hotel to the Shubert Theatre, I was thrilled to see the title of our show on the marquee, but I was surprised by the graphic: silhouettes of a boy and a girl in front of a rising sun. *Was the love story supposed to be the main plotline? That wouldn't have been my choice. Was it the most marketable*? Cal, the outsider, was the character that resonated with me—but which plotline was the main story? Cal and his father? Cal and his brother? Cal and Abra? The two boys competing for their father's love? What was the purpose of the angry, vindictive mother? Who and what were the audience supposed to root for? What was the show really about? I didn't know—but I did know that if I had been Cal, I would have been on the first train out of that stifling town, and none of this drama would have taken place.

In the final scene of the show, Adam, who has had a debilitating stroke, makes a gesture of rapprochement to Cal, but since Adam is now dependent on Cal, I didn't find this a very satisfying ending—although it implied that the Cal/Adam plot was the main story.

At one of the first performances in Philadelphia, just before the overture began, Hanya announced that the opening number, "Sweeping Change," wasn't working, so the dancers playing Mexicans should stay offstage, and the rest of us should plug up the holes. *Yikes*! *Couldn't she have figured this out fifteen minutes earlier and given us time to do a quick rehearsal?* "Sweeping Change" wasn't helped by the fact that Hanya had singers with brooms sweeping the floor, but the song was soon replaced by a new song, "We Are What We Are," which got the show off to a better start.

Preview audiences were small, so we needed good reviews if we wanted to fill the theater. Unfortunately, on press night, an electrical fire broke out in one of the boxes in the balcony. The fire was quickly extinguished, but it certainly upstaged the drama in the show.

The review in the Philadelphia *Bulletin* was titled, "*Here's Where I Belong* Doesn't Belong Here." The reviewer liked Paul Rogers (the father), but thought the show was dreary. The *Inquirer* liked the show and the lead actors, but thought there should be at least one more big dance number, and the *Philadelphia Daily News* announced, "the conflagration was the first real excitement of the musical's initial 45 minutes." *Ouch*!

The first reading of a new musical is usually the first opportunity for the ensemble to judge the quality of the show. (Principals are given scripts before rehearsals begin, but members of the ensemble usually are not.) But even at the first reading, our judgment is colored by the interpretations of the actors (who might later be replaced by actors with very different interpretations), the enthusiasm of the other people in the room, our desire for the show to be a hit, and our hope that all of the weaknesses will be solved by the brilliance of the creative team. During rehearsals and previews, some cuts and changes improve the show; others don't. If we aren't in the new and/or altered scenes, we might not know about the changes until we hear unfamiliar words or music coming from the monitors in the dressing room. The response of the audience, night after night, tells us whether the show is working, and in Philadelphia, the audiences, like the critics, told us that *Here's Where I Belong* needed work.

At the end of the three-week run in Philadelphia, we returned to New York and moved into the Billy Rose Theatre on 41st Street. The Billy Rose was not a prestigious theater like the St. James, where *Hello, Dolly!* was still running and where producer David Merrick had his offices. The Billy Rose was south of 42nd Street, which was gaining a reputation as the most dangerous street in the U.S. Today, 42nd Street is a tourist mecca anchored by Disney's historic New Amsterdam Theatre, but in 1968, it was lined with peep shows and movie theaters that screened XXX-rated films. When I walked up 8th Avenue from the theater to my home at the Washington Jefferson Hotel, I often passed young women in short skirts with their backs plastered against recessed doorways, their wary eyes darting left and right looking out for cops, while men, facing the buildings, their faces hidden, pumped their hips against the girls.

The female ensemble of *Here's Where I Belong* moved into a large dressing room several flights up from the stage. Costume changes required us to run up the stairs, take off our costumes and wigs, put on body paint, get into different costumes and wigs, run down several flights of stairs, dance a little, run upstairs, shed the costumes and wigs, wash off the body paint, put on the next costumes and wigs and run back down to the stage.

During daily rehearsals, I could feel the tension mounting. Mitch Miller put up $100,000 of his own money to delay the press opening from February 20 to March 3. Terrence McNally took his name off the show amid rumors that other writers were working on the book, and the fictitious Alex Gordon became the credited writer. Tony Mordente, who had assisted Gower Champion with *Bye Bye Birdie,* replaced Hanya Holm as choreographer and lifted our spirits with his enthusiasm and energetic choreography.

Finally, after three months of rehearsals and previews, it was opening night on Broadway. My dressing table was covered with opening night gifts and flowers, and some of the male dancers (and Jimmy Coco) popped in to wish us luck. I put on my makeup, my ruffled dress, and my Mary Pickford wig, and went down to the stage.

Outside the theater, Asian actors were picketing the show to protest the casting of Jimmy Coco, and I hoped that the pickets wouldn't affect the size of the house or the response of the audience.

The overture began. The curtain went up, and during the opening number, I could see that we finally had a full house. *Hooray*! The audience laughed at the jokes and applauded the song and dance, and when the curtain fell, the audience jumped to its feet and gave us a standing ovation. *Had the show found its audience*?

I walked to La Fonda del Sol for the opening night party, where the mood was festive—until the reviews came in: Clive Barnes began his review in *The New York Times*: "The most distinguished aspect of *Here's Where I Belong ...* is the scenery by Ming Cho Lee." (Ming Cho Lee created a tree so spectacular that after it was lit, Michael Kahn stopped the rehearsal and asked the entire cast to come into the house to admire the tree.) Clive Barnes doubted that the serious story of a father and his sons was suitable material for a musical. He criticized the juxtaposition of the dark story with jolly song and dance, but wrote that the dance had "more than usual vigor and imagination." He liked the lead actors, but thought they deserved a better show.

Richard Watts, Jr., in the *New York Post,* also questioned the suitability of the source material for a musical and found the story and the song and dance "a clumsy juxtaposition of elements."

At La Fonda del Sol, the crowd rapidly thinned out. I saw Robert Waldman (composer) and Alfred Uhry (lyricist) sitting together in a corner. One looked at the other and said, "Well, we got one on

Broadway." I was cheered by the hopeful tone. The reviews weren't good, but we were on Broadway, and that was a pretty good place to be.

The next evening, I arrived at the theater, and the doorman grumbled, "You're late."

"It's not even seven-thirty."

"The show's closed. You're late to pick up your things."

It took me a moment to process the information. Then I remembered: the closing notice had appeared on the bulletin board a week earlier, but one of the singers had told me, "Forget about it. The notice will come down once the reviews come out." He was wrong—and closing a show, unlike firing individuals, requires only one week's notice.

I climbed the stairs to the girls' dressing room. All of the other dressing tables were bare. I packed up my makeup, my hairpins, and my dressing gown, and I turned out the light. There would be no original cast album and no chance to say goodbye to the cast. Ming Cho Lee's spectacular sets would be destroyed. Soon, the window card for *Here's Where I Belong* would go up on the wall at Joe Allen, and people would debate whether or not *Here's Where I Belong* had replaced *Kelly* as the most expensive one-night flop in Broadway history.

As I walked up 8th Avenue toward the Washington Jefferson Hotel, I looked down 44th Street where audiences were gathering under brightly lit marquees. I saw the excited anticipation of the people lining up at the box office—but I was unemployed. I hoped that my next show would be more cheerful and have more dance—and I hoped it would have a much longer run. I picked up the trade papers at Smiler's Deli, ordered a scoop of mocha chip ice cream at Howard Johnson's, and began the search for my next job.

3

Oklahoma! at the Paper Mill Playhouse and *How Now, Dow Jones* (1968)

The telephone rang in my room at the Washington Jefferson Hotel. "This is Ray Gibbs." I flashed back to *Hello, Dolly!* Shortly after I had joined the cast, Dan Merriman told me about a young opera singer from San Diego who was getting his master's degree from the Manhattan School of Music. Dan wanted to introduce us because he thought we were perfect for each other. I told Dan I wasn't interested. I wanted to focus on my career. Nevertheless, one evening as Dan, June Helmers, and I perused the menu at Joe Allen, a young man bounded over to the table as if we were all expecting him. He was tall, with brown curly hair, and a rakish smile. Dan said, "Lee, this is Ray Gibbs." I muttered something forgettable and glared at Dan. Ray got the message. Nevertheless, I noted that Ray was funny, smart, outgoing, and passionate about music.

Now, months later, Ray was calling me. He was about to make his debut with the New York City Opera in a comprimario role in the New York premiere of *Bomarzo*. He had told Dan that he didn't know anyone he could invite to the opening, and Dan had suggested me—thinking that I might enjoy a night at the opera.

Dan was right. I missed the music and spectacle that had been such an important part of my life during my years with the Metropolitan Opera Ballet.

A few days before the premiere, Ray offered to let me borrow his score, so I stopped by the New York State Theater to pick it up.

Ray told me he would be singing immediately after a short break and invited me to watch a bit of the stage rehearsal. What a glorious voice he had! When he joined me in the house, I whispered, "You have one of the most beautiful tenor voices I've ever heard."

"I'm a baritone," he whispered back—but later, as we got a bite to eat at a nearby restaurant, he told me that he enjoyed singing along with recordings of his favorite tenor, Jussi Björling, a Swede who had died in 1960. *My* favorite tenor was the tall Italian Franco Corelli, who sang regularly at the Metropolitan Opera while I was dancing with the Metropolitan Opera Ballet. Ray had never seen Corelli, nor had he ever been to the Met. Ray had a scholarship to the Manhattan School of Music and a church job at Park Avenue United Methodist Church, but he depended upon a monthly check from his church in San Diego to pay the rent on his fifth-floor walkup in Spanish Harlem. He certainly couldn't afford a ticket to the Met.

The premiere of *Bomarzo* confirmed my opinion of Ray's voice, so I called John Gutman, the assistant general manager in charge of new talent at the Met. I told him about Ray and asked for passes to Corelli's next performance. Two weeks later, Ray and I were at the Met watching Corelli sing the role of Romeo.

I liked Ray, and I enjoyed reconnecting with the world of opera, but I lost no time lining up my next show—a four-week run of *Oklahoma!* at the Paper Mill Playhouse in Millburn, New Jersey. This was a Golden Age musical with a great ballet—exactly the kind of show I wanted to do.

The Paper Mill Playhouse began its life as the Thistle Paper Mill in the late 19th century and was converted into a theater in the 1930s. It was located near a bubbling brook and was only a 45-minute drive from midtown Manhattan.

At the time of the *Oklahoma!* auditions, I didn't know where the Paper Mill Playhouse stood in the hierarchy of musical theater (one notch below Broadway) or how I would get to the theater (carpooling in a rented car), so I sidled over to Graciela Danielle and whispered, "If you get this show, will you take it?" Her emphatic nod reassured me, and I was pleased when we both got the job.

Oklahoma! was the first collaboration of Rodgers and

Hammerstein and was the first Broadway musical in which the songs and dances were fully integrated into the plot. It is an optimistic, joyful show that takes place just after the turn of the 20th century in the Indian territories that were about to become the state of Oklahoma. The glorious score includes "Oh, What a Beautiful Mornin'" and "People Will Say We're in Love," and the first act ends with Laurey's "Dream Ballet," one of the most satisfying ballets in musical theater.

Critics often rave about the music and the ballet, but dismiss the plot of *Oklahoma!* as trivial, cornball, or irrelevant—nothing more than a question of which of two young men will take a farm girl to the box social. I disagree. Laurey is not a pawn. She is the protagonist, and she is not choosing between Curly, the cocky young cowboy she loves, and Jud, the burly farmhand who is stalking her. She is trying to answer two questions that are fundamental to the lives of most American women: Does the man I love have the right stuff to become my life partner? What can I do about a man who terrifies me when no one else believes he's a threat?

Laurey may say "ain't" and "ast" and "skeered," but she is a land owner. She has the highest status and highest net worth of the main characters. Curly is toying with her—will he or won't he take her to the box social only hours away? Laurey decides to put Curly in his place. She arranges to ride to the box social with Jud driving her rig instead of Curly, but she had assumed that Aunt Eller would be with them, and Aunt Eller informs her that she has promised to ride with Curly. Laurey tells Aunt Eller that she is afraid to be alone with Jud—that she hears him pacing outside her bedroom window every night—but Aunt Eller dismisses Laurey's fears and reminds Laurey that Jud does the work of two men, and they can't get along without him. Laurey buys an elixir to help her make up her mind. Some people conclude that "making up her mind" means that she is choosing between two suitors, but I believe that Laurey is choosing between two risky courses of action—riding alone with Jud, who dreams of touching her, or riding with Curly and Aunt Eller and risking Jud's wrath. During Laurey's "Dream Ballet," she makes her choice:

As Laurey breathes in the elixir, she drifts into sleep, and dance counterparts take the places of Laurey, Curly, and Jud. Laurey and

Curly dance a romantic pas de deux. Then, Curly, with his fellow cowboys, and Laurey, with her girlfriends, prepare for their wedding. Surrounded by her friends, Laurey walks down the aisle, but the man who lifts her veil is Jud. Horrified, Laurey looks to her girlfriends and Curly for help, but stone-faced, they all back away. Jud dances briefly with Laurey, but then leaves her to cavort with flashy dance-hall girls, who look like the picture postcards on the walls of Jud's room in the smokehouse. Jud and Curly fight, but when Curly shoots Jud, the bullets have no effect. Jud advances on Curly, grabs him by the throat, and strangles him. Then, he picks up Laurey, holds her high above his head like a trophy, and carries her offstage.

The real Jud approaches the sleeping Laurey and wakes her to go to the party. Curly enters, his eyes pleading for Laurey to go with him, but Laurey, "remembering the disaster of her recent dream … avoids its reality by taking Jud's arm." End of act one.

This 15-minute ballet is a joy to dance. Every step has a purpose; every sequence advances the story. The choreography is classically based, but has a freedom that expresses the wide-open spaces of the Oklahoma territories. The showdown between Curly and Jud perfectly dramatizes Laurey's fear that Curly does not have the right stuff to become her husband and that Jud will have his way. It also prepares the audience for the violence to come.

In act two, Jud and Curly bid against each other for Laurey's box lunch. Jud bids everything he has in the world "all fer Laurey," but Curly sells the tools of his trade as a cowboy—his saddle, his horse, and his gun—everything *he* has in the world—to top Jud's bid and prove to Laurey that he is ready to give up his itinerant cowboy life and become the farmer/husband she needs. Jud accuses Laurey of thinking she's too good for him, and when he threatens her, she fires him. Three weeks later, everyone is celebrating the marriage of Laurey and Curly when Jud crashes the celebration, demands a kiss from the bride, and grabs Laurey; Curly pulls him away; Jud lunges at Curly with a knife, and Curly throws Jud to the ground where Jud falls on his knife and dies. A trial is held on the spot, and Curly is deemed "not guilty."

By the end of this scene, both of Laurey's problems have been solved. Curly has proved that he *does* have the right stuff to be Laurey's partner, and the threat from Jud is gone. The show ends as the young couple departs on their honeymoon—the morning of their life together—while the entire company sings "Oh, What a Beautiful Mornin'."

In the late 1960s, theater critics for the major New York newspapers, who were and are almost exclusively male, ridiculed the story. Even today, in the era of #MeToo, critics don't seem to hear Laurey's voice. However, Laurey's problems resonate with women, and women buy nearly 70 percent of musical theater tickets.

It is worth noting that the civilizing influences in this musical are the women. Laurey is the character who forces Curly to grow up and who confronts the predator Jud by firing him. The farmers and the cowmen are close to violence until Aunt Eller intervenes and reminds them that a healthy society works together and insists that farmers and cowboys can and should be friends. Aunt Eller is also the host of the box social that raises money for the schoolhouse that will educate the next generation. (Curly's selling of his horse, saddle, and gun that some people find unrealistic is not only Curly's declaration that he is ready to settle down and put his future in Laurey's hands, but also an investment in the education of their future children.) *Oklahoma!* presents a community in which women have power—and the community is the better for it.

At the Paper Mill Playhouse, the cast, headed by Linda Bennett, James Hurst, and Michael Kermoyan, was first rate, and director/choreographer Gemze de Lappe, who had worked closely with Agnes de Mille, was a dream to work with as she recreated the original choreography. I loved being part of a show that required no rewrites and no changes in personnel. I loved performing such a well-written, well-choreographed show, and I loved getting out of New York City and spending time surrounded by trees and a bubbling brook.

The four-week run was much too short, but less than 48 hours after *Oklahoma!* closed, I received a telephone call from Charlie Blackwell, production stage manager for David Merrick: "If you're available, we'd like you to join the cast of *How Now, Dow Jones*."

Wow! *That was fast*!

Charlie asked me to come to the theater on Thursday afternoon to meet everyone, read a few lines, and sign a contract.

Wow! What a great way to get a job!

Two days later, I read a few lines and signed the contract for my second David Merrick show, which was playing at the beautiful Lunt-Fontanne Theatre, only six blocks from my hotel.

How Now, Dow Jones, like *Here's Where I Belong*, had been in trouble on the road. Legendary director George Abbott (*Pajama Game*, *Damn Yankees*) had replaced Arthur Penn (*Golden Boy*, *Wait Until Dark*), and choreographer Michael Bennett (uncredited and the future director/co-choreographer of *A Chorus Line*) had replaced Gillian Lynne (the credited choreographer and future choreographer of *Cats* and *Phantom of the Opera*). However, there was a big difference between *Here's Where I Belong* and *How Now, Dow Jones*: *Here's Where I Belong* had almost no advance sales while *How Now, Dow Jones* had an advance of half a million dollars—a big advance at that time.

The interesting thing about the advance for *How Now, Dow Jones* is that it wasn't generated by star names. In 1967, none of the lead actors—Marlyn Mason, Tony Roberts, Brenda Vaccaro, and Hiram Sherman—were stars. Nor was the advance generated by the creative team. Max Shulman (book), Elmer Bernstein (music), and Carolyn Leigh (lyrics) were not a well-known brand like Rodgers & Hammerstein. *How Now, Dow Jones* had a large advance because theater-party ladies liked the title. (Theater-party ladies are the people—nearly all women—who buy blocks of tickets at a discount prior to a show's opening to resell at a mark-up for professional organizations and charities. Theater parties are an insurance policy for producers who get advance income, guaranteed audiences, and [hopefully] good word of mouth even if the reviews turn out to be less than stellar.)

How Now, Dow Jones was a title that sounded like fun—something even tired businessmen would enjoy—and Wall Street was topical because money was flowing into the stock market. When the show opened in December 1967, the percentage of American families' wealth invested in the stock market had nearly doubled since the 1950s, and the Dow Jones Average was approaching the magic number of 1,000. *How Now, Dow Jones* had a huge advance because it was a show that theater-party ladies could sell.

The cast was terrific, but the story didn't make sense: Kate, the young woman who announces the Dow Jones Average on the radio, has been engaged for two years to Herbert, a boring, workaholic broker. Herbert won't marry Kate until the Dow Jones Average hits 1,000. *Why? And what does Kate see in Herbert?* Kate goes to a bar where she meets Charlie, who is also frustrated in love, and they end up in bed. *Hmmm....* Kate discovers that she is pregnant, but by then, Charlie is engaged, so Kate deliberately and inaccurately announces that the Dow Jones Average has broken 1,000. *Really?! Is Kate foolish enough to think she can marry Herbert before her lie is discovered? How is it possible that no one corrected Kate's lie before the market opened the following day? Are we supposed to root for a girl who lies to trap a man into marriage without telling him that she is pregnant by someone else? Yikes!*

As a member of the audience, the show didn't work for me, but as a member of the cast, it was great fun. *How Now, Dow Jones* was my first contemporary show, and I enjoyed wearing the fashionable costumes with shockingly short skirts. The dancing was minimal, but I had a small speaking part as Miss MacKenzie, and I liked the marching song "Step to the Rear," which became the jingle for Lincoln Mercury car commercials. I laughed every night as I stood in the wings and watched Brenda Vaccaro sing "He's Here," the highpoint of a comedic performance that earned her a Tony nomination for Best Actress in a Musical, and brought Hiram Sherman, the object of her affection, the Tony Award for Best Featured Actor in a Musical.

I planned to spend the entire summer performing in *How Now, Dow Jones* and in the fall, look for a more challenging show, but on June 7, Actors' Equity went on strike. David Merrick, who employed roughly one out of every five people on Broadway, announced that he would close one of his shows each day that Equity remained on strike—and he kept his word. First, he axed *I Do, I Do*, then *How Now, Dow Jones*, and on the third day, the strike ended. The new contract gave performers a raise from $130 a week to $155 over three years, but for the fifth time in 12 months, I was unemployed.

When I was a little girl growing up in the suburbs, listening to cast albums, all I knew were the hits. I didn't ask myself, "What is the ratio of hits to flops?" When I left the Metropolitan Opera Ballet, I expected to stay with a show until I was ready to move on. I expected to perform in the evening and spend my days taking dance classes and working on scenes for acting classes. Instead, I spent most of my time auditioning and rehearsing. Nevertheless, I couldn't complain. Less than one year after leaving the Metropolitan Opera Ballet, I had three Broadway shows on my résumé.

Musical theater pushed me toward a personal life outside of the theater. As long as I danced at the Met, the theater was my home, and the people in the company were my extended family. I vocalized and practiced the piano in soundproof rooms at the theater. I spent my free evenings watching performances from the company box. When I attended parties, the hosts were men and women connected with the Metropolitan Opera. I even washed out my practice clothes and took my showers at the theater.

In musical theater, each new show created a new family that banded together quickly and disbanded quickly or slowly depending on the length of the run. I moved from one theater to the next. I no longer had access to pianos in soundproof rooms and world-class, free entertainment in the evenings. My job and my workplace no longer fulfilled my every need.

Dan Merriman was my oldest Broadway friend. He and his wife, Mara Worth, a petite singer who had left *How Now, Dow Jones* before I joined the cast, had taken Ray under their wing. Ray spent many evenings in their seven-room apartment on West 141st Street. When I wasn't working, Dan and Mara invited me to join them. Dan opened a jug of wine, sat at the piano, and played arias and show tunes while Ray sang. Sometimes Ray and Mara sang duets. Mara didn't tell her age, but Dan told me she had been a child bride. Since Dan was 37, I guessed that Mara was in her early thirties.

When I had made the transition from ballet to Broadway, my voice teacher had advised me to shave two years off my age and tell everyone I was 19, and I had followed his advice. At 21, I believed I was getting a late start on my Broadway career. Harvey Evans was five years older than I, but when I joined the cast of *Hello, Dolly!*, Harvey had ten years of Broadway hits on his résumé—shows that included *Gypsy* and *West Side Story*. I told Dan, Mara, and Ray my real age, but Mara advised me to stop telling my age to *anyone*. Dancers were considered old at 30—but I looked young, and Mara said that if people didn't know my age, I could extend my career. Decades later, after Mara's death, I was astonished to discover that Mara had been in her mid-forties when we met.

Ray and I quickly became a couple. Ray came to the opening night of *Oklahoma!* and sent me his rave review when he sang Valentin in *Faust* in Chattanooga. He invited me to his church, and after the service and coffee hour, we walked along Central Park and visited the Metropolitan Museum of Art. We listened to opera singers on my portable record player, read the Tolkien trilogy, and bought each other love beads. I didn't know it yet, but I was on a fast-moving train toward marriage.

4

Gimbels and *Love Match* (1968–1969)

In the summer of 1968, after the demise of *How Now, Dow Jones*, I performed in my first industrial show (a show designed to motivate and excite salespeople about the products they are selling). The fast-paced Theatre Now production showcased the latest children's fashions at Gimbels department store, the chief rival to Macy's. Jill Harmon, J.J. Jepson, and I were the featured dancers, and all three of us could pass for teenagers.

Boyish Barry Manilow, who had just turned 25, was the conductor and rehearsal pianist. Barry was a terrific accompanist and a joy to work with, so I wasn't surprised to hear the producers say that he had a big career ahead of him. He first became known for his memorable jingles: "Like a good neighbor, State Farm is there" and "I am stuck on Band-Aid brand 'cause Band-Aid's stuck on me!" Today, of course, Barry Manilow is a superstar composer and singer with dozens of hit records.

The comedienne in the Gimbels show was also a talent who was not yet on most people's radar: Lily Tomlin, who was very funny and very serious about her work. I didn't get to see her perform because I was changing clothes, but I think she was featuring makeup, and I heard gales of laughter from the audience. Today, a list of Lily Tomlin's awards would fill half a page.

Jill, J.J., and I were the featured dance trio, but all of the young people modeling the clothes were singers and dancers who performed like the ensemble in a Broadway show. We were all contracted for three performances, but after a request from numerous employees, Gimbels added a fourth performance the following week so that cafeteria workers and other employees not involved in sales could see the show. *Backstage* gave us a rave review and suggested that this kind of show might be the future of retail because "When these Equity kids showed the clothes, you really wanted to buy them!"

After the last performance at Gimbels, Ray and I hopped on a train for Wilmington, Delaware, to attend the wedding of my oldest brother, Trick (Joseph Durant Cooper Wilson III). Trick was only 21, but in the late 1960s, the median age of first marriage for men was 22, and for women, 20. Girls of my generation were advised to marry young "before all the good ones are taken," and many girls went to college just long enough to find a husband—"getting an M.R.S. degree." As I watched my brother and his bride, I began to visualize my own, future wedding, which would be quite different from Trick's.

Instead of a formal wedding at noon, I wanted a candlelight ceremony at 8:00 p.m. Instead of a morning coat for the groom and a traditional white gown for the bride, my groom would wear elegant black tie and I would wear a short cocktail dress suitable for opening night parties in the future. Instead of a sit-down dinner, I would have a party at my parents' house with fresh strawberries and scrumptious cake. I wasn't yet ready to cast myself as a bride, but the Sunday night after Trick's wedding, while I was packing to return to New York, Mom told me that my aunt Jean had said she was sure there would be another Wilson wedding within a year—and Mom seemed to like the idea.

My new musical that autumn was *Love Match*, the tumultuous love story of Queen Victoria and Prince Albert. The show was booked into theaters in Phoenix, Los Angeles, and Detroit before the Broadway premiere in February 1969.

I have always loved period shows that take me to a different time and place, and two of the try-out cities were also new cities for me to explore: Phoenix and Los Angeles. While *Love Match* was in Phoenix, Ray would be singing Schaunard in *La Bohème* in his hometown of San Diego. His next engagement was *The Barber of Seville* in Houston in early January, so he told me he would drive up to L.A. for the opening of *Love Match* and stay with me through Christmas.

The book for *Love Match* was by Christian Hamilton, the music by David Shire, and the lyrics by Richard Maltby, Jr. (Maltby and Shire were just beginning their illustrious careers that now include the Broadway musicals *Baby* and *Big*). Danny Daniels, the director and choreographer, had received three Tony nominations for Best Choreography and would later win in that category for *The Tap Dance Kid*, but this was his first Broadway show as a director.

During the first read-through, I thought the show had wonderful moments, but was unfocused and much too long. However, I liked the songs, and Danny Daniels described some terrific dance numbers. As Queen Victoria, Patricia Routledge, who had just won a Tony Award for Best Actress in a Musical for *Darling of the Day*, was an adorable, irrepressible dumpling. Laurence Guittard had a wonderful singing voice and was a handsome, worthy opponent as Prince Albert. Hal Linden was terrific as Albert's brother Ernest, and Rex Robbins and Bill Hinnant were delightful in a comedic subplot. Every actor in the show seemed perfectly cast.

The first of the two big dance numbers was a dress parade in Scottish kilts to celebrate the coronation of Queen Victoria. Danny began rehearsals by showing us a basic Scottish dance step: high cuts. To perform high cuts, a dancer bounces from one foot to the other on demi-pointe while the working leg taps the supporting leg twice in passé position just below the back of the knee. In ballet, passé position requires a pointed foot, but in Scottish dance, the working foot is slightly flexed so that when the dancer is viewed from the front, the working foot disappears behind the calf of the supporting leg.

I had danced only a few high cuts before Danny turned to me and said, "You've done these before."

In fact, when I was in high school, I had competed in Scottish dance competitions all across the Northeast and had won a stack of gold, silver, and bronze medals. I told Danny that I had studied Scottish dance with James Jamieson in Wilmington, Delaware, and Danny's eyes twinkled when he told me he had just returned from Wilmington where he had been working with "Jamie." Danny and I had worked with the best: James Jamieson was the Scottish dance champion who had assisted Agnes de Mille with the Tony Award–winning choreography for *Brigadoon*.

Some of the dancers grumbled that Danny was too strict. When rehearsals began at 10:00 a.m., he expected us to be warmed up and ready to dance—not straggling in at 10:05 with a cheese Danish and a cup of coffee. Since Danny was directing as well as choreographing, I thought his demand was quite reasonable. Danny wasn't the warmest, fuzziest personality, but when he laughed, his face lit up, and many dancers, including me, loved and respected him both as a person and as a choreographer. He was disciplined, imaginative, loyal, and direct.

However, when we did our first run-through, I was astonished: The running time of the show was more than three and a half hours. *Why wasn't Danny making cuts*?

One of the dancers informed me that the producers really wanted British director Noel Willman to direct the show. (Willman's Broadway credits included *A Man for All Seasons, The Lion in Winter*, and *Darling of the Day*, the short-lived musical that had brought Patricia Routledge her Tony Award.) However, Willman wasn't available until November, so they elevated Danny from choreographer to director/choreographer and gave Noel Willman the title of "production supervisor." According to my informant, Danny wasn't allowed to make any significant changes until Noel Willman had seen the show—and Willman couldn't see the show until after we opened in Phoenix.

I could only imagine how frustrated Danny must have been. Shaping a new show is a process of trial and error, and Danny was being denied that process. He was, however, eliciting beautiful performances. I could only hope that when Noel Willman arrived in Phoenix, he and Danny would quickly agree on what they wanted to do and use the 12 weeks in Los Angeles and Detroit to cut and shape the material into a gem that sparkled.

Our tech rehearsal at the Palace West in Phoenix lasted two days—obscenely long in the days before falling chandeliers and hovering helicopters—but finally, it was opening night and time to hear the response of the critics.

Left: **Patricia Routledge played Queen Victoria in the Broadway-bound musical *Love Match,* and I played Young Victoria prior to her coronation at the age of 18.** ***Right:*** **For the Coronation Parade, I wore a MacLeod tartan kilt.**

Larry Rummel's review in the *Phoenix Gazette* stated, "The opening performance may be compared to a jigsaw puzzle in which the separate pieces were scattered about helter-skelter." However, "The cast of this production is outstanding and Patricia Routledge's performance is a superb tour de force." Larry Rummel also praised the sets and costumes and the Scottish dance number, the "Coronation Parade."

The *Variety* review began, "*The Love Match* ... is in trouble. It's too much of a very good thing. It ran a tortuous, meandering three hours and 35 minutes." However, "The company is populated with a cast of huge capabilities, the settings superb, and the choreography spectacularly extravagant." The review ended with additional praise for Danny Daniels' sensational choreography.

In addition to the Highland dance with its authentic choreography and intricate patterns, there was a comedic dance at a palace ball. Victoria and Albert led the dance, but each wanted to lead—Victoria because she was queen, and Albert because he was the man.

The subtle pulling and tugging between the two of them became more pronounced as it progressed down the line of dancers behind them, and by the time it reached the last couple (J.J. Jepson and me), our desperation to follow the queen was broad comedy. The audiences loved it.

We played only one week in Phoenix before opening in Los Angeles. In the *Los Angeles Times,* reviewer Cecil Smith wrote that Patricia Routledge was "the happiest thing to happen to the American stage since the invention of the spotlight" and that Danny's choreography had "the most imaginative and stylish dances in recent years." As for the play: "Victoria and Albert, who really cares?"

Ouch.

In spite of the problems with the show, I was enjoying my time in the Southwest. I liked everyone in the cast, and before we opened in Phoenix, the producers told me they were afraid Hollywood might snatch me away, so they offered me a nice bump in salary for signing a six-months' rider to my contract—an addendum that prohibited me from leaving the show during the first six months. I also signed a rider that gave me additional pay for my non-speaking role as young Victoria. In Los Angeles, my temporary home in the Hotel Clark was only a short walk from the Ahmanson Theatre where, eight shows a week, I reveled in the brilliant choreography, and audiences responded with enthusiastic applause. At one performance, the "Coronation Parade," early in the first act, received a standing ovation.

While Ray was performing in San Diego, he bought an old car for 100 dollars, and after his last performance, drove up to L.A. to attend the opening of *Love Match* with a star-studded audience. At the opening night party, I was delighted to meet Ann Miller. As a little girl, I had admired her tap dancing in musicals like "On the Town" and "Easter Parade," which I had watched on TV. In person, her presence seemed much larger than it was on the small screen.

Between rehearsals and performances, Ray and I explored the Central Market and the Los Angeles Public Library. One sunny day off, Ray drove me to San Diego to show me his hometown. I met his parents, saw the Pacific Ocean, and had dinner at a Mexican restaurant in Old Town. On another day off, Ray cooked tacos for some of the cast at a cast member's apartment, and some nights after the show, we'd go to a piano bar, where Ray would sing show tunes, and people would send us so many drinks it was ridiculous. For Christmas, we bought a small Christmas tree and decorated it with strings of popcorn and tiny candy canes that melted and dripped in the heat. By the time Ray left for Houston to begin rehearsals for *The Barber of Seville*, we had decided to get married.

I felt underprepared for marriage, but I had felt underprepared for every major step in my life. At 15, I had felt underprepared to live by myself in New York City—until I moved into the Martha Washington Hotel and took to New York like a duckling to a lake. At 17, I felt underprepared to become première danseuse of the Bordeaux Opera Ballet, but I trusted Rosella Hightower to know what I could handle, and the following year, after I had declined to spend another year in Bordeaux, I trusted her again when she suggested I return to America to work with Dame Alicia Markova at the Metropolitan Opera Ballet.

I had done well by trusting people more experienced than I, and my parents and my aunt seemed to think that I was ready for marriage, and that Ray was the right choice. One of my younger brothers (and most girls my age) were already married, but for me, the main reasons to marry then (and not wait until Ray was better established) were the laws that discriminated against unmarried couples: In Los Angeles, Ray could stay in my hotel room, but in much of the country, including New York, it was illegal for unmarried couples to share an apartment or spend a night together at a hotel. In New York, Ray had moved into a hotel across the street from Lincoln Center, which was a short walk from my hotel, but we couldn't spend the night together in either of our homes, or the host would be evicted. (The doormen in both hotels didn't hide the fact that they watched our comings and goings.)

Ray and I planned to fly all over the country to watch each other work, and we didn't want to waste money on two hotel rooms when we only needed one. In some states, it was even illegal for unmarried women to use birth control. And, of course, if a single woman became pregnant, she had four choices: get married immediately while people snickered and took odds on how long the marriage would last; risk an illegal abortion; give birth to a child who would be stigmatized for being born out of wedlock; or cut all ties with family and friends and move to another town where she could pretend that her husband had died in a tragic accident and left her alone with the dear little one. Option number four was impossible if she wanted to dance on Broadway.

I loved Ray, and he loved me. He was handsome and talented and had a boyish enthusiasm that made even mundane things fun. Ray also seemed to understand that my career was of paramount importance to me. We agreed that no matter which of us became more successful, we would consider both careers equally important.

I've never believed that the value of a career is a function of money or fame. Dance gave me freedom and joy—two things far more important to me than money or fame—and I knew that Ray found joy and purpose through music, so he could understand my passion for dance. In 1968, it was a rare man who didn't insist that *his* career was more important, and many men demanded that their wives stop working as soon as one paycheck could support the family. A stay-at-home wife was a status symbol for men.

To my surprise and delight, Danny Daniels and his lovely wife Bea invited all of the *Love Match* dancers to a beautiful restaurant for a pre–Christmas dinner. We laughed and talked and shared stories about other shows, but at the end of the meal, Danny dropped a bombshell: He was leaving the show.

I was stunned.

Danny explained that his contract stated that he was the "sole and only director," wording he had negotiated to make sure he would not be second-guessed by Noel Willman, but, in fact, Danny had not been allowed to do the work he thought necessary. Noel Willman, he said, had seen the show and decided it should *not* have big dance numbers.

What?!

Danny told us that he personally owned the rights to his

choreography. *Love Match* could use the choreography in its entirety, but no one except Danny could make cuts or changes. In a previous show, Danny said, another choreographer had replaced him and cut his work to shreds, but because Danny was the credited choreographer, *he* had received the terrible reviews. To make sure that didn't happen again, Danny had negotiated a contract in which he owned his choreography.

My heart sank. Danny's brilliant dance numbers would never be seen in New York. The dancers would have to start over.

In a rehearsal room at the Ahmanson Theatre, a new choreographer began work on a new "Coronation Parade." Average 10-year-old children could have performed the steps. Rehearsals were excruciating for the dancers—and probably for the choreographer. He must have known how good the work was that he was forced to replace—but the coup de grace came quickly. The run in Detroit was cancelled, and *Love Match* closed in Los Angeles on January 4.

On January 5, most of the company flew back to New York to look for new jobs. I flew to Houston where Ray was rehearsing the role of Figaro in *The Barber of Seville* with the Houston Grand Opera. Ray's sister and her husband shuffled around their four young children so Ray and I each had our own rooms. Ray's sister, like my parents, asked Ray and me to promise that we would not tiptoe between our rooms at night since we were not yet married—a promise we kept.

After the final performance of *The Barber of Seville*, Ray and I drove across the South and up the East Coast. In New Orleans, we spent an evening in the French Quarter and enjoyed a delicious dinner at Antoine's, the oldest French-Creole restaurant in the city. We drove through Georgia and up to Virginia Beach, where my family had once fled a hurricane. I loved the travel, the sights, and spending time with Ray, but my heart was in my throat every night when we checked into a hotel as Mr. and Mrs. Gibbs. We were in the South where cohabitation was illegal, and the penalties could be 500 dollars (six months' rent) or 60 days in jail.

Ray and I arrived in Delaware just before dinner. At the end of the meal, we told my parents that we planned to marry in the spring, and Dad deadpanned, "What a surprise." We asked Mom if she would like to produce and direct the event, and she was thrilled. We set the date for April 19, 1969.

5

Oklahoma! at Lincoln Center (1969)

I began to prepare for my new role as a wife. I read Amy Vanderbilt, Emily Post, bridal magazines, and books about marriage. Everything I read stressed the importance of cooking, and Mom gracefully allowed me to practice in her kitchen. One of my first dinners featured veal cutlets Niçoise. I looked at Mom as she took her first bite and watched her eyes widen.

"That's a lot of garlic," she said.

"The recipe called for one clove of garlic," I said, "so that's what I used."

"No," said my youngest brother, Tuck, as he stabbed a clove with his fork. "This is a clove. You used a butt."

Oops!

Mom and her sister Jean gave me a kitchen shower. I picked up a circular metal pan and chirped with delight, "For bundt cakes!"

"No, that's a Jello mold," said Mom. She handed me a larger pan. "*That's* for bundt cakes."

I had a lot to learn—but I found excellent recipes in *The Art of French Cooking*, and my specialties soon included beef bourguignon, chicken Bordeaux, and crème caramel.

My search for an apartment was more immediately successful. I found a perfect home on 72nd Street between Broadway and West End Avenue—a short walk from Lincoln Center and 25 blocks from the heart of the theater district. The apartment was in the Westover, an air-conditioned, newly renovated building with two elevators and a 24-hour doorman. The spacious third-floor apartment had a huge living/dining room, a small, separate kitchen, and a large, walk-in pantry. The bedroom was almost as big as the living room and had a newly renovated bathroom and another walk-in closet. Four large windows (two in each of the main rooms) looked south across 72nd Street.

I also found a perfect living room set: a mid-century walnut and black Naugahyde sofa and chair with a coffee table and end tables that were walnut with black slate tops. I took Ray to the showroom without telling him which furniture I liked, and I was delighted when he walked briskly through the showroom, stopped at the black Naugahyde sofa and announced that this was the one. We agreed that black Naugahyde and walnut would look very theatrical on red wall-to-wall carpeting.

The pièce de résistance for the living room was a brand new, ebony-finish, studio upright piano. Ever since I had left the Met, I had missed having access to a piano. Before making a choice, I played a Steinway (the brand I had played at the Wilmington Music School), a Mason & Hamlin (the brand my former piano teacher preferred and had in her home), and a Baldwin (a piano that was getting a lot of buzz because it was the choice of Leonard Bernstein). The Steinway had the brightest sound; the Mason & Hamlin had the most muted sound, and the Baldwin, somewhere in the middle, was my favorite. I told the salesman at Baldwin that I would pay in full with a money order, but he advised me to pay in monthly installments, so I could establish credit.

At the time, I couldn't imagine why I would ever need credit. Everyone I knew paid with cash, check, or money order. In Delaware, most telephone orders from Sears arrived COD (cash on delivery), although people with Sears accounts, like Mom, could pay by check. Anywhere in the country, I could make a plane reservation by telephone weeks in advance, pay cash at the airport minutes before take-off, and go on my merry way. I had heard about the new, all-purpose credit cards that allowed people to defer payment, but it seemed to me that whenever you add a middleman, prices go up, so I doubted the general public would embrace all-purpose credit cards. How wrong I was! I hadn't considered that businesses, not individuals, would set payment policy. As for the piano, since there were no interest charges, I compromised with the salesman and paid for the piano in two installments.

Finally, my wedding day arrived, and it was exactly what I had envisioned seven months earlier. The intimate candlelight ceremony began at 8:00 p.m. in Grace Episcopal Church, only a few minutes' drive from my parents' home. I wore a pale grey Bill Blass dress with silver and emerald trim that was shockingly short by Delaware standards and that I later wore to dozens of parties and opening nights (and shortened again when hemlines continued to rise). My matron of honor (Trick's wife) and both mothers looked beautiful in pale green cocktail dresses of their own choosing, and the men in the wedding party (Ray's older brother, my three younger brothers, and Dad) all looked elegant in black tie. Ray chose the music, and at Mom's request, sang at the beginning of the ceremony. The reception in my parents' home featured tea sandwiches, fresh strawberries, scrumptious wedding cake, and cases of champagne. Mom made sure there was punch for the teenagers, but their red faces suggested they were sneaking champagne.

For my first summer as a married woman, I signed on for a limited engagement of *Oklahoma!* at the New York State Theater in Lincoln Center—a ten-minute walk from my new home. The New York State Theater (now the David H. Koch Theater) was built for dance, and Agnes de Mille's exuberant choreography with its expansive leaps and runs couldn't have had a better showcase. I loved running and grand jetéing across the wide stage.

Oklahoma! was also a happy reunion with some of my favorite people. Gemze de Lappe again recreated Agnes de Mille's original choreography; Graciela Daniele was one of the dancers, and June Helmers (from *Hello, Dolly!*) and her husband, Alex Orfaly, were two of the singers. I played the role created by Bambi Linn in the original 1943 production—the role of the little girl who bursts into tears at Laurey's wedding in the "Dream Ballet."

I hadn't previously worked with any of the principals, but Lee Beery, a pretty brunette who later played Joanna Mills on the television series *Dark Shadows*, was a lovely Laurey; Bruce Yarnell, who played Frank Butler opposite Ethel Merman in the revival of *Annie Get Your Gun*, was an impressive Curly; Spiro Malas, a leading bass with the New York City Opera, was a rich-voiced, threatening Jud; and Margaret Hamilton, a Broadway veteran best known as the Wicked Witch of the West in the film *The Wizard of Oz*, was a terrific Aunt Eller.

One day, Gemze walked into rehearsal accompanied by Agnes de Mille, a vibrant woman in her sixties. Agnes de Mille was best known for her Broadway choreography, which included *Oklahoma!*, *Carousel*, *Brigadoon*, *Gentlemen Prefer Blondes*, and *Paint Your Wagon*, but it was her choreography for ballet companies that opened the door to Broadway.

In 1940, her first ballet for Ballet Theatre was *Black Ritual*, a ballet with a cast of 16 Black dancers, but it was not a success and disappeared from the repertoire. The following year, she staged a very successful comedic ballet, *Three Virgins and a Devil*, in which she played The Priggish Virgin, one of three virgins whose weaknesses are exploited by the devil. But de Mille's biggest success—and the ballet that gained her the job of choreographer for *Oklahoma!*—was *Rodeo*, a ballet she choreographed for the Ballet Russe de Monte Carlo in 1942. The choreography in *Rodeo* depicts the everyday lives of cowboys as they rope and ride and woo. In the original production, de Mille played the lead role of the young cowgirl who acts like a boy to be liked by the boys, but discovers that the way to get their attention is to put on a dress. On opening night, *Rodeo* received 22 curtain calls, and Rogers and Hammerstein decided to hire Agnes de Mille to choreograph *Oklahoma!*.

As I write this in 2023, there is a terrific one-minute 56-second clip on YouTube (posted by the Rodgers & Hammerstein channel) of Agnes de Mille describing how she came up with some of the movements in *Rodeo*, and then showing how they should be danced—a perfect example of a choreographer who can explain and demonstrate exactly what she wants.

In the summer of 1969, in a rehearsal room at the New York State Theater, Agnes de Mille demonstrated the subtle hand movements in "Many a New Day," and explained the everyday rituals they represented—smoothing out corsets, fluffing up lace, and making sure every hair was in place. She performed the pulsing arm movements during the long runs across the stage in the "Dream Ballet" and looked like a bird about to take wing. What a treat to work with her!

During tech rehearsals, Margaret Hamilton regaled us with stories about the filming of *The Wizard of Oz*. One story, however, was a cautionary tale: During a special effect for the Wicked Witch of the West, her broom burst into flames, and she was badly burned. Six weeks later, when she returned to the set, she had to wear gloves to cover the burns on her hands. The producers assured her that the effect was safe—that they had worked out all of the problems—and tried to bully her into doing the stunt. She flatly refused. Her stand-in did the shot, and as Margaret Hamilton feared, her stand-in was burned and rushed to the hospital.

Today, unions for the performing arts have negotiated safety provisions for many situations, but it still isn't uncommon for producers, directors, and choreographers to bully, cajole, or rush performers into doing things that aren't safe. Performers must stop and ask themselves, "What is the risk? Is it a risk I am willing to take?" Whenever I was placed in potentially dangerous situations, I reminded myself that jobs are temporary, but damage to my body could last a lifetime. At the Met, when I learned that stage rehearsals for the dancers had been delayed because some of the stage elevators were malfunctioning, I informed Dame Alicia, who promptly took the dancers out of the scene. At auditions, on the rare occasions I was paired with a dancer who posed a hazard, I asked for a different partner; both times that I can recollect, I got the job. I was willing to try anything when I had a strong partner and someone to spot us (catch anyone who needs catching), but I preferred to err on the side of safety.

The opening night of *Oklahoma!* at the New York State Theater didn't have the high stakes of a new show that would live or die on its reviews, but Ray and I made the evening special by having a late dinner after the show at Sardi's restaurant on West 44th Street.

Sardi's was and is a show business institution that dates back to the 1920s. The interior décor, like the front awning, is burgundy, and the restaurant walls are covered with caricatures of Broadway personalities. The first 700 caricatures were drawn by Alex Gard in return for one meal a day at the restaurant, and Sardi's became a popular place for press releases and announcements, including the Tony nominations.

In 1969, *The New York Times* was located on West 43rd Street. On opening nights, someone from the producer's office would wait outside the building, buy one of the first copies of the morning paper, and run to Sardi's where the producer would read the review out loud. Everyone in the restaurant would celebrate or commiserate depending on the review. On the opening night of *Oklahoma!*, reviews came in from various newspapers throughout the evening, and every review was positive. Most critics loved the ballet, loved the music, and loved or liked the cast. I was thrilled to hear the producer read Jerry Tallmer's review in the *New York Post*, in which Tallmer wrote, "I was also taken with an adorable little thing named Lee Wilson." However, most reviewers described the plot as "a bit inane," "antiseptic," and a "fairytale" that "didn't seem relevant."

It seemed to me that *Oklahoma!* was a happy company, and one of the brightest rays of sunshine was Lee Roy Reams, who played Will Parker. One day, Lee Roy told me he had invited ballerina Suzanne Farrell to see the show and would bring her backstage so I could meet her. Everyone in the dance world was buzzing about Suzanne Farrell. She had been a star ballerina and the latest muse of choreographer George Balanchine at the New York City Ballet until earlier that year when she had married Paul Mejia, another dancer in the company. Balanchine, who wanted Farrell for himself, had made life at NYCB impossible for the young couple who were now unemployed. *Where would Suzanne dance? Would her rift with Balanchine terminate her career?* I was eager to meet the young woman who had dared to defy the god of American ballet, a man 41 years her senior, her employer from the time she was in her mid-teens, and a man accustomed to getting his own way.

However, when Lee Roy Reams and Suzanne Farrell arrived at the stage door, the security guards refused to allow Farrell backstage.

Lee Roy explained that Suzanne was a childhood friend and that she was his guest, but security was adamant. George Balanchine had given the order not to allow Suzanne Farrell backstage. It didn't matter that *our* company was in residence, and Balanchine's was not. It didn't matter that Suzanne Farrell was an acclaimed ballerina whose picture had been on the cover of *Life* magazine and that the company of *Oklahoma!* wanted to meet her.

Eventually, Suzanne Farrell was forced to leave the country to find a steady job. In her memoir, *Holding On to the Air,* she wrote, "I knew my career might change when I married Paul, but I honestly didn't believe it would."

Like Suzanne, I knew my career might change with marriage. I certainly anticipated taking more time between jobs to travel with Ray—like flying to Houston after the demise of *Love Match* instead of flying home to New York—but I too underestimated the effect of marriage on my career.

6

La Strada (1969)

Like most dancers, I auditioned for new shows as soon as I knew the closing date of my current show, and, like most dancers, I usually took the first job I was offered. Some performers seemed to go from one hit to the next; others went from flop to flop, but it was impossible to know in advance which shows would be hits and which would be flops.

In 1966, the new Broadway musical *Breakfast at Tiffany's* seemed a sure-fire success. The Truman Capote novella on which the musical was based had already become an Oscar-winning film. The music and lyrics were by Bob Merrill (music and lyrics for *Carnival!*, lyrics for *Funny Girl*), and the cast was headed by Mary Tyler Moore (*The Dick Van Dyke Show*), Richard Chamberlain (*Dr. Kildare*), and Larry Kert (*West Side Story*). The show even had a huge advance. However, to avoid disastrous reviews and angry audiences, producer David Merrick closed *Breakfast at Tiffany's* after only four previews in New York.

On the other hand, nine years later, a musical about dancers, with no above-the-title stars, opened at the Public Theater Off Broadway with book, music, and lyrics by people with no previous Broadway musical credits in those categories. This show became the Tony– and Pulitzer Prize–winning sensation *A Chorus Line*.

Every new show is a crapshoot.

In September 1969, after the limited engagement of *Oklahoma!* at the New York State Theater, I began rehearsals for a new Broadway musical, *La Strada*. The show was written and produced by Oscar– and Emmy–nominated writer/producer Charles K. Peck, Jr., based on the original screenplay for the Oscar-winning Italian film *La Strada*. The music and lyrics were by Lionel Bart (*Oliver!*).

In 1969, there were no VHS tapes or DVDs. Films played in theaters, and then some of them played on TV. *La Strada* had opened in the U.S. in 1956, when I was only 10 years old, so I hadn't seen it, and I didn't know anyone who had. However, I knew and liked Bernadette Peters (née Lazzara), who was in my acting classes with David LeGrant and was playing the lead role of Gelsomina. Bernadette was only 21 years old, but she had been performing since she was a child and had recently won awards for playing Ruby in *Dames at Sea* Off Broadway and Josie Cohan in *George M!* on Broadway—both upbeat roles with tap-dancing. She was talented, cute as a button, and easy to work with. Gelsomina was her first leading role in a Broadway musical.

The only other person I had worked with was the show's choreographer, Alvin Ailey, the great American dancer and choreographer who had founded the Alvin Ailey American Dance Theater. Three years earlier, while I was dancing with the Metropolitan Opera Ballet, Alvin had choreographed *Antony and Cleopatra*, the extravagantly budgeted opera that had opened the new Metropolitan Opera House in Lincoln Center. I admired Alvin's choreography and loved his sense of humor, so I wanted to work with him again.

At the audition for *La Strada*, Alvin gave a rousing dance combination that ended with knee slides to the footlights. I had never done knee slides, didn't own a pair of kneepads, and didn't want to risk my knees, so while the other dancers slid on their knees toward the footlights, I jogged downstage, put both hands onto the floor, got onto my knees, and with a big grin on my face, threw my arms into the air with everyone else. That choice could have cost me the job, but it didn't. Alvin placed me in the lineup of dancers he was hiring for the show.

As soon as the dancers were dismissed, I asked the stage manager if there were any small roles I might read for. He conferred with the director, Alan Schneider, and informed me that I could play the role of Sister Claudia, a young nun who had several nice scenes with Bernadette.

Really?! "Don't I have to read for it?"

"No," said the stage manager. "The role is yours. However,

you can't *tell* anyone that you're playing Sister Claudia because it's been promised to one of the singers, and the director is planning to rehearse her for a few weeks and then switch to you before the opening in Detroit."

Yikes!

This maneuver was terribly unfair to the other girl. It would also deprive me of rehearsal time—but I could imagine Alan Schneider's strategy: He wanted a soprano with glorious high notes, and the soprano wanted a speaking part, so he offered her the role of Sister Claudia. He also wanted me. If the soprano and I both believed we had the role, we would sign our contracts. The soprano would be disappointed when I replaced her, but would probably think it was her own fault. She probably wouldn't give two weeks' notice because by then, she would be emotionally invested in the show, and if she quit, she couldn't go back on unemployment insurance. Of course, if Alan Schneider could do this to the singer, he could do it to me. What if he were promising a third girl that she could open the show in New York?

In any event, I had no doubt that if he liked the singer's performance better than mine, he would put her back into the role. Alan Schneider would start rehearsals with a dancer who didn't trust him, and shortly thereafter, he would have an unhappy singer who would probably be furious if she learned that I had been promised the role before she had signed her contract. This was not an auspicious beginning, but I decided to take the job.

Rehearsals began with a reading of the script: Gelsomina is a sweet, but slow-witted girl whose destitute mother sells her to Zampano, a strongman, who travels from town to town performing one trick—breaking a chain by expanding his chest. Zampano dresses Gelsomina like a clown, and teaches her to blow on a trumpet, beat a drum, and pass a hat to collect the tips on which they live. Zampano abuses the girl, who is fascinated by Mario, a tightrope-walking clown who makes fun of Zampano. In a fit of anger, Zampano hits Mario and kills him. Gelsomina becomes a whimpering wreck, so Zampano leaves her behind. Several years later, Zampano, haunted by the memory of Gelsomina, is devastated to learn that she is dead.

At the end of the reading, I flashed back to the first reading of *Here's Where I Belong.* After the earlier reading, one cast member had whispered to another, "We're in another flop." At the time, I had wondered: *how can anyone judge a show from one reading—before the show is even staged*? Now, less than two years later, I was almost sure I was in another flop. However, my two contrasting roles as Sister Claudia and Eva (one of Gelsomina's sisters) gave me a good showcase.

The producer arranged for the cast to see a screening of the Italian-language film. The black and white cinematography underscored the bleakness of the story; the close-ups of Giulietta Masina as Gelsomina were haunting, and the Italian streets, the Italian language, the religious parade, and the bleak seaside and snow-covered landscapes transported viewers to another country. However, none of that would appear in the musical. On stage, everything would be in color; there wouldn't be haunting close-ups of Gelsomina; the language would be English, and even Ming Cho Lee couldn't create expansive Italian landscapes behind the proscenium arch.

Bernadette was perfectly cast as Gelsomina and proved she could play drama as well as comedy. Vincent Beck (*Gypsy, Bells Are Ringing*) had the rugged sex appeal of Anthony Quinn, who had played Zampano in the film. Offstage, Vinnie was soft-spoken and warm—a big contrast with his character. Larry Kert, the original Tony in *West Side Story*, was perfect for Mario, the agile, tightrope-walking clown. The fourth important role was Marita, a woman who loves Mario despite his infidelities and who lives in fear that Mario might fall to his death. Patricia Marand, who had created the role of Lois Lane in *It's a Bird... It's a Plane... It's Superman* and had played Aldonza in *Man of La Mancha*, was a powerful presence with a powerhouse voice. Her song "My Turn to Fall" was heart-wrenching. However, Patricia Marand disappeared in the blink of an eye. *Did she quit*? *Was she fired*? Nobody seemed to know. The role of Marita was greatly diminished, and "My Turn to Fall" was cut.

We were told that Lionel Bart, the composer and lyricist, was wrestling with drug and alcohol problems in England and would not be able to participate in rehearsals or the out-of-town run in

Detroit—discouraging news. New songs, written by Elliot Lawrence (music) and Martin Charnin (lyrics), would later supplement and replace songs by Bart.

Director Alan Schneider, known for his direction of dark plays with small casts, like *Waiting for Godot* and *Entertaining Mr. Sloane*, had never directed a Broadway musical. During rehearsals, he whispered his direction to individual actors while everyone else wondered what he was saying and how it might affect them.

I was officially the understudy for Sister Claudia, but Alan wouldn't allow me to watch rehearsals of the Sister Claudia scenes, so I had to learn the blocking from the singer I was supposed to replace. (She was, as I had anticipated, a soprano with glorious high notes.) When I asked her if she had been given any direction other than blocking, she said, "None."

Just before the first run-through, the stage manager informed me that I was playing Sister Claudia in the run-through. *Yikes*! This was my audition, and the entire creative team was watching—including the set, lighting, and costume designers. I did what I had rehearsed at home, and after my scenes, Larry Kert told me that he loved the walk I had created for the character. I was thrilled. I had decided to move like the female dancers in the Moiseyev Ballet—as if gliding on roller skates—so that my graceful movement in the nun's habit would contrast with the awkwardness of Gelsomina. Alan Schneider said nothing to me, but the role was apparently mine—at least for now.

In October, *La Strada* began a short run at the Fisher Theatre in Detroit, Michigan. Detroit was cold and bleak, and the stage manager warned us to travel in groups to avoid being mugged. A feeling of impending danger followed us into the theater because we never knew what to expect.

Alan moved Bernadette from stage left to stage right just before a big dance number, but didn't tell the ensemble, so we charged onto the stage and nearly trampled the star. There was dance chaos until we adjusted our positions around her.

In one of the last scenes in the show, I looked for my sight cue—the entrance of another girl—but she didn't appear. When the curtain came down, I learned that the stage manager had grabbed her in the wings just before her entrance and informed her that she had been fired.

The stage manager gave me a handwritten note from Alan for Sister Claudia: "I can't see you. I can't hear you." Bernadette had a body mic, and I didn't, so I couldn't judge our relative volumes, but the mother of the little girl in the show told me that she could see my face clearly and that my volume was the same as Bernadette's. Nevertheless, I increased my volume and cheated front. Alan gave me the note again: "I can't see you. I can't hear you." I asked him what he meant. "Exactly what I said. I can't see you. I can't hear you." He replaced me as Sister Claudia.

Alvin Ailey created a romantic pas de deux for one of the male dancers and me—a ballet that showed Gelsomina what her relationship with Zampano was lacking—the warmth of love. One evening, as I left for dinner, I overheard Alan tell the stage manager, "Make sure Hal [Hal Hastings, the conductor] knows the ballet is cut. When those two are dancing, no one's looking at Bernadette."

Like Noel Willman, Alan Schneider didn't seem to appreciate the function of dance. Like Danny Daniels' brilliant choreography for *Love Match*, Alvin's beautiful pas de deux for *La Strada* wouldn't make it to New York.

I wasn't the only person who had problems with Alan Schneider. Larry Kert learned some acrobatics for the show and insisted, against Alan's wishes, on having a padded mat for safety during one of his tricks. At one performance, there was no mat. Larry hesitated, but did the trick. As he exited into the wings, he whispered to the stage manager, "What happened to the mat?"

"Alan said you don't need it."

Larry froze, then replied with a tense smile. "If the mat is missing again, I'll walk off stage." He walked away, then turned back. "And I probably won't come back."

The mat was never missing again.

The most dramatic clash was between Alan and Vinnie Beck, our Zampano. At the end of an afternoon rehearsal, minutes before the mandatory dinner break prior to a performance, Alan announced from his seat in the house that while Vinnie was singing new lyrics he had been given that afternoon, he would also be driving his motorized bike onto the large circular turntable. He would begin upstage right and drive counterclockwise against the clockwise movement of the turntable; he would exit the turntable downstage left and stop at the very edge of the orchestra pit. Vinnie was nervous about the maneuver and asked for a rehearsal with the bike. Alan said there wasn't time. The stage manager sided with Vinnie and set up the scene. The turntable began to move. Vinnie drove onto the turntable, but he didn't drive fast enough to reach downstage left before a billboard on the moving turntable blocked his exit.

Alan yelled from the audience. "Stop! Get off the bike! Stan will do it!"

Stan Page, a dancer and assistant stage manager, executed the maneuver perfectly.

"See?" Alan called out to Vinnie. "That's what you'll do tonight." Alan ran down the aisle, hopped onto the stage, put his arm around Vinnie, and whispered into his ear.

Zampano's booming voice filled the theater. "GET YOUR HANDS OFF ME, OR I'LL BASH IN YOUR FUCKING FACE!"

Everyone froze.

Alan let go of Vinnie, shrugged, tugged on his baseball cap, and put his arm back on Vinnie's shoulder.

Vinnie brushed Alan's hand away as if it were a bug, marched out of the theater, and we never saw Vinnie again.

Stephen Pearlman, Vinnie's understudy, became the new Zampano.

When I talked to Ray at night, I shared my frustration with the show, and Ray shared his frustration with me. He was lonely. He didn't understand why his wife would rather be in a dangerous city with a flop musical than home in bed with him. We were newlyweds, and he was sleeping alone.

In the past, when Ray and I had been working in different cities, I had hung up the telephone with a happy glow, but now, every time we talked, I felt torn between my responsibility to the show and my responsibility to my husband.

Alan Schneider's wife came to Detroit, and when she left to go home, Alan saw her off at the stage door, got into the elevator with another girl and me, put his arm around the other girl and asked her if she would come to his room that night after the performance. She wiggled and giggled and said she would. Alan looked at me with a swagger.

I knew that Ray could find company as easily as Alan Schneider, and Ray had made it clear that he felt neglected, so I gave two weeks' notice to the show. Almost immediately, I had trouble keeping food in my stomach. *Had I caught a bug, or was my body reacting to my decision to leave the show*? I sat on the sidelines during rehearsals and watched my replacement, Odette Panaccione, learn new choreography that I performed in the evening. When Odette looked secure, I asked Alvin when she would be ready to perform. Alvin said she could do the matinee the following day. We agreed that it didn't make sense for me to continue performing just to serve out my notice when Odette could benefit from stage time before previews in New York.

However, 15 minutes before the matinee, the dance captain informed me that *someone* had overruled Alvin, and I was doing the matinee. I slapped on make-up, and while I watched Gelsomina beat her little drum, a tree flew in and almost hit me on the head. I finished the performance and made a plane reservation for New York.

As I left my hotel room with my suitcases and a note for the stage manager, I came face to face with Alvin. I told him I was ill and was flying back to New York, and he laughed. "Good for you! Come say goodbye. Everyone's in a meeting right there." He gestured to a room between my room and the elevator.

I hesitated. As much as I liked Alvin, I didn't want to antagonize Alan and the producer.

"You really should," he said. "I can't wait to see Alan's face when he finds out you're leaving."

Alvin and I walked into the room, and conversation stopped. I told a sea of astonished faces that I was sick and was flying home. Alvin burst out laughing.

Bernadette Peters (center stage) played the lead role of Gelsomina in *La Strada*. Susan Goeppinger (holding the rope) and I (on my knees) played two of her sisters—until I gave my notice and left the show in Detroit. Photo by Martha Swope ©The New York Public Library.

As I walked down the hall to the elevator, I could still hear Alvin's laugh.

La Strada opened and closed on December 14, 1969. That night, I watched a television review that showed rehearsal footage of the opening scene, and there I was playing Gelsomina's sister Eva. I could almost hear Alvin laugh, but I felt a pang of regret. I had given up an opening night on Broadway, a Broadway credit, additional paychecks and per diem, and the right to collect unemployment insurance after the show closed. I had made a career choice that I would never have considered if I had been single.

7

Commercials, Milliken, and *The Sound of Music* (1969–1970)

I wanted it all: health, happiness, a good career, and a good marriage. I was born with good health, and my career made me happy. Marriage was the final ingredient in my life soup. I had always assumed that one day I would marry. While I was growing up, all of the women I knew were married—except my piano teacher, Miss Littell. Miss Littell was a wonderful teacher who sent me picture postcards from Switzerland during her summer vacations, but her teenaged students snickered behind her back that she was an old maid. My brothers and I grew up playing the card game Old Maid, and the Old Maid was the ugly card that defined the loser. I didn't see myself as an object of ridicule or a loser, so I always planned to get married, but adjusting to marriage was a challenge.

I was five years old when my middle brother was born. In anticipation of his birth, my father added two bedrooms and a bathroom to our home in Wilmington, Delaware. From that day forward, with the exception of a few months in Cannes, I had had a room of my own. Someone else had always cleaned my room and laundered the sheets and towels. Now, I had to share space and housekeeping duties with Ray. Ray was good about sharing the work, but when I was out of town, Ray had to do it all, and when he was out of town, I had to do it all. For many years prior to my marriage, I had made decisions based on what I thought was best for me and my career. Now I had to consider someone else. Marriage had made my life exponentially more complex.

When I arrived in New York from the disaster of *La Strada*, I was the sickest I had ever been. I didn't have a family doctor, but I remembered that every *Playbill* listed the name of a doctor who was on call for Actors' Equity performances on Broadway, and I asked Ray to call him and tell him that I was a member of Actors' Equity. The doctor came to our apartment and gave me an injection that allowed me to keep food in my stomach and sleep for hours.

This was the second time in two weeks that I had relied upon Actors' Equity. The first was after writing out my notice. I didn't know whom to give it to. Did I have to track down the producer and deliver my notice in person, or could I give it to the stage manager? Months earlier, I had met Gina Belkin, who was on the board of Actors' Equity, and she had given me her business card with the assurance that if I ever needed help—anytime, anywhere—I could call her. So, I did. As soon as I told her that I was in Detroit with *La Strada*, she said, "Poor baby! How can we help?" Within minutes, she had assured me that my notice contained all the necessary information and that I could give it to the stage manager.

For the remaining weeks of 1969, I was content to play wife. Ray was performing at City Center in *Help, Help, the Globolinks!*, a comic opera by Gian Carlo Menotti that was a perfect antidote to the gloom of *La Strada*. On Ray's nights off, we would listen to opera or watch our new Sony color TV that a bank had given me for opening a CD. (In those days, banks competed for business with gifts of appliances and TV sets, and none of my banks had minimum balance fees, photocopy fees, money order fees, fees for printing checks, or any of the other fees that banks charge today. My checks and money orders were free, and bank employees cheerfully made photocopies.)

With the dawn of a new decade, I was ready to go back to work, but I was determined to work in New York until Ray was better established and more secure. Right on cue, Ray's career took a big jump forward. In January, he auditioned for the Metropolitan Opera, and in February, made his debut as a baritone soloist—although by then, he was considering a transition to tenor. Ray liked the steady paychecks, but was unsure he had made the right decision by joining the Met. Shortly after we had begun dating, Ray had told me that he hoped to sing at the Met when he was 40 or 45, but here he was—just 27—probably the youngest baritone soloist on the roster.

One of his first days at the theater, he came home distraught because he had been assigned a bass-baritone role.

"Can you sing it?" I asked.

"Yes, but it won't be good for my voice."

"Then tell them the role is too low."

"I can't do that! They're paying me so much money!"

"The people assigning the roles don't know the tessitura of every new singer. You have to tell them. Let them know you're a very high baritone—maybe someday a tenor."

He did, and the Met gave him higher roles. Next came the challenge of *La Traviata*. "They want me to walk across the stage holding two champagne glasses and then shake hands. It's impossible."

I took two champagne glasses out of a cabinet. "Hold out your left hand—palm up." I put one glass between his second and third fingers and another between his fourth and fifth. "Can you shake hands?" He could. (I had seen more than one *Traviata*.)

New York City was not only the most important city in America for musical theater and opera—it was also the hub of the advertising business, which included TV commercials. TV commercials could be lucrative, and many of them were filmed in New York City. I could work without leaving the city and also get acting credits that didn't define me as a dancer.

At that time, most commercial actors in New York worked with many agents. A good manager could cobble together a network of agents to make sure her clients got as many auditions as possible. A good manager could also smooth the ruffled feathers of agents who wanted to submit an actress only to find out that another agent had already submitted her.

A girl I saw regularly at auditions recommended her manager, Fifi Tanzy. Fifi's daughter Jeanne had performed in several Broadway shows, and Fifi had acted as her daughter's manager before adding additional clients. Fifi was warm, honest, organized, and well-connected. Her clients were welcome to drop into her office at any time, and I enjoyed chatting with her about the latest Broadway

In the early 1970s, actors handed out 8 × 10 headshots for theater auditions. However, "composites" with multiple photographs were becoming popular for commercials. Photos by Joan Weaver.

shows. I hired Fifi in January and within a week, half a dozen agents were submitting me for commercials.

My most memorable agent meeting was with Gus Schirmer, an

agent, manager, and director who had represented Ethel Merman and Lee Remick, and was then representing Sandy Duncan. Fifi told me that Gus Schirmer was the best person to submit me for the role of Liesl in *The Sound of Music* at the Jones Beach Marine Theater—a coveted summer job that began casting in early February. When I walked into Gus's office, he barked, "You can't play Liesl. You're not blonde."

"The original Liesl on Broadway wasn't blonde—nor was the girl in the movie."

"Can you sing?"

"Yes."

"Can you dance?"

"Yes."

"Tell them you have a blonde wig."

Gus immediately submitted me for a TV commercial for Skandi, a new beverage from Pepsico. All of the other actresses in the waiting room were blonde. I was wondering why Gus had submitted me until I booked the job and the producers bought me a blonde wig.

Unfortunately, Skandi didn't sell, and to the best of my knowledge, the commercial never aired. However, from time to time, Skandi bottles pop up on rare memorabilia sites.

I enjoyed shooting commercials, including spots for press-on earrings and Hour after Hour deodorant, but I was eager to get back on stage. I lined up two terrific shows in quick succession: the Milliken Show at the Waldorf Astoria hotel, followed by the role of Liesl in *The Sound of Music* at the Jones Beach Marine Theater.

The Milliken Show was a breakfast show that hired Broadway talent and paid Broadway salaries. Competition was fierce because the show could employ not only performers who were unemployed, but also performers who were currently working on Broadway. More than 1,500 people attended each performance in which the performers wore the latest fashions made of Milliken fabrics. The plot was different every year, but every show ended with the cast singing: "If the tag on the fabric says Milliken, it's a material success."

In the spring of 1970, Danny Daniels was the choreographer, and the stars included Dorothy Loudon (who later won the Tony Award for Best Actress in a Musical playing Miss Hannigan in *Annie*), and René Auberjonois (who had played Father Mulcahy in the film *MASH* and was about to win the Tony Award as Best Featured Actor in a Musical for *Coco*).

I was too small to be an adult dancer, so I auditioned as a Milli-kiddie, children's size 10, and was hired along with two 11-year-olds and a 14-year-old.

I loved dancing in the Milliken show. Danny's choreography was exuberant, and it was fun to be one of the kids. Everyone worked hard to make the show as good as it could be, but there were no worries about whether the show would run or what the critics might say. We rehearsed at the Diplomat Hotel, which was much nicer than rehearsal studios, and in the morning, the producers provided an array of pastries, juice, and coffee. In the afternoon, there were boxes of Russell Stover chocolates. On performance days, we arrived at the Waldorf Astoria hotel to find a Continental breakfast buffet with waiters to serve us. The audiences were enthusiastic, and every seat was filled. At the end of the run, the performers could keep all of their clothes. For many dancers, the Milliken Show was a highlight of the year.

After my last performance in the Milliken show, I went directly to my first rehearsal for *The Sound of Music,* a musical based on the lives of the Trapp Family Singers. The show is set in Austria in early 1938—just before the Nazis take over the country. Like *Oklahoma!*, *The Sound of Music* is a Rodgers and Hammerstein musical that has charming dialogue (book by Howard Lindsay and Russel Crouse), tunefully delicious songs, and a plot that resonates with women.

Maria, ever since she was a little girl, has dreamed of becoming a nun and living in Nonnberg Abbey. She is a postulant when the Mother Abbess assigns her a temporary job as a governess to seven children who have no mother and an absent father. Maria falls in love with the children, then with their father, and has to choose between the life/career she has always wanted and marriage to the man she loves.

When the show opened in 1959, it was legal and common for employers to fire women when they married, and the vast majority of women with small children didn't work outside the home, but even in the 21st century, women struggle with marriage/career choices, and many, like Maria, find that the career they wanted when they were children is unrealistic—or not the best use of their talents—and they end up doing something entirely different. *The Sound of Music* is sold on cute children singing "Do Re Mi" and "The Lonely Goatherd," and critics often describe the show as "saccharine," but the marriage/career plotline keeps the story grounded and relevant. There is also the imminent Nazi annexation of Austria that hangs over the family like the sword of Damocles. When the Nazis finally take control of the country, the family escapes to Switzerland to the sound of the inspirational song "Climb Every Mountain." Yes, the von Trapps have escaped—but they have left behind their beautiful home, their friends, and their possessions. They are now refugees—immigrants who will have to start over in a new country—and Americans, immigrants themselves, can relate to that experience.

I had wanted to play 16-year-old Liesl, the oldest of the seven children, ever since I had seen the show on Broadway during my senior year of high school, and my desire increased in 1965 as I watched the Julie Andrews/Christopher Plummer film because I was dismayed that the innocent Liesl on stage had been transformed into an aggressive flirt on screen. Where would Liesl have learned to tiptoe her fingers up a man's arm, and twirl locks of his hair? Liesl has been raised by a strict father and a series of governesses on an estate that has not hosted a party in years. Rolf, the telegram delivery boy, knows what is happening politically—he warns Liesl that her father is in danger—but Liesl has no clue. She proudly and naively tells Rolf, "Don't worry about Father. He was decorated for bravery."

Throughout their dialogue and the song "You Are Sixteen," Rolf takes the lead, and Liesl follows. The kiss that ends the scene is most charming when it comes as a surprise to both, as it did in the Jones Beach production when I spun toward Rolf, stopped abruptly so as not to run into him, but cantilevered at the hips, so my lips met his. Then, according to the script, Liesl and Rolf "break away in confusion." Rolf jumps on his bicycle and rides off. Liesl "shouts with joy and runs off in the opposite direction." Liesl doesn't shout in triumph after achieving a goal, but with joy at the realization that she has just been kissed by a boy. Oh, wow!

Liesl's innocence at the beginning of the show allows her to grow, and contrasts with the cynicism and sophistication of Captain von Trapp's friends, Max and Elsa. When Liesl is innocent, her discovery that Rolf is collaborating with the Nazis is a devastating revelation. A worldly Liesl undercuts the power of that moment.

Constance Towers, who had starred in *Anya* on Broadway, was our beautiful Maria with a lovely singing voice and emotional depth. Everyone in the cast adored her. John Michael King, who had created the role of Freddy Eynsford-Hill in the original cast of *My Fair Lady*, was a stern Captain with a warm heart and a rich singing voice. He and Connie made a telegenic couple. Christopher Hewett (a Broadway veteran and later Mr. Belvedere on TV) was an outstanding Max. He was so delightfully entertaining and informative about what the Nazis were doing that it was easy to understand why the Captain allowed Max to freeload at his home—even though he knew that Max was cooperating with the Nazis. Vincent Alexander, who had played 14-year-old Friedrich in the national tour, choreographed the Jones Beach production and played Rolf, the telegram delivery boy who works with the Nazis, but saves the lives of the von Trapp family.

The Jones Beach Marine Theater was an outdoor theater that seated more than eight thousand people. At night, under the stars, the view could be magical. From July 1 through September 6, we performed seven nights a week—with only one rainout the entire summer. Every night at 6:00 p.m., a bus picked us up on 42nd Street and drove us to the theater in Long Island; after the performance, it brought us back to 42nd Street.

The seats in the theater overlooked the water. Directly in front of the audience was the orchestra and then a wide dock where Rolf and I sang and danced "You Are Sixteen." The Abbey and the dressing rooms were on an island in the bay. Between the dock and the island was "the moat." Actors could travel between the dock and the island by swinging bridges or by boat. Floating sets, including the von Trapp family home, would float into the moat and attach to the dock. During the intermission, the floating sets were cleared; a bridge swung open, and Guy Lombardo came speeding into the moat on his boat to perform for the crowd.

I loved playing Liesl. Every night as Rolf sang, "You Are Sixteen," I felt a bounce of excitement in my belly, and my heart beat faster. I loved being part of a large family, learning to trust and then love Maria, mourning her loss when she left, celebrating her return, and regaining the closeness with my father. Even today, when I read the scene in which Liesl feels betrayed by Rolf, tears form in my eyes. For Liesl, the show is an emotional rollercoaster within the cocoon of a loving family.

Decades later, I read a *Performances* magazine interview with Connie Towers in which she said that her favorite moment in *The Sound of Music* is the reprise of "You Are Sixteen" in which Maria advises Liesl to "wait a year or two." Connie's warmth and love and understanding enveloped me like a warm blanket. If only every girl could have a mother like that!

Shortly after the show opened, the stage manager told me that Richard Rodgers had enjoyed my performance and wanted me to sing for him because he thought I might be right for the role of the youngest daughter in a new musical he was writing.

Wow! Oh! Eek!

I was a dancer who sang, not a singer, and composers generally want highly trained singers who can make their music soar. On the other hand, Mr. Rodgers had heard me sing Liesl, so he had some idea of the quality of my voice. The audition was at Mr. Rodgers apartment on a weekday morning.

I had met Mr. Rodgers briefly five years earlier. At that time, I had already signed a contract for the Metropolitan Opera spring tour that gave the Met an option for the following season. However, I didn't know for sure that the Met would pick up the option, so, as a backup job, I auditioned for the summer run of *Carousel* at the New York State Theater.

When I arrived at the stage door, two security men in uniform told me to sign in and take the self-service elevator upstairs. When I got off the elevator, I didn't know where to go. I saw a middle-aged man seated on a chair across from the elevator. No one else was in sight, so I asked him if he knew where the ladies' dressing room was. He offered to show me the way and asked if I might be auditioning for *Carousel*. I said that I was, and he wished me luck as he pointed out the door to the dressing room.

A few minutes later, I walked into the audition room, and one of the dancers whispered, "Richard Rodgers is here."

"Where?"

"Right there." She pointed to the nice man who had escorted me down the hall.

At the end of the audition, I was offered the show, but I had to turn it down when the Met picked up my option.

By 1970, I knew that Richard Rodgers, like David Merrick, had a reputation for having a girl in every show, and I had heard that Mr. Rodgers liked his girls young, but I didn't consider that a problem. If Mr. Rodgers was looking for romance or high notes, I was the wrong girl; if he was looking for a dancer who could sing, I might fit the bill.

On the morning of my audition, Ray was agitated and obstructive. He informed me that it was inappropriate for a married woman to go to a man's apartment.

What?! I pointed out that my voice teachers and singing coaches were all men, and they all worked out of their apartments. I had never had a problem. "That's different," he said.

"If you were a world-famous composer and you wanted to hear a girl sing, would you ask her to come to your apartment where you have a perfectly tuned grand piano, or would you trek downtown and pay for a studio?" (I was guessing about the grand piano, but I was right.) "Richard Rodgers is at least 65 years old, and he walks with a cane. What do you think he's going to do? Hit me over the head with his cane?" I was not giving up the opportunity to sing for Richard Rodgers.

Nevertheless, my nerves were on edge when I arrived at his apartment. Mr. Rodgers answered the door himself, and while we exchanged "good mornings," I listened for the sound of someone else in the apartment. I heard nothing. Mr. Rodgers asked me if I wanted something to drink—coffee or water. I declined.

Mr. Rodgers walked slowly toward the grand piano in the far, right corner of the room. He placed his cane upright in the corner as he sat on the piano bench. I stood in the middle of the room facing him. He tapped the bench and told me to sit beside him.

Does he want me to sight read music, or is this his first move?

My alert system went from yellow to orange, but I sat on the bench to his right. I still had a clear escape route to the door. Mr. Rodgers played an arpeggio, and I sang. On the second arpeggio, he shifted to his right so his body was touching mine. I shifted right to give him room. He shifted right. I shifted right. Soon, I was squatting at the end of the bench with my left cheek barely touching the bench. I felt ridiculous. I was pretending to sit, and Mr. Rodgers knew I was pretending—but I wasn't going to be the one to give up. I slid my right foot to the side and stabilized my squatting position. I have no idea what sounds were coming out of my mouth, but I suspect they might have resembled the cries of a cat when someone steps on its tail. Mr. Rodgers informed me that he had heard enough, and I left.

As I walked to the bus stop, I wondered: *Is the role of the youngest daughter reserved for "his girl"? Is the role even available? Will I ever again be allowed to work in a show written or produced by Richard Rodgers?*

That last question, "Will I ever again be allowed to work in a show written or produced by Richard Rodgers?" may seem melodramatic—especially since my next job was playing Liesl in the Paper Mill Playhouse production of *The Sound of Music*—but I had no way of knowing what Mr. Rodgers might or might not do. Some powerful men simply do not allow young women (or young men) to evade their advances without repercussions.

A well-publicized example occurred in the film industry when actresses Mira Sorvino and Ashley Judd went public with their belief that producer Harvey Weinstein had launched a smear campaign against them because they had rejected his advances. Weinstein denied the allegations. However, as reported in *Variety, The Guardian, Time* magazine, and many other news outlets, producer/director Peter Jackson later confirmed that Miramax, Harvey Weinstein's company, had told him that Sorvino and Judd were "a nightmare to work with and we should avoid them at all costs." As a result, Peter Jackson took their names off the casting list for the blockbuster film series *The Lord of the Rings*, which he produced and directed. In 2020, Harvey Weinstein was convicted of rape and sentenced to prison, but like many powerful men, he had an organization that protected him for decades.

Sometimes, careers stall, and there can be many reasons for that, but one all-too-common reason is that the actor, singer, or dancer said "no" to a very powerful man.

The Sound of Music was well publicized, and throughout the summer, photographs of Maria, the Captain, and the children appeared in various newspapers. Two pages in my portfolio were now filled with photos and wonderful reviews both for the show and for me. One night, the stage manager walked over to my dressing table with a stack of mail. "Boy, are you popular," he said. That night when I got home, I opened the letters. Most were from companies that sold wedding gifts, sterling flatware, china, crystal, and honeymoon packages, but some were from charities thanking me for volunteering to sponsor African children. My best guess was that someone was filling out ads from magazines using my name and the Jones Beach Marine Theater as my address. I hoped it was a juvenile prank, not a stalker who was envisioning a future with me.

For the rest of the summer, every night after the company bus dropped me off in Times Square, instead of taking the quicker subway, I took the slower, but (I thought) safer, bus up to 72nd Street. Instead of reading a book as I traveled, I watched the people around me. When I walked the single block from the bus stop to the Westover, I walked close to the storefronts, so it would be difficult to push me into traffic or into a parked car. I was grateful for the brightly lit deli halfway down the block that stayed open until 2:00 a.m., and the 24-hour doorman at my building. The mail continued throughout the run, but I never found out who was behind it.

As the summer drew to a close, Christopher Hewett (Uncle Max) told me that he had been hired to direct an upcoming production of *The Sound of Music* at the Paper Mill Playhouse, and he wanted me to play Liesl. I accepted immediately and was honored when Chris invited me to attend the Rolf auditions and help choose the Rolf. (Vincent Alexander, my wonderful Rolf at Jones Beach, was choreographing the production before going back to college.) I enjoyed seeing the different interpretations of the young men who auditioned, and, of course, my reading with the prospective Rolfs allowed Chris to see how we worked together. Chris and I compared notes and agreed on our first choice and a backup. I could now visualize the new Rolf, and he could visualize me—not the girl in the movie whose Liesl was so different from mine.

Our feisty young Maria was Barbara Meister, who had played the role on the national tour and was a standby on Broadway. The Captain von Trapp was Erik Silju, who looked like a Norse god and was famous for his cigar commercial for Erik cigars (viewable on YouTube). Many people knew Erik only as an actor and were surprised at how well he sang, but Erik first came to the United States as a soloist with the Singing Boys of Norway, and had a long list of musical theater credits.

Harry Packwood, my new Rolf, drove the carpool with three of the nuns and me. We laughed all the way from New York to New Jersey and referred to ourselves as "Harry and his harem." When we had time, we stopped at the Dairy Queen for ice cream sundaes before the show. That fall, I reveled in Dairy Queen pineapple sundaes.

Liesl was not only a role I loved; it was also a supporting role on my résumé that people recognized. After tiny roles in Broadway and Broadway-bound flops, I hoped that the role of Liesl and several commercials for well-known products might give me more credibility as an actress and greater access to principal roles.

At the end of the run, I joined Ray in Houston where he sang Dr. Falke in *Die Fledermaus*, and the opera angels took us on tours of NASA and the Astrodome. It was inspiring to look at the control room of NASA where only seven months earlier, scientists had heard the chilling words, "Houston, we've had a problem here." At that time, Dad was one of the people NASA called to help—not, Dad told me, because he could fix the problem—he couldn't—not his field—but he knew who could. I have no idea whether or not Dad's referral helped NASA bring the astronauts home safely, but I was impressed that mission control had contacted him.

After Houston, we traveled to Boston, one of my favorite cities, where Ray sang the *Messiah* with the Handel and Haydn Society. It seemed to me that our marriage was on steadier ground. By mid-December, in plenty of time to enjoy the holidays, I lined up my next Broadway show, a new Alan Jay Lerner musical based on Vladimir Nabokov's brilliant and controversial novel *Lolita*.

8

Lolita, My Love (1971)

The Broadway audience was and is predominantly affluent, well-educated, and white. In the late 1960s, living conditions in the city were deteriorating. New York City had a transit strike, a teachers' strike, and a sanitation strike. Peep shows and movie theaters with XXX-rated films lined 42nd Street. Pimps, prostitutes, and drug dealers prowled the streets, and a growing number of homeless families huddled in doorways and slept in subways. Serious crimes reached historic highs, and Vincent Sardi, Jr., hired a private security firm to protect his employees as they came to and from work at his 44th Street restaurant. Members of the affluent, white, well-educated audience fled the city.

The deterioration of the city was not the only reason that Broadway ticket sales were plummeting. In 1968, the Dow Jones Average had approached the magic number of 1,000, but during the early 1970s, it dropped below 600. Audiences had less money to buy tickets, and angels had less money to invest. In 1970 and 1971, there were so few shows that the Tony Awards Nominating Committee selected only three nominees to compete for Best Musical instead of the usual four.

Also, during the 1960s, tastes in music were changing. Pop and rock music replaced show tunes on the radio, and show tunes lost their visibility. *The Ed Sullivan Show*, a reliable showcase for Broadway performers for more than two decades, went off the air in 1971.

By the end of the 1960s, the long, illustrious careers of writer/director George Abbott (*On Your Toes*, *Where's Charley?*, *The Pajama Game*) and composer/lyricist Irving Berlin (*Call Me Madam*, *Annie*

Get Your Gun) were coming to an end. The long, successful partnerships of Rodgers & Hammerstein and Lerner and Loewe had ended. In 1960, Oscar Hammerstein died, and Frederick Loewe retired to Palm Springs. In the following decade, Richard Rodgers wrote the music for three Broadway shows (*No Strings*, *Do I Hear a Waltz?*, and *Two by Two*), and Alan Jay Lerner wrote the book and lyrics for two (*On a Clear Day You Can See Forever* and *Coco*). Only *No Strings* in 1962 had a run of more than a year. By the early 1970s, it was unclear if either Rodgers or Lerner could equal his former success with a new collaborator.

In 1971, Alan Jay Lerner's new musical was *Lolita, My Love*. The show was based on Vladimir Nabokov's novel *Lolita*, the story of Humbert Humbert, a middle-aged European professor who is sexually obsessed with Dolores Haze, a 12-year-old girl, whom he calls "Lolita." Humbert marries Lolita's mother, Charlotte, to be close to her child, but when Charlotte reads Humbert's journal and discovers that Humbert is repulsed by her and lusts for her daughter, she is horrified, runs into the street, and is killed by an oncoming car. Humbert takes Lolita on a long road trip, suspects they are being followed, and Lolita disappears. Two years later, Lolita contacts Humbert because she needs money. She tells Humbert that she left him for Clare Quilty (who was, in fact, coordinating itineraries with Lolita), but she left Quilty when he wanted her to take part in an orgy. Humbert begs Lolita to come back to him, but Lolita is happily married and refuses. Humbert tracks down Quilty, and shoots him dead.

The novel is written from Humbert's point of view, and the pre-teen, auburn-haired Lolita is sketchily drawn as Humbert attempts to seduce readers into believing that his love for Lolita has elevated an ordinary, prepubescent child to the transcendent status of nymphet.

However, in the 1962 film that starred James Mason and Sue Lyon, Lolita's age was increased to 14, and she was played by a voluptuous, 15-year-old blonde, who was dressed and photographed to look older. In the film, the moment Lolita lowers her heart-shaped sunglasses to get a better look at Humbert, she defines herself as a worthy adversary, and her low-pitched, authoritative voice reinforces that perception. After the premiere of the film, the name "Lolita" was often used to describe a teenage temptress, rather than a child victim.

The creative team for the musical was provocative. The book and lyrics were by Alan Jay Lerner, who, like Nabokov, had dazzling verbal dexterity. The music was by John Barry, the Academy Award–winning composer of *Born Free* and the James Bond films. The director was Tito Capobianco, an Argentine who resembled the Italian movie star Giancarlo Giannini and was known for productions in which the acting, the movement, the staging, and the singing were coordinated for dramatic effect. The choreographer was the legendary Jack Cole (*Kismet, A Funny Thing Happened on the Way to the Forum, Man of La Mancha*), who was still wiry and energetic as he approached the age of 60.

At the dance auditions, after Jack Cole had chosen his dancers, including me, producer Norman Twain introduced the voluptuous 15-year-old blonde who was cast as Lolita—Annette Ferra. Annette's hair was styled like Sue Lyon's hair in the film, so it looked as if the Broadway *Lolita* might be following in the footsteps of the film.

I asked Norman if there were any small roles I might play, and he told me I could understudy the role of Lolita's best friend Mona, who would be played by Judy Garland's younger daughter, Lorna Luft. I told Norman that I was ambivalent about taking a chorus job, and Norman said he would look through the script to see if there might be anything he had overlooked—but he doubted it. He asked me to have lunch with him that Saturday at the Russian Tea Room so he could tell me more about the show and convince me to be a part of it.

The Russian Tea Room was a famous and expensive restaurant on West 57th Street near Carnegie Hall that was founded in the 1920s by members of the Russian Imperial Ballet (now the Mariinsky Ballet). I had walked by its red awning hundreds of times, but this was the first time I had seen the gloriously theatrical red and gold interior. Norman told me he had looked through the script and there was nothing for me except the Mona understudy. However, he thought *Lolita, My Love* was the best show ever written, and the cast was outstanding: John Neville, an acclaimed British actor whose

Broadway roles included Romeo and Hamlet, was playing Humbert Humbert. René Auberjonois was cast as Clare Quilty, and Dorothy Loudon was playing Charlotte, Lolita's mother.

I had worked with René and Dorothy in the Milliken Show, and I thought they were terrific. Norman also told me that Lorna Luft was no longer in the show, but a friend of mine, Mary Case, would play the role of Mona and understudy the role of Lolita. Mary was a pretty blonde, less voluptuous than Annette, who lived in my apartment building. Mary had ID that allowed her to buy wine, so I assumed she was at least 18—although I thought she could play younger. I told Norman I thought Mary might be an excellent Lolita. "She's too old," he said. I told him I thought an actress who was over 18, but looked younger, might give the role more depth and make audiences more comfortable than an underage girl, but Norman insisted that Lolita absolutely had to be a child. Norman asked me what it would take for me to sign on for the show. I asked for a modest amount above Equity scale, and he agreed.

The chaos of *Lolita, My Love* began on the first day of rehearsal. Leonard Frey, not René Auberjonois, was playing the role of Quilty, and Lorna Luft was back in the role of Mona. Choreographer Jack Cole told the dancers that the dance music for the girls wasn't written, so the girls sat on the floor the entire morning while the boys worked on eight bars of music. After the lunch break, Jack Cole returned to the studio 45 minutes late and grumpy. That night, Mary Case told me that she didn't know whether she was in the show. She said she was supposed to have lunch with Norman Twain at the Russian Tea Room (the same day and time that I had had lunch with him), but he had cancelled and she had heard nothing further. I said nothing about my lunch with Norman.

The next morning, Norman announced that Danny Daniels was replacing Jack Cole. One of Danny's conditions was that he could bring in some of his own dancers, so all of the current dancers would have to audition for Danny. As we left the studio, Norman pulled me aside and said, "Danny knows you. He loves you. You don't have to audition—but don't spread that around." My heart went out to the other dancers. They had signed contracts for a Broadway show and had probably celebrated with their friends. Now, they had to audition for a new choreographer, and many of them would soon be unemployed—and good shows were getting harder and harder to find.

During the next few days, dancers came and went. I asked Danny what had attracted him to *Lolita, My Love*, and he said, "Usually I get rave reviews for my choreography, but the show closes out of town. This time, there's almost no choreography, but I think I have a hit." His assessment of the show was encouraging.

My manager, Fifi Tanzy, added drama to the rehearsal period when she informed me that Gus Schirmer, the agent who had submitted me for *The Sound of Music* at Jones Beach the previous summer, had accepted the role of Liesl for the following summer on my behalf. I was flabbergasted. Agents were required by Actors' Equity to inform their clients before accepting or rejecting offers. I asked Fifi to tell Gus that I was rehearsing a new Broadway show and couldn't accept the job. Gus was furious and told me that *nobody* turns down Jones Beach. If I didn't do the show, our relationship was over.

Indeed, it was. I called Arnold Spector, the managing director at Jones Beach, to apologize and explain the situation. Arnold spoke gently: "Your show is going to bomb."

"Even if it does," I said, "I played Liesl in two productions last year. I'd like to do something new."

"You may feel differently when you're out of work," he said. "I won't lie to you. I'll audition other girls, but I won't cast anyone until you're back in town. Give me a call then."

I thanked him and promised I would call.

On the sixth day of rehearsals, we finally had a reading of the script, and my gut feeling was that Arnold Spector was right. I had landed another flop. Most of the cast was terrific. Dorothy Loudon was funny and touching and had a potentially show-stopping song, "Sur Les Quais," but her character died halfway through the first act. John Neville was a tortured Humbert who sang some beautiful ballads, and Leonard Frey was gleefully sleazy as Quilty, but Lolita was not well-defined. When she sang "Mother Needs a Boyfriend," I didn't know what she was trying to communicate. Was she a child imploring this older man to get her mother off her back, or was she aware of his prurient interest and teasing him with her underage status? ("Mother Needs a Boyfriend" would later be replaced by "Saturday," a child's celebration of a day with no homework.) The tone of the show veered from broad comedy to psychological drama.

After two weeks of rehearsals, Alan Jay Lerner apologized for not having one of the second act songs. He thought we needed a break from plot with a rousing song like "Oklahoma!" or "Get Me to the Church on Time" to get the audience fired up before returning to plot, but he simply didn't have the song.

We were rehearsing at Stage 73 in a cramped space with little heat. Most of the cast had colds, and after two weeks, Lorna Luft still didn't know her lines. On day 18, Mary Case took over the role of Mona, and Lorna Luft disappeared. We had our first run-through, and Danny told me he was horrified to see how much of the show hadn't been staged.

In six-degree weather, we moved from Stage 73 to the stage of the Belasco Theatre, which had no heat and hadn't been cleaned since the last show had packed out. We rehearsed the opening number, "Going Going Gone," the "orgy scene" in which Quilty auctions off scantily clad girls who stand on pedestals and perform provocative movements while the men swirl around them and bid for their services. At the Belasco, we stood on our pedestals and shivered in our winter coats, wool scarves, wool hats, and fur-lined gloves while the male dancers tried to pirouette without losing their earmuffs. Kendall March, a brunette in her mid-twenties, replaced Mary Case as Mona, and Leonard Frye blew up at Norman about the filthy stage. A member of the ensemble telephoned Actors' Equity during our lunch break, and Equity got the heat turned on. *Oh, the glamorous life of a Broadway dancer*!

On February 10, we assembled at the Belasco Theatre to take the bus to Philadelphia—except the bus didn't have enough seats. We sat around trying to keep warm while Norman Twain booked a larger bus.

In Philadelphia, the reviews were generally negative and conflicting. *The Evening Bulletin* thought John Neville was terrific. The *Inquirer* found him "anemic," and the *Daily News* thought the role of Humbert was too repulsive. Two critics thought Annette's Lolita *looked* right, but was superficial. Another critic thought she dominated her scenes. However, critics and audiences agreed that Dorothy Loudon as Charlotte was wonderful, and as long as Charlotte was alive, the audience was enthusiastic.

After opening night in Philadelphia, Tito Capobianco disappeared, and Alan Jay Lerner took over the direction. Lerner was a colorful personality. He was blind in one eye from a boxing incident and wore dark lenses in his eyeglasses. On his hands, he wore white cotton gloves, and his fingers fidgeted and picked at the gloves as if they were trying to break though the cotton and attack his nails. He chain-smoked, and at the time of *Lolita* was married to the fifth of his eight wives.

During the day, Lerner rehearsed the cast; in the evening, he watched the show and took notes. Every morning, he had pages and pages of new material. I was astonished by his productivity. Lerner expanded the role of Charlotte so that her death came late in the first act, and that act played quite well, but after Charlotte's death, the comedy became a drama. Lerner told the company he couldn't continue as director because he needed to focus on the script. The show would close early in Philadelphia and return to New York for revisions and rehearsals with a new director before going to Boston.

I overheard some of the all-male creative team discussing Annette's performance. They didn't know whether Annette understood what the show was about, but no one wanted to broach the subject. *Yikes! Why did they hire an actress without being sure that she understood the role? Why had they hired a minor without discussing the role and the communication ground rules with her mother and her sister/manager?* When we returned to New York, the creative team held auditions for a new Lolita. They chose Denise Nickerson, a petite 13-year-old who had just played 10-year-old Violet in the soon-to-be-released film *Willy Wonka & the Chocolate Factory.* Denise had the body of a child, and the high-pitched voice of a child. This Lolita would not be a worthy adversary, but a child victim, played by a child. Jill Streisant, a 15-year-old member of the ensemble with a huge belt voice, replaced Kendall March as Mona and understudied Lolita. Noel Willman, Danny's nemesis from *Love Match*, was announced as the new director, and Danny walked out mid-rehearsal. Dan Siretta, one of the male dancers who had previously worked with Danny in *Walking Happy*, took charge of the choreography.

I was sorry to lose Danny, but I didn't mind losing the choreography of the number he was staging: "How Far Is It to the Next Town?" This pulsing number came near the end of the second act when Humbert is driving Lolita from town to town. Humbert knows they are being followed, but by whom? The police? Lolita feeds Humbert's fear by reminding him that he is taking a minor across state lines. Humbert catches a glimpse of Lolita talking to the driver of the car that is following them, but when Lolita disappears, she always returns with glib explanations for where she has been and what she has done. "How Far Is It to the Next Town?" had a menacing sound, with interwoven dialogue.

Danny decided that the dancers should be drivers on the road. Each of us had to decide what model car we were driving and how fast we were traveling. John Mineo drove an imaginary Porsche that zoomed around the stage swerving around other drivers. I drove a VW Beetle and obeyed the imaginary traffic signs. I have no idea what costumes and lighting Danny had in mind, but in rehearsals, we had to squat as low as we could, hold our arms in front of us as if holding a steering wheel, and scoot around the stage. I suspect that the chaos of the interweaving cars reflected the chaos in Humbert's mind, as he tried to evade the car that was following him, but all I could think about was the searing pain in my thighs after hours of squatting—never low enough for Danny—and running around in the squatting position for what seemed like an eternity. I wasn't looking forward to doing that eight shows a week.

On March 16, 1971, the company climbed into the bus to travel from New York to Boston. We were still within city limits when Denise chirped from her seat in the center of the bus, "I smell grass!" Indeed, she did. John Neville, in the back of the bus, had lit up a joint, and Denise, unlike me, had recognized the smell. Denise looked more like Nabokov's pre-teen Lolita than Annette—and she was certainly more sophisticated than Annette—but I thought that a younger, less-voluptuous Lolita was a huge mistake for the musical.

On the evening of the first preview in Boston, someone telephoned the theater with a bomb threat that delayed the performance, but when the curtain finally went up, the audience loved Dorothy Loudon. However, when Charlotte died, and the comedic barrier between Humbert and Lolita was gone, virtual daggers of ice came shooting across the footlights.

In spite of the audience response, I was eager to read the reviews because Boston reviewers had the reputation of being knowledgeable and supportive. They generally didn't take cheap shots to make a name for themselves, but tried to tell their readers what to expect from the show and tell the creative team what was working and what wasn't. All of the critics agreed that the show didn't work.

Elliot Norton in the *Record American* wrote that the show lacked a consistent style and that Denise Nickerson sounded like a sweet 10-year-old.

Samuel Hirsch in the *Boston Herald Traveler* wrote that the show worked when it was light, but not when it became serious, and that Loudon's "massive contribution to the excellent first act makes you sorely miss her in the second."

Kevin Kelly in *The Boston Globe* wrote, "John Neville plays Hubert [sic] with a kind of erotically eloquent pain, always aware of the hysteria in his hunger and, somehow, doomed in the awareness. Dorothy Loudon, as Charlotte, is frantically funny, elaborately coy gestures decorated in atrocious French, and then very, very touching in her final exit to death." However, the character of Lolita "is hardly more than an outline."

In fact, the sketchily drawn Lolita that worked so well in the book by keeping the focus on Humbert and *his* feelings, was a huge problem for the show. Lolita wasn't a three-dimensional character that audiences could embrace, and they certainly couldn't root for Humbert or Quilty. They could and did root for the frantically funny middle-aged widow who set her sights on a handsome professor and tried to be everything he might desire in a wife. Charlotte was the

Rosie Ricci and I played classmates of Lolita at the Beardsley School for Girls in *Lolita, My Love.* The show was a lovely reunion with Rosie, who was my best friend at the Ballet Theatre School and at the Professional Children's School when she was a junior, and I was a senior.

heart of the musical, and when Charlotte died, so did the show. *Lolita, My Love* closed at the end of the week.

Alan Jay Lerner told the cast that he would continue to work on the show—that he was determined to make it work—and Norman Twain also seemed enthusiastic about a future production, but I wonder: Who is the target audience for a musical about a middle-aged man who has sex with his pre-teen stepdaughter? It seems to me that if *Lolita* is going to work as a musical—and I'm not sure that it should—Lolita must be the protagonist, and Lerner's Lolita was not.

As soon as I got back to New York, I called Arnold Spector and told him that I appreciated his holding open the role of Liesl at Jones Beach, but I wanted a new challenge. Arnold graciously wished me well and invited me to see *The Sound of Music* that summer.

A few days later, I went to the Diplomat Hotel to audition as a Millikiddie size ten for the new Milliken Breakfast Show. I looked forward to a show that would roll out like a well-oiled machine. Just as in the previous year, hordes of young girls sang and danced, and the last six or eight girls in each size were escorted one by one into a private area where they were weighed and measured. As the producer and I walked into the measuring booth, she noted that I was thinner than I had been the previous year.

"Is that good?" I asked. "Yes," she said.

My spirits soared as I stepped onto the scale. I weighed 89 pounds fully dressed in my short skirt and white go-go boots. My measurements were roughly 30-18-30. I fit the clothes perfectly.

While I was growing up during the 1950s, Marilyn Monroe was at the pinnacle of her career, and the ideal figure was an hourglass. Women wore pointy bras to emphasize their breasts, and girdles to decrease the size of their waists, but during the 1960s, the British model Twiggy, with her boyish haircut and slim, androgynous body, introduced a new ideal, and many young women aspired to be stick-thin like Twiggy. Because of my ballet background, I had always aspired to be thin, and I had finally achieved that goal.

The Milliken producer and I returned to the ballroom, where I lined up with the other potential Millikiddies. The creative team whispered and pointed and shuffled résumés. Finally, the producer chose four children size 10 and offered me the job of swing dancer (understudy) for the four girls. *Ouch, ouch, ouch! I was thinner this year. The producer said that was better.* I wanted to be singing and dancing onstage—not learning four parts and standing in the wings. However, I knew that the producer's decision made sense. I wasn't a tween. I was 25 years old, and I was a head taller than the other girls. However, the producer knew I was reliable. I could learn four parts and be ready to perform at a moment's notice, so hiring me made sense for them.

But did the job make sense for me? I had just finished a show in which there was very little dancing, and I wanted to perform. I also knew that Ray wanted me to join him as he flew in and out of the cities on the Metropolitan Opera spring tour. *How would Ray feel if I stayed in New York to stand in the wings as an understudy for four pre-teen girls? How would I feel? Would I enjoy being part of the Milliken family and taking home a good paycheck, or would I feel rejected and old*? I asked the producer if I could have a few minutes to call my husband, and after the call, I turned down the job.

In just four days, I had turned down two terrific jobs—Liesl at Jones Beach and the Milliken Show at the Waldorf Astoria Hotel. In turning down Liesl, I had given up a well-established agent and the highest salary of my career to date. At the Milliken Show, I had probably closed a door forever. *Was I making sound business decisions or was I slipping off the tightrope between career and marriage and falling into the marriage? Was it realistic to think I could find another role as good as Liesl*?

With *La Strada* and *Lolita,* I had been engulfed in stories about powerful middle-aged men who abused helpless young girls. Every day during rehearsals and every night on stage, I saw the physical and verbal abuse. I was starved for a show in which people are kind. Abuse—even when it isn't real—takes its toll, and joy—even in fiction—lifts my spirits. After *Lolita,* I wanted joy.

During the next few weeks, I had plenty of time to second-guess my decisions to turn down Liesl and the Milliken Breakfast Show. I watched Ray's performances in New York and on tour with the Met. I went to social functions, got new headshots, and did my taxes. Finally, one long month after the closing of *Lolita,* I saw a beacon of light on the horizon. The show gleaming before me had been a hit Off Broadway, so there would be no missing songs and no rewrites.

It needed no out-of-town tryout, and it was a happy show—a show about the joys of everyday life, the power of the imagination, and the importance of forgiving the flaws of others as they forgive ours. It was a show with name recognition all across the country because it was based on the comic strip *Peanuts*. The upcoming show was *You're a Good Man, Charlie Brown*, and the role of Patty was exactly what I was looking for. Patty was a joyful, principal role on Broadway.

Would the creative team want *me* as much as I wanted to be part of their show?

9

You're a Good Man, Charlie Brown (1971)

In the spring of 1971, *You're a Good Man, Charlie Brown* had played Off Broadway for four years, and its producers, Arthur Whitelaw and Gene Persson, had closed the show downtown to mount a new production on Broadway with a new cast. The music and lyrics were by Clark Gesner, and the book (according to Gesner in the Fawcett Crest script of March 1970) was attributed to John Gordon, a pseudonym for all the people who had worked to create the Off Broadway show, including the cast, the producers, and Clark Gesner himself. The characters are young children and a beagle, but in most professional productions, they are played by adults.

The action takes place in one day, an average day in the life of 6-year-old Charlie Brown. There are six characters: Charlie Brown (a boy with a good heart who fails at everything, but never gives up); Lucy (a girl who is part bully, part psychologist, and wants everything her own way); Linus (Lucy's baby brother who is a philosopher and has anxiety attacks when separated from his security blanket); Schroeder (a loner who plays Beethoven on the piano and ignores Lucy's plans to make him her future husband); Patty (a happy, optimistic follower who has no filter and says exactly what she thinks), and Snoopy (a beagle whose imagination allows him to be everything from a World War I flying ace to a vulture—and who celebrates "Suppertime" as if it were the 11 o'clock number that it is).

The term "11 o'clock number" dates back to the era when the advertised curtain time for Broadway shows was 8:30 p.m. and most musicals had a high energy and/or dramatic number at 11 o'clock to propel the audience into the final minutes of the show—numbers like "Rose's Turn" in *Gypsy* and "Oklahoma!" in *Oklahoma!*. Today, it's hard to imagine *Oklahoma!* without the title song, but as Todd S. Purdum wrote in his book *Something Wonderful: Rodgers and Hammerstein's Broadway Revolution*, it was only during backers' auditions that producer Terry Helburn (co-founder of the Theatre Guild) told Oscar Hammerstein that she hoped he and Rodgers would write a song about the earth. That idea came out of the blue to Hammerstein, but two days later, he had written the lyrics for "Oklahoma!."

Terry Helburn actually set that groundbreaking musical in motion when she approached Richard Rodgers with the idea of turning Lynn Riggs' play *Green Grow the Lilacs*, which the Theatre Guild had produced, into a musical. She also identified Agnes de Mille as the perfect choreographer. To convince Rodgers and Hammerstein to hire de Mille, she invited them to the opening night of the ballet *Rodeo* at the Metropolitan Opera to see the charismatic dancer, the brilliant choreography, and the 22 curtain calls. As time goes by, the collaborators people remember become fewer and fewer, but in 1942, *Oklahoma!* (then called *Away We Go*) was also known as "Helburn's Folly." Without Terry Helburn, *Oklahoma!* might never have been written or had the success it had.

I like to audition early in the day. If I am right for the role and one of the first people to audition, I can become the measuring stick—the actress to whom all others are compared until someone better comes along. Also, early in the day, producers are less likely to be running behind schedule and rushing the actors to catch up.

I will never forget one commercial audition in Los Angeles when the casting director was almost an hour behind schedule. (At commercial auditions, the Screen Actors' Guild requires actors to be paid an hourly rate if they have not auditioned within one hour of their appointment times.) This audition was a final callback for the director, the ad agency, the production company, and the client. I was on deck when I learned that the decision-makers were ravenous and lunch had *finally* arrived. I told the casting director I would sign out immediately (indicating that I had auditioned within one hour of my scheduled time) if she would please allow me to audition after lunch—but she pushed me into the front of the room just as lunch arrived through the back door. I looked at the decision-makers, but all I saw were the backs of their heads as they reached for boxes of food. I was ordered to begin and did my best over the sounds of "Who has the pasta?" and "Where's my tuna?"

When I left the room, I still hadn't seen anyone's face. I didn't get the job.

The morning of the auditions for *You're a Good Man, Charlie Brown,* I had begun my day at a commercial audition, so by the time I arrived at the Edison Theatre, the street in front of the theater and the lobby were jammed with actors. I signed in and was given an index card on which to write my name, address, telephone number, and relevant credits. A number at the top of the card implied that just over 1,000 people had signed in ahead of me. Because of the huge crowd, the producers were "typing" (deciding who would be allowed to sing based on physical appearance). The stage managers called out a range of 20 numbers and lined up the actors in numerical order. The actors then filed onto the stage. The few who were asked to sing auditioned one by one while the stage managers rounded up the next groups of 20.

It was late afternoon before I was typed in. Finally, it was my turn to sing. I walked onto the stage and stated my name and the title of my song.

"Which role are you here for?" asked a voice in the dark.

I was surprised that it wasn't obvious. "Oh! I'm Patty," I said.

"Yes, we think you probably are," said the voice in the dark.

Wow! What an encouraging way to begin an audition!

I sang my song, chatted with the voices for several minutes, and was asked to come to the Golden Theatre on Wednesday.

The following Wednesday, I sang and read and talked while one of the producers dashed from the middle of the orchestra to the back of the balcony to make sure my voice could fill the 800-seat theater without amplification. At that time, most Broadway shows had microphones spaced across the front of the stage near the footlights, but *You're a Good Man, Charlie Brown* would have no microphones. The actors would have to project.

At the end of the day, the producers cast three people: Liz O'Neal as Lucy, Stephen Fenning as Linus, and me as Patty. I was finally in a hit show—a show that gave me my best role to date on Broadway.

The following day, Thursday, the producers held more auditions for the roles of Snoopy, Schroeder, and Charlie Brown. Liz, Stephen, and I were summoned to the theater late that afternoon so the producers could see us with the top candidates for the other three roles. On Friday—exactly two weeks before our first preview—I picked up my script. On Sunday, Gene Persson took a few photos for publicity, but there were still only three actors—-Liz, Stephen, and me. (We later had an official photo call with the acclaimed theater photographer Martha Swope.) Carter Cole, who had played Schroeder Off Broadway, and Grant Cowan, who had played Snoopy in Montreal, Chicago, and Las Vegas, joined the cast—but we still didn't have a Charlie Brown.

Finally, one of the producers thought of Dean Stolber. Dean had performed on Broadway in *Bye Bye Birdie,* but had since become a lawyer. The producers tracked him down, and Dean worked it out with his law firm to get every afternoon off for rehearsal week and Wednesday afternoons for the run of the show. Our cast was complete, and our performance schedule seemed like a dream: Wednesday at 2:00 p.m. and 7:30 p.m., Thursday and Friday at 7:30 p.m., Saturday at 2:00 p.m. and 7:30 p.m., and Sunday at 2:00 p.m. and 5:00 p.m. I hoped the show would run for years.

However, I knew there were several challenges to a long run. Many people had seen the show Off Broadway, and many more had seen the show advertised as an Off Broadway show at Off Broadway prices. *Would people be willing to pay Broadway prices to see the show on Broadway*? I didn't know. Also, there were no star names to drive the box office, and no central conflict to drive the show. The forward momentum of *You're a Good Man, Charlie Brown* did not come from rising conflict between a protagonist and an antagonist, but from the passage of time—from morning until evening. *Charlie Brown* relied on charm, and charm usually works better in intimate environments.

We had only one week of rehearsal, which was very unusual for a Broadway musical—especially since two-thirds of the cast was new to the show. Also, to my surprise, our rehearsal day began around 1:00 p.m. —not the usual 10:00 a.m. In summer stock, it was common to rehearse one show during the day and perform another at night with a new show every week, but on Broadway, a cast usually had six weeks of all-day rehearsals. Fortunately, director Joseph Hardy and choreographer Patricia Birch knew exactly what they wanted, and our cast was a quick study.

Joe Hardy had won awards for directing *You're a Good Man, Charlie Brown* Off Broadway, and his Broadway credits included *Play It Again, Sam* (Tony nomination) and *Child's Play* (Tony Award). Choreographer Patricia Birch had staged the musical numbers for the Off Broadway production and had made a splash on Broadway with her musical staging for *The Me Nobody Knows*, a show about kids in the New York ghetto. In the next few years her eclectic choreography would include *Grease*, *A Little Night Music*, and *Over Here*.

At one rehearsal, after we had run the first act, Stephen Fenning, who was making his professional debut as Linus, pushed one of the set pieces to set up for the second act.

"Don't do that!" barked a voice from the wings.

"It's not heavy," said Stephen. "I can do it."

"No, you can't," said the stagehand as he lumbered onto the stage. "Union rules."

The stagehand was right. In a Broadway house, only stagehands are allowed to move set pieces (unless the movement is part of the choreography), and the number of stagehands a producer must hire is determined by negotiations between the theater owners and the stagehands' union.

You're a Good Man, Charlie Brown had little work for stagehands. The curtain went up and down for each of the two acts, and during the intermission, two lightweight set pieces were moved a few feet. There were no drops, scrims, turntables, or elaborate set pieces. However, shows at the Golden Theatre were required to pay a minimum of four or five stagehands, so a group of stagehands showed up for every performance and played poker in the basement.

The number of musicians a producer must pay at each theater is also established by negotiation, so producers sometimes had to pay more musicians than they actually wanted. There is a wonderful story that when Harold Prince produced and directed *Candide* at the Broadway Theatre in 1974, he wanted the sound of 13 musicians, but the union required him to pay 25. On opening night, he was still so steamed about the extra 12 musicians that he ordered them to perform in the men's room—an order the musicians' union immediately overruled.

At the Golden Theatre, I had a huge dressing room all to myself. To give my home away from home some warmth and personality, I purchased turquoise and white striped sheets and made curtains for the windows and matching tablecloths for the dressing tables. I bought black wooden picture frames and hung some of my favorite theatrical photos. Nevertheless, the room felt much too big, and I missed the chatter and the laughter that had always surrounded me as I put on my makeup. On stage, as Patty, I basked in the warmth of my friends, but before and after the show, I was lonely.

I had little time to chat with other members of the cast, but I did have one memorable conversation with Dean Stolber when he called out from the hallway, "Does anybody know the director Alan Schneider?"

Silence.

"Has anybody ever worked with Alan Schneider?"

"I did," I said. "He directed *La Strada*."

"Great!" he said. "My law firm is representing him in an altercation with a policeman, and we're looking for a character witness."

"You don't want me," I said. I wasn't the first person who had declined to be a character witness for Alan Schneider.

Many years later, I was talking with a group of actors, and Alan's name came up. "He's dead," said one of the actors. "Killed by a motorcycle in London. Hit and run."

"The driver was probably an actor," said someone else, and everybody laughed.

A man was dead—a Tony Award–winning director—but at the news of his death, I felt nothing.

During the run of *You're a Good Man, Charlie Brown*, I missed the camaraderie of other girls in the dressing room, but the show itself was a joy. I loved squeaking high notes in the title song, chasing rabbits with Snoopy, and performing the intricate drama of "Glee Club Rehearsal."

During previews, many of my friends came to see the show, including Dan and Mara, Mary Case, and some of my commercial agents. Mom, Dad, and Ray were in the audience on opening night, and everyone seemed to enjoy the show. Later in the run, I was pleased when Ray told me that the woman behind him had announced to her companion at intermission, "The best one up there is the little girl." During one matinee, an actor in the show next door stepped into the alley during our concurrent intermissions, frowned at me, and said, "Little girl. You can't be back here. This is only for the actors." The youth and innocence of Patty (and the phrase "Good grief!") were following me into my offstage life.

On Sundays, some of the actors stayed in the theater between the two o'clock and five o'clock shows, but even when I didn't go out for dinner, I usually changed out of costume and stepped outside to sign autographs. Many of the children who came to the matinees were seeing their first Broadway show and were thrilled to see some of the actors up close and take home their autographs.

In addition to the children, there was an autograph hound named Dave who patrolled the theater district. When people exited stage doors, Dave shoved his autograph book in front of them and asked, "Are you anybody?" I had given Dave numerous autographs at the stage doors of *Hello, Dolly!*, *Here's Where I Belong*, and *How Now, Dow Jones*, so whenever he accosted me at Colony Records or the Drama Book Shop, I said I was nobody and kept walking. Shortly after the opening of *You're a Good Man, Charlie Brown*, I came out of the Drama Book Shop, and Dave thrust his autograph book in front of me and asked, "Are you anybody?"

"No," I said and kept walking.

"Yes, you are!" he said. "You're Lee Wilson! *Hello, Dolly!*, *Here's Where I Belong*, *How Now, Dow Jones*, *You're a Good Man, Charlie Brown*!" He planted himself in front of me and held out his autograph book. I had progressed from "Are you anybody?" to "You're Lee Wilson!"

In *You're a Good Man, Charlie Brown,* Snoopy (Grant Cowan) has an imagination that allows him to be anything from a World War I flying ace to a vulture, but my Patty wasn't prepared for a smooch from a beagle. Photo by Martha Swope ©The New York Public Library.

The most important review for any Broadway show was (and is) the review in *The New York Times*. Clive Barnes, a dance and theater critic at *The New York Times*, was a fan of *You're a Good Man,*

Charlie Brown, so the producers invited him to see one of the previews, and Barnes gave us a great review on WQXR radio, stating that "the musical fills the bigger house as amply as it did the smaller house.... I think 'Charlie Brown' will be as successful on Broadway as it ever was off."

However, *The New York Times* assigned one of their other critics, Mel Gussow, to write the review for the newspaper. Gussow wrote that he liked the show better downtown because "At the Golden—same director, same scenery, same basic staging—one looks over an orchestra pit and up to a stage. Intimacy is abandoned." Before Gussow's review was published, our producers learned that it wasn't a rave, so they ran the Clive Barnes review as an advertisement on the same day that the Gussow review appeared. Gene Persson was gleeful when he told me that some people at the *Times* were *very* annoyed, but there was nothing they could do.

Mel Gussow wasn't the only critic who had reservations about the Broadway production. Douglas Watt in the *Daily News* wished the show had been updated to include Woodstock; Richard Watts in the *Post* missed the intimacy of the smaller theater and wished that Woodstock had been added. Another critic wrote that he preferred the production downtown because there weren't so many musicians. Only Clive Barnes and the reviewer for *The Record* gave us unequivocal raves with the *Record* giving me a quotable review: "Lee Wilson is a pert Patty, miraculously turning a minor role into a major one."

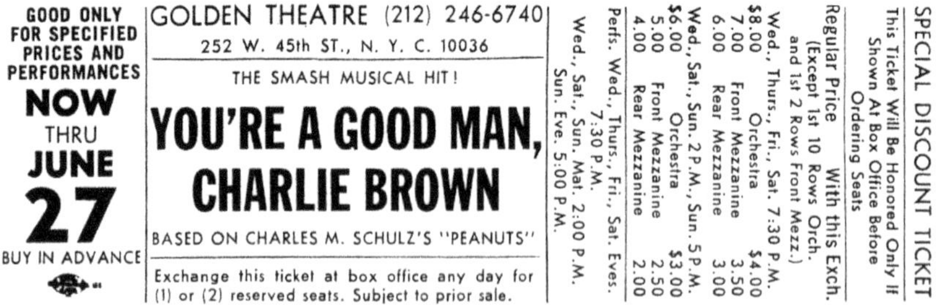
GOOD ONLY FOR SPECIFIED PRICES AND PERFORMANCES
NOW THRU JUNE 27
BUY IN ADVANCE

GOLDEN THEATRE (212) 246-6740
252 W. 45th ST., N. Y. C. 10036
THE SMASH MUSICAL HIT!
YOU'RE A GOOD MAN, CHARLIE BROWN
BASED ON CHARLES M. SCHULZ'S "PEANUTS"
Exchange this ticket at box office any day for (1) or (2) reserved seats. Subject to prior sale.

SPECIAL DISCOUNT TICKET
This Ticket Will Be Honored Only If Shown At Box Office Before Ordering Seats

Regular Price		With this Exch.
	(Except 1st 10 Rows Orch. and 1st 2 Rows Front Mezz.)	
	Wed., Thurs., Fri., Sat. 7:30 P.M.	
$8.00	Orchestra	$4.00
7.00	Front Mezzanine	3.50
6.00	Rear Mezzanine	3.00
	Wed., Sat., Sun. 2 P.M., Sun. 5 P.M.	
$6.00	Orchestra	$3.00
5.00	Front Mezzanine	2.50
4.00	Rear Mezzanine	2.00

Perfs. Wed., Thurs., Fri., Sat. Eves. 7:30 P.M.
Wed., Sat., Sun. Mat. 2:00 P.M.
Sun. Eve. 5:00 P.M.

Twofers brought the price down to four dollars for 11th row center (three dollars for matinees), but, like many shows in the early 1970s, we still couldn't fill the theater.

Our producers put out twofers, small paper coupons that allowed people to buy tickets at half price for all seats except the first ten rows of the orchestra and the first two rows of the mezzanine, but they didn't help. On June 27, after 15 previews and 32 performances, *You're A Good Man, Charlie Brown* ended its Broadway run. I packed up my curtains and my photographs, said goodbye to the rest of the company, and bought the trade papers to look for my next job.

I had left the Metropolitan Opera Ballet four years earlier to dance on Broadway, and I had achieved my goal, but my life was very different from the life I had envisioned. I had expected Broadway to give me more free time than ballet companies because ballet companies are constantly rehearsing, whereas hit Broadway shows have only occasional clean-up or put-in rehearsals. Unfortunately, I couldn't find a hit. My longest run, less than 12 weeks, was *Hello, Dolly!*. When I danced with ballet companies, my Sundays were always a day of rest, and I often spent the entire day lying flat on my bed, eating ice cream, and reading a book. However, on Broadway, some of the shows, like *Charlie Brown*, switched their workweek from Monday through Saturday to a schedule that included Sunday, so performers like me were working seven days a week.

For example, on the last Monday before the closing of *You're a Good Man, Charlie Brown*, my alarm clock jolted me awake at 6:00 a.m. I tiptoed around the bedroom, trying not to disturb Ray while I prepared for an 8:30 a.m. call to act in a hair care commercial. I worked right up to my guaranteed release time of 1:00 p.m., took a taxi to another TV studio, changed clothes, and at 2:00 p.m., taped the *Joe Franklin Show*, a late-night talk show, where I promoted the final week of *You're a Good Man, Charlie Brown*. After the taping, I dashed over to Madison Avenue for a 3:50 p.m. commercial audition before taking the bus home to spend the evening with Ray. This was a far cry from lying on my bed with a book at the Washington Jefferson Hotel.

The opportunity to rest and recharge my batteries was one attraction of the Olde West Dinner Theatre in Little Rock, Arkansas. Another was the opportunity to do my first leading role in a straight play—the role of Robin in *Under the Yum-Yum Tree*. However, the main reason I wanted the job was that Veronica Lake, the 1940s movie star, was already cast in the other female role—the role of my aunt Irene.

Veronica Lake had starred in *This Gun for Hire*, *I Wanted Wings*, and *Sullivan's Travels*, and she was the rare pin-up girl whose photos usually showed her from the shoulders up. When I was a little girl, Mom told me that Veronica Lake's peek-a-boo hairstyle was so popular during World War II that the U.S. Government asked her to pin back her hair so that working women who copied her style wouldn't get their hair caught in machinery. Veronica Lake had been part of the glamorous old Hollywood that had disappeared, and I was thrilled by the opportunity to work with her. I signed an eight-week contract with the Olde West Dinner Theatre to play the ingénue leads in two plays: *Under the Yum-Yum Tree* and *Natalie Needs a Nightie.*

Nevertheless, I wondered: *Why is a former movie star performing in Little Rock rather than starring on Broadway? Did she retire to Little Rock, or is there something I don't know?*

I would soon find out.

10

Veronica Lake, Cruising the Caribbean, and Chateau de Ville (1971–1972)

Under the Yum-Yum Tree is a romantic comedy that premiered on Broadway in 1960 with Sandra Church (the original Louise in *Gypsy*) as Robin, Dean Jones (later the original Bobby in *Company*) as her fiancé Dave, Academy Award–winning Gig Young as the playboy landlord Hogan, and Broadway veteran Nan Martin as Robin's aunt Irene. At the Olde West Dinner Theatre, Veronica Lake was the only star, and although I knew her as a *film* star, the producers told me that she had recently received rave reviews in England for her stage portrayal of Blanche DuBois in *A Streetcar Named Desire.*

I met Miss Lake the morning of our first rehearsal. She was tiny—4 feet 11—and unassuming in her tailored slacks, conservative shirt, and loafers. She was 48 years old, still pretty, and still blonde. She was polite, but reserved.

In the first scene of the play, Irene is moving out of her San Francisco apartment, and Robin is moving in. The director, who co-owned the theater with the actor playing Hogan, blocked the scene. (The word "blocking" pays homage to the 19th-century directors who planned actors' movements by using blocks of wood to represent the actors. The word was *not* chosen, as some people have speculated, to reflect a director's opinion of the intelligence of actors.) I wrote the moves into my script. Miss Lake did not. After we had blocked four pages, the director asked to see what we had done so far. Miss Lake read her lines, but didn't move until the director prompted her. After a few prompts, the director asked Miss Lake if she might prefer moving somewhere else. "No," she said vaguely. "It's fine." The director went through the first four pages again, move by move, but when he asked us to play the scene, Miss Lake seemed confused. We took a bathroom break and started over.

The next day the producers hired a local actress, Judy Fields, to serve as a dialogue coach for Miss Lake, but Miss Lake still couldn't learn her lines. I was told that her frequent bathroom breaks involved a flask with an alcoholic beverage. Judy, who was a quick study, was formally cast as Irene, and Veronica Lake, whose name and photograph were in all of the advertising, agreed to stay on as mistress of ceremonies to greet the guests.

On opening night, Miss Lake greeted the guests before and after the show, and the reviewers gave conflicting stories to explain her absence from the stage. The *Arkansas Gazette* stated that the best thing about the show was "the attractive and able cast that does not include Veronica Lake (out ailing, probably for the run)." Another reviewer said, "Olde West's production is directed by Veronica Lake." *Oops*! Another review is the one I remembered decades later: "The 'Yum Yum Tree' is yummy, although star Veronica Lake, due to illness, had to drop out.... Miss Lake does greet the guests before the play begins and last week at least, also greeted them in the foyer as they left. It was a fine way for the men, who remembered the peek-a-boo girl, to take themselves back in time and dreams to the 40's and for their spouses to remind their husbands and friends, that time does creep up on everyone—even a dream girl of the 40's and World War II. She is a very attractive matron, just as the mates of many men attending the production."

Veronica Lake. Attractive matron. If a forty-eight-year-old former MVP of Major League Baseball had made an appearance in Little Rock, would any sports writer have described him as "a very attractive husband, just like the mates of many Little Rock women"? I doubt it.

Veronica Lake left Little Rock within days of our opening, and I never saw her again, but years later, I realized we had something else in common. In her autobiography, *Veronica*, written with Donald

Bain, Miss Lake wrote, "It seems everyone remembers when Veronica Lake was discovered working as a cocktail waitress in the Martha Washington Hotel in New York. It made headlines all over the world." The news that Veronica Lake was living and working at the hotel broke in early 1962, and according to her autobiography, she lived and worked at the hotel for four months, so she had arrived only months after I had left: The Martha Washington was where I had lived during the summer of 1961 while I was attending the summer program at the Ballet Theatre School. My mother chose the hotel for the same reason as Veronica Lake. It was less expensive than the Barbizon.

My second show in Little Rock, *Natalie Needs a Nightie,* is a farce that one reviewer described as "hilarious ... one of the most astronomically, monumentally, heroically silly shows of all time." In contrast, another reviewer wrote, "Farce is the lowest form of drama, and 'Natalie Needs a Nightie' ... is one of the lowest of all.... It is made slightly palatable because Lee Wilson, a cute thing with the widest eyes this side of Little Orphan Annie ... appears in her underwear." In spite of the opinion that our show was "the lowest form of drama," the run was extended for a week.

The productions in Little Rock were very low budget, but I had accomplished several things. I had gained my first credits as a lead actress in straight plays; I had received excellent reviews to put in my portfolio—especially for *Yum-Yum Tree*—and I had worked outside of New York for two months for the first time since *La Strada.* I had asked for and received a rider to my contract that allowed me to leave after the first play if I wanted to do so, but Ray had spent part of October in Delaware with my parents and had told me that he was looking forward to visiting Little Rock and seeing me in the second play in early November (which he did), so I felt I had jumped a hurdle in my marriage.

Back in New York, I shot more TV commercials and then booked a job that sounded like heaven on earth—eight weeks as an entertainer aboard a Norwegian cruise ship, the M.S. *Skyward,* cruising the Caribbean with all expenses paid and a salary that would cover my half of the expenses in New York with a margin to spare. I was one of four performers (two girls and two boys) in a Broadway revue that included songs from *Cabaret, Fiddler on the Roof,* and *Mame.* We were scheduled to perform one night a week during each of the eight cruises, and the rest of the time we were free to enjoy all of the activities. The ship would stop in Nassau, St. Thomas, San Juan, and Bermuda—all glamorous resorts I had never seen.

During rehearsals, I received a call from Vince Alexander, who had choreographed the Jones Beach production of *The Sound of Music* and played Rolf. He had been hired to choreograph and play Rolf that summer at the Chateau de Ville dinner theaters in the Boston area and wanted to know why I hadn't come to the audition. I told him about the cruise show, and he asked if I could get out after four weeks. I had an oral agreement to do the cruises for eight weeks, so I told Vince I would have to discuss that with the producer.

"Great!" said Vince. "Come up to the Ansonia Hotel after your rehearsal."

"I can't," I said. "I have tickets for *Two Gentlemen of Verona.*"

"You'll love it," he said. "I saw it last week. If the producers can come back after the show, will you audition then? We're only two blocks from your apartment."

How could I resist?

That night, when I arrived at the Ansonia, Vince introduced me to Gerry Roberts, the producer for the Chateau de Ville theaters, and I liked him immediately. His wife Bunni, the casting director, was charming and funny, and I was impressed that they were willing to see me so close to midnight. I sang and danced and read with Vince and told them I would get back to them about my availability.

When I talked with the producer of the cruise show, he told me that he had asked everyone to sign on for eight weeks, but the other girl he had hired, the last person cast, was only available for four, so he didn't mind if I left at the same time. He could replace two girls for the same cost as one. I called Gerry Roberts, who offered me a choice between living near each of the two theaters—one in Framingham and the other in Saugus—or living in Boston with a van picking me up at my hotel prior to the performances. I chose to live in Boston.

It was still winter in New York, so I was looking forward to four weeks of cruising the Caribbean, a short break to join Ray on the Metropolitan Opera spring tour, and a summer in Boston.

The M.S. *Skyward* departed from Baltimore, Maryland, for the first three cruises, and Charleston, South Carolina, for the fourth. To my surprise and delight, I was assigned the large stateroom reserved for the assistant cruise director because there was no assistant cruise director at the time. Ten years earlier, when my family had sailed to Europe, I had loved every minute aboard the S.S. *United States*, but the *Skyward* was a smaller ship, and each time it rounded Cape Hatteras, the rolling of the ship made me queasy.

We spent most of the week at sea, and the food was superb—from the tender, juicy filet mignon to the luscious millefeuilles. Every day, I did a ballet barre, vocalized, walked the deck, and watched the other entertainers' performances, but the days on board seemed long.

The cruise ship was its own community, and the rest of the world seemed far away. When I called Ray from the ship, the connection was poor; I was facing people on the other side of a glass window who may or may not have been listening in, and I had to shout for Ray to hear me. Even though Ray could meet me between cruises, I was glad I had decided to leave the ship after four weeks.

Our time in port was limited, but each destination was different. The beach in Nassau was clean and beautiful. The beach in St. Thomas was dirty and crowded with people selling souvenirs, and I was sorry I hadn't signed up for a tour of the island. In San Juan, I wandered around the casino where elegantly-dressed men and women gambled and drank. (The casual, even sloppy, attire of gamblers in Las Vegas would come as a big surprise after the elegance of San Juan.) My favorite destination was the last—Bermuda. As the ship sailed into port, I saw beautiful pastel-colored houses along the waterfront, and all afternoon, I enjoyed walking the car-free, tree-lined streets where bicycles circled policemen in Bermuda shorts.

After the last cruise and a party-filled week in Cleveland with Ray, I returned to New York for my reunion with Christopher Hewett (director), Vince Alexander, and several other cast members from earlier productions of *The Sound of Music*. I had grown as an actress since the 1970 productions, and playing Liesl was like reestablishing a good friendship that has deepened with time.

The Chateau de Ville dinner theaters in Framingham and Saugus were the most formal dinner theaters in the Northeast, with crystal chandeliers in the lobbies, and booths that recalled the old-time showrooms in Las Vegas. Most dinner theaters had buffets, but Chateau de Ville had maître d's and table service.

The cast for *The Sound of Music* was excellent. Willi Burke (who had starred on Broadway in *Fiorello*) was Maria, and Erik Silju (our Captain at the Paper Mill Playhouse) was Captain von Trapp. Erik still looked like a Norse god. He and Willi made a very attractive couple, and the show got terrific reviews.

My home for the summer was the Copley Square Hotel, a boutique hotel built in the late 19th century that had an excellent Hungarian restaurant that served delicious cold cherry soup, exotic meat dishes spiced with paprika, and crisp apple strudel. The hotel had a few rooms without private baths that were priced far below the other rooms, and I didn't mind the walk down the hall to have the amenities of the upscale hotel and the perfect location—close to the majestic Boston Public Library, and a scenic one-mile walk to the Boston Museum of Fine Arts.

During the day, I walked the Freedom Trail, visited the Isabella Stewart Gardner Museum, and took the T (the subway) out to Cambridge to explore the campus of Harvard College. I took a side trip to Plymouth to see Plymouth Rock, which hadn't impressed me when I was a child and was equally unimpressive to me as an adult.

Boston restaurants were superb and ranged from the elegant Locke-Ober, with French cuisine and fresh seafood, to the boisterous Durgin-Park, which had communal tables, thick slabs of prime rib, and soup bowls of Indian pudding topped with vanilla ice cream. For everyday dining, I enjoyed La Crepe with giant, lighter-than-air crepes filled with creamed spinach or chunks of ham and Swiss cheese, Brigham's ice cream parlors with comfort food and chunky chocolate chip ice cream, and Dunkin' Donuts with flaky biscuits and honey-glazed chocolate cake donuts. Even Jordan Marsh, a department store, was famous for its giant blueberry muffins—although the bran muffins packed with dried fruit were equally delicious. I loved living, eating, and performing in Boston, and it was quick and easy to fly into New York on my day off.

Gerry Roberts called me during the run in Framingham and told me he wanted me to leave *The Sound of Music* two weeks prior to its closing in Saugus to play Louise in *Carousel* in Framingham for eight weeks. He had already signed John Raitt, the original Billy Bigelow on Broadway, to reprise his leading role and direct the production. I was delighted. I had wanted to play Louise ever since I had seen the Lincoln Center production of *Carousel* in the summer of 1965. I looked forward to dancing "Louise's Ballet," and I wanted a closer look at a musical in which the lead characters, Julie Jordan and Billy Bigelow, seem doomed from the outset.

Julie Jordan loves Billy Bigelow—even after Billy is fired from his job, refuses to look for work, hangs out all night with a lowlife, hits Julie, bungles a robbery, commits suicide, and, when sent back to Earth to atone for his sins, slaps his daughter. Nevertheless, audiences like him. Why?

In *Something Wonderful*, Todd Purdum wrote that producer Terry Helburn (the producer who brought Rodgers and Hammerstein the play *Green Grow the Lilacs*, the source material for *Oklahoma!*, and the Hungarian play *Liliom*, the source material for *Carousel*) asked people why they liked Billy even though he was "such a bastard." People responded that he was "so human" or "such a cute bastard." Certainly, John Raitt was a handsome man with great charm whose voice soared in the romantic "If I Loved You" and thrilled in the tour de force "Soliloquy," but I don't believe that audiences root for Billy because of his looks or his voice. I believe that audiences root for Billy because of what they learn about him in the prologue—an overture with no singing, no dancing, and no dialogue—just movement timed to music:

The curtain rises on an amusement park in a small town in New England where everyone from sailors and millworkers to the richest man in town enjoy the sights. Mr. Bascombe is the rich man; he flaunts his wealth, and people greet him with deference. Mrs. Mullin sits beneath a sign that reads "Mullin's Carousel," and sells tickets for the carousel. Billy Bigelow, the barker for the carousel, mingles with the crowd and flirts with the girls. He begins his spiel, and everyone turns away from the other attractions to watch Billy. Soon, everyone is swaying in unison—everyone except Julie, who stands motionless as she watches the charismatic barker. Billy is distracted by Julie, and everyone turns to follow his gaze. Mrs. Mullin chastises Billy, who regains his focus and captivates the crowd. When he finishes his spiel, all of the girls stampede for the carousel. By the time Julie gets her ticket, the carousel is already moving, and she is afraid to step on board, so Billy lifts her onto the only remaining horse and then hops off the carousel. Mrs. Mullin gives Billy an icy glare. Billy looks back at Julie and waves; Julie is so thrilled she almost falls off the horse. Billy laughs, hops back onto the carousel, and leans against her horse. The furious Mrs. Mullin shuts down her booth and paces angrily. The carousel gains speed as Billy leans closer to Julie.

Billy hasn't said a word, but we know three things about him that are confirmed in later scenes: He loves his job. He excels at his job, and he is sexually harassed by his employer. In 1945, the term "sexual harassment" had not yet been coined, and audiences hadn't read studies indicating that anxiety, depression, and low self-esteem correlate highly with victims of sexual harassment, but people then and now recognize the truth of Billy's character and they understand the unfairness of his situation.

Carousel is a musical about class. Billy does the work of attracting girls to the carousel and lifting them onto the horses, but Mrs. Mullin sits on an elevated perch and collects the money. As an employer, she can demand sex in return for a job. Mr. Bascombe carries huge sums of money from the mill he owns to the ship he owns, but the people working their fingers to the bone are the mill workers like Julie who are required to live in dormitories with an early evening curfew that limits their future prospects and chains them to the mill.

Carousel was written in 1945, but it is timely in 21st-century America when income inequality is increasing, upward mobility is decreasing, and people who have been sexually harassed are shouting, "Time's up!" "Enough is enough!"

I loved playing Louise, the daughter of Billy and Julie, who is introduced near the end of the show in a ballet that Billy watches from outside the back door to heaven. Louise's emotions ricochet like a silver ball in a pinball machine: joy as she runs barefoot on the beach, frustration when the other children won't play with her, gloating satisfaction when she grabs the flashy hat of a tormentor, awakening passion as she dances with a carnival boy, heartbreak when he walks away, and fury because she is an outcast through no fault of her own. Louise is a show-stealing role that gives *Carousel* its somewhat hopeful ending when Billy, unseen by anyone at Louise's graduation, reinforces the words of the graduation speaker who tells the children not to rely on the success of their parents or be held back by their failures, but to stand on their own two feet. "Believe him," Billy whispers to his daughter while the entire company sings the inspirational song "You'll Never Walk Alone."

Carousel asks us to look at the people who were not born to wealth, who did not have the good fortune to live in a good school district, or who were stigmatized at birth. The show reminds us that society works better when the fortunate do not leverage their power to take advantage of the less fortunate, but give them a helping hand. (Imagine if Mrs. Mullin, after telling Billy that the girls at the carousel missed him and that attendance was down, had offered to let Billy return to his job without the demand that he leave his wife and come back to her. Imagine how different the lives of Julie and Billy and Louise would have been: Billy would have had his dream job; Julie, a happy, productive husband, and Louise would have frolicked in the park and watched her father excel in his job.)

At the end of the show, Louise has potential—*if* society helps her—*if* she never walks alone. In the Molnar play, Billy doesn't get the second chance to go back and help Louise; he must walk into the offstage fires. *Carousel* is more optimistic, but I think part of the reason that some of the audience is in tears at the end is because audiences know that in the real world, Louise barely has a chance.

The Chateau de Ville production of *Carousel* was a rousing

success. John Raitt thrilled audiences with his high notes at the end of the "Soliloquy"; reviews for the ballet were superb, and at the end of the show, some of the audience was in tears.

What a wonderful summer! With the doubleheader of *The Sound of Music* and *Carousel,* I had performed non-stop for 14 weeks—my longest stretch of performances to date. Liesl and Louise were satisfying roles in very good productions. I had accumulated production photos and quotable reviews for my portfolio, and for the first time in a long time, I felt young.

11

The Fantasticks (1972)

How important is age? In the early 21st century, SAG-AFTRA backed a law to make it illegal for "commercial online entertainment employment providers" that charge a subscriber's fee to publish actors' ages. Why? Because women who played younger than their actual ages claimed that when IMDB published their ages, their incomes dropped.

According to a 2015 *Time* magazine analysis, jobs for film actresses peak when they are 30. This is not true for men. At age 30, men and women get the same number of jobs, but after 30, jobs for women drop 25 percent by age 40 and continue their decline while jobs for men at age 30 *increase* by 25 percent over the next 16 years until they peak at age 46. Only when men are in their mid-sixties do their jobs fall to a number that equals the women's best year at age 30. When you consider that many women of 30 can still pass for early 20s, you get an idea of how young a woman must *look* for maximum employment.

In New York, I carefully guarded the secret of my age, but when I visited my parents in Delaware, my mother constantly reminded me of my age. After playing Liesl at Jones Beach and at the Paper Mill Playhouse, I told Mom that in ten years, I wanted to play Maria. "Ten years?!" she said with a horrified look. "It should be two. How long do you think you can play sixteen?"

"Probably ten or twenty years," was the correct response, but I didn't know that at the time. I *did* know that no one would hire me to play Maria in two years—not in a professional production. I was five-feet-one-and-a-quarter inches tall, 90 pounds, and had a baby face. If I were Maria, how on earth would you cast Liesl and six younger children (keeping in mind that the youngest must learn lines and choreography and sing harmony)? Yes, the real Maria had married Captain von Trapp when she was 22, but the original Maria on Broadway had been in her mid-forties. I knew I wouldn't be cast as Maria for a long time, and I worried that if people knew my real age, I wouldn't get cast at all.

I looked young, and in Boston, there was no one to remind me of the ticking clock. When Ray came to visit, we were "Lee and Ray," not "Mr. and Mrs." When I went to the movies, if I failed to specify that I wanted an adult ticket, the cashier would ask, "Are you under sixteen?" At the Boston Museum of Fine Arts, one of the docents asked why I wasn't in school—but seemed satisfied when I told her I had graduated from high school when I was 16. In Boston, the time ahead of me seemed to expand.

After *Carousel* closed and I returned to New York, I quickly identified what I hoped would be my next show: *Butterflies Are Free* at the Beverly Dinner Playhouse in New Orleans. I had seen the play on Broadway, and the character description of the ingénue suited me perfectly. Jill Tanner is 19 with a "delicate, little-girl quality about her." However, when I went to the Equity interviews, the producers told me that the movie of *Butterflies Are Free* would be playing in New Orleans that fall, so they had decided to replace the play with a musical, *The Fantasticks*. They thought I would be perfect for the role of 16-year-old Luisa. I told them I didn't have the voice for Luisa. "Come sing for us," they said. I declined. They insisted. I didn't want to offend the producers—especially in a city I had briefly glimpsed and longed to explore—so I agreed.

My goal at the audition was *not* to land the role, but to impress the producers as an actress for future plays, so I began with Luisa's monologue that leads into the song "Much More." I could identify with Luisa, a girl who wants "much more than keeping house," who longs "to go to town in a golden gown.... Just once. Just once. Just once before I'm old."

I finished the song, and the producers offered me the role on the spot.

"I really can't sing this role," I said. I walked over to the piano and played the obbligato for "Round and Round" and squeaked the high notes as if I were Patty in *You're a Good Man, Charlie Brown.*

They said my singing was lovely. Then they told me about New Orleans. The weather in October, November, and December would be warm, and I would live in an apartment complex with two swimming pools walking distance from the historic Beverly Dinner Playhouse. The cast would have access to a company car to drive into the city and explore the French Quarter, the world-class restaurants, and the jazz clubs. After the performances (only seven per week), the actors were invited to the piano bar where the first drink was free and additional drinks were half price. *The Fantasticks* was scheduled to run for seven weeks, and I would be home two weeks before Christmas.

Their pitch was irresistible. I said "yes."

In the 19th century, the Beverly Dinner Playhouse, a white building with stately columns, was part of the Labarre family plantation. In the 1920s, it became a roadhouse, and in the late 1940s, in its most famous incarnation, it was The Beverly Country Club, a glamorous casino with entertainers like Sophie Tucker, Carmen Miranda, and Rudy Vallee. The owners of The Beverly Country Club included Meyer Lansky, Frank Costello, and Carlos Marcello—men who are now "notable names" in The Mob Museum in Las Vegas. When the Kefauver Committee began investigating organized crime, the Beverly closed its doors.

In May 1972, producers Storer Boone and Charles Wisdom re-opened the Beverly as a dinner theater with a piano bar. The china, crystal, and silver all dated back to the days of the casino, and the waiters and waitresses were dressed as croupiers and cigarette girls.

Storer, Charlie, and director Pat Baldauff were wonderful hosts and made living and working in New Orleans a joy. They took the cast to brunch at Brennan's and to dinner at Commander's Palace. When I told Pat that cigarette smoking during rehearsals irritated my throat, he banned smoking in the rehearsal room even though he was one of the smokers.

The original Off Broadway production of *The Fantasticks* ran for

42 years. The cast is small, and the few props include a cardboard moon and a wall represented by a mime holding a stick.

The Fantasticks plays like a sweet fairy tale set in a simpler time when fathers knew best, girls fell in love with the boys next door, and there was no place like home. However, in telling the tale, *The Fantasticks* deconstructs the sexist society of the 1950s and shows that when the boy and the girl finally get together, they don't always live happily ever after.

El Gallo ("The Cock") is the omniscient narrator and also a character in the play. He introduces Luisa, age 16, who is giddily in love with love, personified by Matt, the boy next door. Matt, 19, has been to college and proclaims that he is grown-up because he has been inside a lab and dissected violets. Matt and Luisa imagine they are Romeo and Juliet when they sneak out at night to declare their love across the wall their fathers built to keep them apart—or so they think. In fact, the two fathers built the wall because they want their children to marry each other, and they know that children do exactly what you tell them *not* to do. Once Luisa and Matt have fallen in love, the fathers must find a way to end their fictitious feud, so they hire El Gallo to abduct Luisa and allow Matt to save her. This reunites the families for a happy ending to act one.

There are hints in act one that *The Fantasticks* is not a simple fairy tale. El Gallo begins the show with the lyric "Try to remember the kind of September…." If this is a story about young love, why is the month September? I think it is September because Luisa's childhood dreams—dreams formed by books that glamorize romantic love—are about to die—like the leaves in September. When Matt woos Luisa, he compares her to Juliet, Beatrice, and Guinevere—women whose lives are defined by the men who loved them. The two fathers hire El Gallo, the Cock, to abduct Luisa and reinforce what she has read—that romance requires helpless women and older men to rescue them—a charade that builds up the self-esteem of the boy and reduces the girl to a pawn. Luisa's father prefers to call the abduction "*attempted* rape," but El Gallo insists on the proper term: "Rape First Class," for which he and his associates will be paid "regular Union rates." The audience usually laughs at the words "Rape

First Class" and "regular Union rates," because Luisa is not in physical danger. However, the rape of Luisa is the rape of her self-esteem, the rape of her belief in her own abilities—a rape that is institutionalized in our society, so it has "Union rates."

In act two, the deconstruction of the fairy tale and of society moves into the foreground. Luisa and Matt see each other by daylight rather than moonlight, and they don't like what they see. They learn that they have been puppets in a charade financed by their fathers, and they are angry. Matt and Luisa decide to go their separate ways to see the world for themselves, but El Gallo, the voice of society, announces, "A boy may go. The girl must stay." Matt travels the world to find out what he wants out of life, but Luisa is not allowed the same freedom. Luisa can see only what El Gallo shows her—glimpses of a cruel world to make her fearful of the outside world. El Gallo shows Luisa how to hold up a smiling mask that alters her feelings and distorts her view—just as doctors in the 1950s gave desperate housewives hundreds of millions of tranquilizers ("mother's little helper") to dull women's frustration and drug them into a state of "happy homemakers." However, Luisa still longs for adventure, so El Gallo promises he will take her away. While she packs, he requires her to give him her prized possession and her only link to her deceased mother—a necklace—as proof she'll return. El Gallo takes the necklace and abandons Luisa just as Matt returns home.

Luisa and Matt admit to each other that they've been foolish and declare their love in the song "You Are Love." Luisa has been transformed from a girl who sings the rangy, aspirational song "Much More" into a girl who sings simple lyrics to a simple melody: "Without you near me / I can't see. / When you're near me / Wonderful things come to be." Luisa's dreams of a bigger life have been systematically destroyed. She will keep house for Matt, and, most likely, for the two fathers. This is the manifest destiny, the "happy ending," that was sold to young girls in the 1950s. Nevertheless, the writers of *The Fantasticks* leave us with hope for Luisa. Luisa and Matt do love each other, and Matt thinks for himself. Perhaps Luisa's dreams of a bigger life will not stay buried in the snow of December. Just as spring follows winter, the 1960s will follow the 1950s, and the Luisas of the world will demand more—and some of the Matts will stand up for them.

To my surprise, my reviews were actually pretty good. One reviewer wrote, "Lee Wilson, as the girl, embodies the Princess mystique. She is sugar and spice and everything nice.... She avoids the caramel trap that awaits actresses who have to be cute." The *Vieux Carré Courier* stated, "Lee Wilson is the cutest, perkiest sugar-and-spice little elf on her tiptoes to starched pinafore and the tears she cries are real tears; thus I forgive the fact that she sometimes tends to stray from the notes as strictly written by the composer. (Edith Piaf didn't hit 'em all the time, either.)"

Straying from the notes was probably accurate, but *Edith Piaf*?! Only in my wildest dreams could I sing like Piaf!

When I wasn't performing, I explored the streets of the bustling French Quarter. I admired the wrought iron balconies on Royal Street, the paintings of the artists in Jackson Square, and the ornate gold crosses in the jewelry store windows. I enjoyed trumpeter Al Hirt, clarinetist Pete Fountain, and the Preservation Hall Jazz Band. I savored chicken creole at Galatoire's and topped off the evening with café au lait and beignets at the Café du Monde. I luxuriated in the warm weather as I read about pouring rain and below average temperatures in New York.

Ray had visited during rehearsals, and I looked forward to showing him the city now that the show was running smoothly and my days were free. He arrived at night. The stage manager drove me to the airport. She and I stood in the terminal and watched Ray's plane land. A rolling staircase was pushed into position at the side of the airplane. The door to the airplane opened, and Ray was one of the first people in the doorway. As he began to walk down the stairs, I knew with absolute certainty that my marriage was in trouble.

12

Playing Wife
(1973)

I had been playing wonderful roles in classic musicals, exploring the stimulating cities of Boston and New Orleans, enjoying quick flights to New York on my day off, and hosting Ray for longer visits at my out-of-town lodging. We had played tourist and shared romantic dinners—but Ray felt lonely and abandoned in our New York apartment, and he wasn't good at being alone.

Ray was also making the transition from baritone to tenor. By the end of 1972, he had signed contracts to sing the lyric tenor role of Romeo in Gounod's *Romeo and Juliet* in San Diego and Omaha early the next year. He wanted 100 percent of my time, attention, and encouragement. I agreed to take 12 months off from my own career and work fulltime on his.

It seemed there was no better time to take a year off than 1973. Broadway was in turmoil. There was a power struggle at the Shubert Organization between Lawrence Shubert and the two lawyers, Bernie Jacobs and Gerald Schoenfeld, who had been running the organization while Lawrence Shubert spent his days at the bar in Sardi's. In the summer of 1972, Jacobs and Schoenfeld had staged a coup, but that December, Lawrence Shubert filed a lawsuit that prolonged the conflict. Jacobs and Schoenfeld tried to get a line of credit for one million dollars with 17 Broadway theaters as collateral, but their offer was rejected—demonstrating to the theatrical and financial communities the plummeting value of Broadway. Back in 1968, Broadway theatergoers had bought 9.5 million tickets, but in 1972, they had bought only 5.4 million tickets. Pessimists predicted the imminent demise of Broadway. Producers were mounting "ethnic" shows to attract minority audiences, rock musicals to attract the young, and shows with nudity to attract randy businessmen, peep show devotees, and iconoclasts. I wasn't Black; rock wasn't my forte, and I wouldn't perform nude.

In 1972, the composer/lyricist often identified as the future of Broadway was Stephen Sondheim, and that was not encouraging news for me. Stephen Sondheim was a protégé of Oscar Hammerstein, but Hammerstein shows were optimistic, and Sondheim shows were not. Hammerstein wrote shows in which dance was essential and helped tell the story. Sondheim did not.

Sondheim first popped onto my radar in the late 1950s when he wrote the lyrics for *West Side Story* and *Gypsy*—two cast albums I loved—and two shows with lots of dance. During the 1960s, Sondheim gained his first Broadway credits for writing both music and lyrics, and in 1970 and 1971, he began the new decade by writing the music and lyrics for *Company* and *Follies*, two shows I admired, but which didn't make my heart sing.

The theme of *Company* is marriage, but the minimal plot (book by George Furth) is murky: Do the birthday party scenes represent one birthday party, or more? Does Bobby change his point of view about marriage at the end? Is the show pro-marriage or anti-marriage? *Company* is a Rorschach test—a series of scenes for the viewer to interpret. In Craig Zadan's book *Sondheim & Co.*, Sondheim is quoted as saying, "people were mistaking our saying that relationships are *difficult* for relationships are *impossible*. What we clearly said over and over again was two is difficult but one is impossible. We said it over and over again, and yet a lot of people missed it."

I saw the original production of *Company* twice—first with Dean Jones as Bobby, and shortly thereafter, with Larry Kert. I have read the script for *Company* and have seen other productions, but I don't see what Sondheim described. I see that two is difficult, but I don't see that one is impossible. In fact, compared to the marriages in *Company*, the single life seems slam-dunk better.

The climax of *Company* is the song "Being Alive." Bobby begins the song by asking what people actually get from marriage. Then he sings a long list of the ways that married people annoy and hurt each other. One of his married friends tells him that he seems to have many reasons for *not* being with someone, but not a single reason for being alone. To me, this sounds like "You've got lots of good reasons for not jumping out of an airplane without a parachute, but not one good reason for sitting in the plane." Well, it's the alternative to being alone that doesn't attract Bobby. The marriages that surround him are filled with conflict. As the song continues, Bobby's married friends encourage (bully?) Bobby and remind him that he's not getting any younger. By the end of "Being Alive," Bobby is singing that he wants someone to hurt him too much and put him through hell to make him alive.

Why would a 35-year-old man have an epiphany about marriage without a specific person or situation in mind—especially since he expects marriage to put him through hell? Is he feeling like an "old maid" at 35? Is his embrace of marriage a momentary enthusiasm? Is it a ruse to pacify his friends? How can I root for Bobby when I don't know what will make him happy?

"Being Alive" leads into the final scene in which Bobby's married friends assemble in his apartment with a birthday cake, but, unlike the earlier party scenes, there is no sign of Bobby, and the friends decide to leave. They all say, "Happy birthday" and then, blow out the candles on the cake. The script reads: "ROBERT has stood center stage; HE now smiles." I concluded that Bobby was smiling because he had evaded his bickering friends and could spend the evening by himself, free to do whatever he pleased.

According to *Sondheim & Co.*, Sondheim recognized that the ending did not have the effect he had hoped: "When Bobby suddenly realizes that he shouldn't be alone at the end of the scene, it's too small a moment and you don't believe it." I was one of the many who didn't believe that Bobby would embrace marriage, but I didn't conclude, as some people did, that Bobby is gay. I walked out of the theater admiring the performances and the songs and trying to figure out the multiple birthday parties:

In *Sense of Occasion*, Harold Prince (the producer and director of the show) wrote: "Since Robert never arrives for the final celebration, there was some question whether they represented one birthday or a succession of them. I am certain they were one. I wouldn't be surprised if George Furth believes there were four. It doesn't matter." It mattered to me, and I wondered: *How can I make sense of these different parties*? My best guess was that the entire show takes place in Bobby's head as he decides how to deal with the upcoming "surprise" birthday party: He imagines himself arriving at the party, pretending to be surprised, and half-heartedly blowing at the candles on the cake. He thinks about his married friends who will be at the party—and the single girls he has dated—none of them interesting mates. He envisions what his friends might do if he doesn't show up for the party, and he decides to skip the party. *Company* is a puzzle that people can solve in different ways.

In the original production, the sets, the staging, the lyrics, and the music were smart and sophisticated, and the original cast (with Dean Jones and later with Larry Kert) was terrific, but *Company* was a show that didn't engage me emotionally, and it had only one number for a trained dancer—the sexy "Tick Tock" dance for Donna McKechnie that illustrated the passionate love-making between Bobby and the flight attendant April. This was not a show in which I could see myself in the near future.

Sondheim's 1971 musical was *Follies*. I went to see the show shortly after it opened—after *Lolita* had bombed in Boston and I had turned down the Milliken Show and the reprise of Liesl at Jones Beach. I doubted there would be a role for me in a show about showgirls, and there wasn't.

The brightly colored, predominately orange *Follies* poster informed me that the show was not light vaudeville. It featured the Mount Rushmore–like face and torso of a showgirl in full makeup, with a FOLLIES crown on her head, a worried look on her face, and waves of blue and purple hair flowing onto her shoulders. Below her shoulders, her body became a flat, light-orange-to-dark-orange background for the name of the show and the credits. The most striking part of the image was a diagonal crack that began in the young woman's crown, widened as it grazed her left eye, and broke into multiple cracks on her chin. Something terrible had happened to this girl and to the art she represents.

When the curtain rose in the Winter Garden Theatre, it revealed the stage and catwalk of a once-opulent, now-crumbling theater. Ghosts of glamorous showgirls roamed the stage while middle-aged, former showgirls arrived with their consorts for a final reunion in the temple of their youth. Only one of the five stars was a Broadway veteran familiar to younger audiences—John McMartin. The others—Alexis Smith, Dorothy Collins, Gene Nelson, and Yvonne De Carlo—were primarily TV and/or movie stars. The glory days of the actors (like their characters) were in the past. As the stars made their choreographed entrances, some received a smattering of applause along with whispers of "Who is that? Which one is she?" None of the leading ladies had actually been showgirls, and their descent down a staircase to the song "Beautiful Girls" underscored the fact that they were no longer girls and that they didn't have the style of the ghosts who floated across the stage.

Thirty years earlier, Sally and Phyllis (Dorothy Collins and Alexis Smith) had been fun-loving showgirls who were dating stage-door johnnies Buddy and Ben (Gene Nelson and John McMartin), whom they later married. Young counterparts played the stars in their happy, carefree youth, but at the time of the reunion, the characters are bitter, unhappily married couples. On the other hand, Carlotta (Yvonne De Carlo), has worked through good times and bad, and is now acting in a TV series and enjoying a "thing" with a young man of 26. The happy people in the musical—the young quartet and the older women who continued their careers—are juxtaposed with the two unhappily married couples.

Some people described *Follies* as an extravagantly produced story about unhappy marriages, and Walter Kerr wrote in *The New York Times*: "'FOLLIES' is intermissionless and exhausting, an extravaganza that becomes tedious for two simple reasons: Its extravagances have nothing to do with its pebble of a plot; and the plot, which could be wrapped up in approximately two songs, dawdles through 22 before it declares itself done."

It seemed to me that *Follies* was a showcase for Sondheim's talent (22 songs in diverse styles) and a eulogy for the Golden Age of Broadway—a tribute to the good old days when opulent theaters showcased optimistic entertainment, dancers flirted with stage-door johnnies, and composers wrote emotional torch songs like "Losing My Mind." I thought it ironic that Sondheim (often described as "the future of Broadway") had written a show that implied that the best days of Broadway were in the past, and that the vibrant, optimistic entertainment of thirty years earlier had become bitter and cynical. I wondered if Sondheim might fear that at age 41, his greatest success was already in the past. In fact, the only Sondheim show that has reached the two-year mark on Broadway is the exuberant *A Funny Thing Happened on the Way to the Forum* (book by Burt Shevelove and Larry Gelbart) that opened in 1962.

Follies had a wide-ranging score, excellent performances, imaginative choreography, and extravagant production values, but there were many discouraging features from my point of view: a minimal plot; lead characters without defined, realistic goals; dance numbers performed by non-dancers; and the characterization of women in their forties as over-the-hill.

Alexis Smith was 49 when *Follies* opened; Yvonne De Carlo was 48, and Dorothy Collins was 44. Collins was two years younger than Mary Martin was when she played Maria in *The Sound of Music*, 15 years younger than Betty Grable when Miss Grable danced through *Hello, Dolly!*, and 26 years younger than Betty Garrett when Betty danced an exuberant Irish jig on a kitchen table in *Meet Me in St. Louis*. For more than two decades, year after year, the *Fabulous Palm Springs Follies* proved that women in their sixties and seventies can strut like showgirls in their twenties—provided they stay in shape. Many of the women in Broadway's *Follies* were struggling with the choreography—not because women their age couldn't perform that choreography—but because they weren't dancers, and because the creative team, including the costume designer, had set them up to look old.

Frank Rich reviewed the show for the *Harvard Crimson* while it was in its pre–Broadway try-out in Boston. His review began: "THESE ARE old women coming down the staircase. They are dumpy, their hair is dyed, they don't exactly keep time with the music. They are not very secure, and, for that matter, neither is the staircase they are descending. It is ratty. But it doesn't make any difference. The staircase is on the stage of a theatre that is about to become a parking lot, and the women—well, the women don't have much farther to go before they die." Rich raved about the book, music, lyrics, choreography, direction, and the actors "all of whom are at once wonderful and sad." He wrote, "*Follies* is a musical about the death of the musical and everything musicals represented for the people who saw and enjoyed them when such entertainment flourished in this country." *When such entertainment flourished. Past tense*! Rich concluded, "there is no getting around the fact that a large part of the chilling fascination of *Follies* is that its creators are in essence presenting their own funeral."

If Sondheim was the future of Broadway, I was out of step. I loved the optimistic Rodgers and Hammerstein musicals in which the lead characters took risks to achieve their goals. It took guts for Laurey to drive alone with Jud, and when Jud slowed the horses, Laurey grabbed the reins and urged the horses to run toward their destination. When Jud became physically aggressive, Laurey fired him. Even in *Carousel*, the darkest Rodgers and Hammerstein musical, Billy and Julie risked everything for love and a family; Billy was too damaged to save his own life, but by the end of the show, he understood and conveyed to his daughter the simple fact that although society is unjust, there are good people within it, and if you can identify the better angels and align yourself with them, you can succeed. In *Company* and *Follies*, the unhappy or ambivalent protagonists ended up where they had begun. (Even if you believe that Bobby has progressed or regressed from "marriage isn't what I want" to "marriage *is* what I want," he has done nothing to change his circumstances, and the unhappily married couples in *Follies* know that they are miserable, but wallow and rant and wail rather than taking action.)

The shows I loved were being produced in regional theater, but they were few and far between on Broadway. I looked to my contemporaries for inspiration. I had identified two young women who I believed had the talent and the work ethic to become Broadway stars: Sandy Duncan and Bernadette Peters. Their career trajectories were not encouraging.

Sandy Duncan was a triple threat with star quality. In 1969, people were buzzing about Sandy when she played multiple roles in the musical *Canterbury Tales.* She received a Tony nomination for Best Featured Actress in a Musical, but the show ran only a few months. Then she starred in the two-character play *Love Is a Time of Day* that ran one week. In 1970, her agent, Gus Schirmer, directed a revival of *The Boy Friend* with Sandy as Maisie, which brought her a second Tony nomination—this time for Leading Actress in a Musical—but the show closed after two months. The following year, 1971, Sandy starred in two feature films (*The Million Dollar Duck* and *Star Spangled Girl*) as well as the TV series *Funny Face,* which in 1972, was reworked and renamed *The Sandy Duncan Show.* Sandy returned to Broadway in 1979 as a brilliant Peter Pan—another Tony nomination for Best Actress in a Musical—and has since starred in other Broadway musicals, but in 1972, it seemed that Sandy had defected to Hollywood.

In the fall of 1967, while I was performing in *Hello, Dolly!,* Bernadette Peters opened on Broadway in the play *Johnny No-Trump,* which ran one night. Then she played Josie Cohan in *George M* for a few months, followed by the one-night run of *La Strada* in 1969. In his *New York Times* review of *La Strada,* Clive Barnes wrote, "In a different show the birdlike and croaky Bernadette Peters would have become a star overnight." Bernadette's performance in her next Broadway show, a revival of *On the Town,* garnered another rave review and her first Tony nomination (Best Featured Actress in a Musical), but ran only two months. By 1972, Bernadette had performed in a couple of musicals for TV. It appeared that she was another talented Broadway performer who was headed to Hollywood, where she later starred in the TV series *All's Fair* and in the feature films, *The Jerk* and *Pennies from Heaven* opposite Steve Martin. In 1974, Bernadette was terrific in the short-lived Broadway musical *Mack & Mabel* (Tony nomination for Best Actress in a Musical), but it wasn't until 1984 with *Sunday in the Park with George* (another Tony nomination for Best Actress in a Musical) that Bernadette had a leading role in a Broadway success—fifteen years after her first leading role in *La Strada.* Her wins for Best Actress in a

Musical (*Song and Dance* and *Annie Get Your Gun*) were still in the future.

These two women were my guiding lights, and they were working in film and TV, but I couldn't visualize myself in Hollywood—primarily because Ray was based in New York, but also because I didn't see myself working in a community where middle-aged moguls chased young actresses around their desks, and producers and directors judged actresses on their "fuckability" ("Fuckability": the instant an actress appears on screen, how urgently do the men in the audience want to have sex with her?).

In New York, I had never been chased around a desk. Most of the propositions I had received had been more sophisticated—like the one from Rudolf Bing: Shortly after my first Metropolitan Opera spring tour in 1965, Bob Herman, an assistant general manager at the Met, gave a pool party for the ballet at his home. One of the girls in the company advised me to leave before sundown. After dark, she said, naked young men would be tiptoeing through the shrubbery. Early in the evening, well before sundown, I thanked Mr. Herman for the delightful afternoon and asked to be in the next car leaving for the train station. Mr. Herman told me that Mr. Bing (the general manager of the company) was driving back into the city and could give me a lift.

"Where in the city is he going?" I asked.

"The Essex House."

"Perfect. I live a short walk away."

During the drive into the city, Mr. Bing, an elegant, articulate man in his sixties, asked me about my ballet career in Europe and told me that he was married to a former ballet dancer. As we discussed our love for ballet and opera, he asked me if I had a favorite opera. "*Otello*" I said promptly, and he told me that *Otello* was one of his two favorites, along with *Die Zauberflöte*. The Mozart opera was not one of my favorites, but Mr. Bing assured me it would grow on me as I got to know it better and got to know the language better. (I must confess that I loved the new production at the Met two years later, but that was primarily because of the Chagall sets and costumes, which some music-lovers believed overwhelmed the music.)

When we arrived at the Essex House, Mr. Bing said he was all alone for dinner and would like me to join him at the hotel restaurant. I was dressed for a pool party, not for dinner at the Essex House, but Mr. Bing assured me that I looked lovely and that we'd have a quiet booth in the back, so I accepted his invitation.

After a very nice dinner and more conversation about the arts, Mr. Bing invited me to see the spectacular view from his apartment. I had never seen New York at night from a tall building, and my intuition (plus Mr. Bing's reputation as a gentleman) told me I had nothing to fear, so I accepted—and the view was spectacular. As I admired the twinkling lights, Mr. Bing began reading a love poem that included the words "dear Lee."

I wondered: *What was the original line? Dear love? Dear Jane? How often had he read that poem to other girls with other names?*

Mr. Bing said he had been watching me for some time. He was a busy man and didn't have much time to woo, but he wanted me to become his mistress. He acknowledged that he was much older than I, but he thought we had a great deal to offer each other. He said I should not think that becoming his mistress would help my career. The ballet was the domain of Dame Alicia Markova, and he would never interfere. Also, as he had told me earlier, he was married, so I would have to disappear when his wife came into the city—but that wasn't often.

I thought it would be awkward to reject the general manager of the Metropolitan Opera, a man I would see regularly at the theater, so I lied and gave him a compelling reason to withdraw his offer. "Mr. Bing," I said. "Do you know how old I am? I'm only seventeen."

"That doesn't matter," he said. "You're surely not a virgin."

Gulp.

"Actually, I am," I said truthfully. "And I plan to stay that way for the foreseeable future." (Another truth.)

"I'm sorry to hear that."

I wondered if he knew I had lied about my age.

He encouraged me to stay the night, but I declined. He wrote a telephone number on a piece of notepaper. "This is my private number that bypasses my secretary. If you change your mind in the next week or so, please call."

I almost giggled. *One week. Or so.*

Mr. Bing asked if I would mind terribly if he put me into a taxi instead of driving me home. I assured him I could walk a few blocks, but he insisted on putting me into a cab. After I was inside the taxi, he handed me a bill. When I saw it was a twenty-—more than a week's rent—I tried to give it back, but he backed away.

I never called the number.

Mr. Bing had set my expectations for how rich and powerful men might proposition young women, but in the following years, I had heard that successful men in Hollywood were much more aggressive and that "being available" for the star or the producer was often part of the job. That was not a world in which I wanted to live.

In December 1972, I didn't know what the future of my marriage might be, but I believed in Ray's talent, and I wanted his transition to tenor to be a success. During 1973, my focus would be on Ray and his career, beginning with the role of Romeo in San Diego, California. The book *Sun Signs* by Linda Goodman was a best seller about the characteristics of people born under different signs of the zodiac, and we used the profiles in *Sun Signs* to jumpstart our discussions about the character of Romeo. We decided that Romeo was an Aries, the baby of the zodiac, who is driven by emotion, jumps quickly from one all-consuming infatuation to the next, and doesn't consider the implications of his actions. Director Jim de Blasis did a terrific job of staging the opera and generously allowed me to watch rehearsals and take notes for Ray. I recall only one time when Ray was doubtful about one of my notes. It was during the ball scene when Romeo first sees Juliet. In rehearsal, when Juliet entered, Ray raised an arm in her direction. I asked Ray why he had raised his arm, and he said it was to acknowledge Juliet—and give her the focus.

"A spotlight will give her the focus," I said. "And I don't think you're *acknowledging* Juliet; I think you're falling in love with her."

"But that's what Romeos do."

Ray was covering the role at the Met, and apparently, the tenor had chosen, or had been directed, to raise his arm.

"When you hold out your hand, you look as if you're inviting Juliet to join you. But she doesn't. I don't think that's what you want."

"So, what do you want me to do?"

"Nothing. The instant you see Juliet, you are in such awe of her beauty, you can't move, you can't think, you can't breathe."

Ray was dubious. He said he felt awkward just standing there, but I assured him that the moment played beautifully. In retrospect, I think I probably got this idea from Agnes de Mille's staging of the prologue of *Carousel.* When Billy Bigelow gives his spiel, Julie is facing upstage, but the audience knows that Julie is in love with Billy because everyone else is swaying while she stands perfectly still. In *Romeo and Juliet,* Ray, in a spotlight, was the only person standing perfectly still.

Throughout rehearsals, Ray was fighting a cold and sang very little, but before the first performance, the doctor said there was no reason Ray *shouldn't* sing—if he could. *Would his voice hold up? Could he hit the high notes? Would he have to cancel mid-performance?* Another tenor was standing by.

In Ray's dressing room, I made hot tea and checked the water level in the humidifier. I ran to the drugstore and bought cough drops. Shortly before curtain time, I slipped a small cassette recorder into the pouch I had made to match my dress, and took my seat in the orchestra section of the theater. The opening night audience included Martin Bernheimer, the music critic for the *Los Angeles Times,* and David McIntyre of the San Diego *Evening Tribune.*

The conductor stepped onto the podium and bowed to the audience. As the applause waned, I sneaked the end of my tape recorder out of the pouch, aimed the microphone at the stage, and pressed the record button. Recording was illegal, but it was routine for opera singers who wanted immediate, accurate feedback.

After each act, I went backstage and assured Ray he was singing well. We rewound the tape and listened to passages that concerned him. At the end of the intermission, I inserted a new cassette, put the recorder back into the pouch, and took my seat.

Ray was on edge as we waited for the most important review—that of Martin Bernheimer in the *Los Angeles Times.* A few days after the first performance, the review was published. The title read: "A Romeo for Juliets to Dream of." Bernheimer wrote that the performance "introduced a singer who, unless something ridiculous happens, soon should have the operatic world at his feet.... His voice, after all, is warm and poised and firm, and he applies it to the Gallic line gracefully.... He acts with forthright intelligence, and even knows how to stand still on stage without losing dramatic tension."

Ray acknowledged that I must have been right about standing still.

The *Evening Tribune* stated that Juliet "is topped by Raymond Gibbs, who appears as the impetuous Montague who wants to have Juliet as his own. Gibbs is forceful dramatically, and this is what makes this production go."

In Omaha, the following month, the reviews were equally enthusiastic. James Bresette wrote in the *Omaha World-Herald* that Ray had a "fresh, boyish handsomeness that belied the strength and maturity of his singing and the sureness of his acting" and that he and the soprano performed their love scenes "with a grandly physical passion that was most effective."

Ray's tenor career was off to a great start. On a rainy night in early April, Ray sang his first Romeo at the Met, and later that month, I accompanied Ray on the Metropolitan Opera spring tour. There were parties and luncheons and interviews. The cities and activities were familiar from the years I had danced with the Metropolitan Opera Ballet, but in 1973, instead of taking private trains as we had in the mid–1960s, we took commercial flights, which were not as much fun. Instead of performing myself, I sat in the audience and watched Ray perform, which was not as much fun.

During the week in Atlanta, we drove to Tullahoma, Tennessee, to attend a celebration for the sixtieth wedding anniversary of my paternal grandparents, Gampie and Nana. Gampie, an Episcopal minister, looked angelic in his collar as he gave an after-dinner speech about the loving woman who had stood by his side for 60 years, and Nana stood beside him and looked up at him in adoration. The effectiveness of the speech was mitigated by the fact that Mom had told me that the dinner almost didn't take place—because a few hours earlier, one member of the adoring couple had thrown a frozen ham at the other.

Long before *The Good Wife* became a hit television series, I wondered what supportive wives standing beside their successful husbands were actually thinking.

Being married in the opera world was a challenge. Tenors generally played the romantic leads, and tenors were the male voices most likely to become superstars. Some tenors' wives stayed in the suburbs and raised their children while their husbands had casual and not-so-casual affairs. In contrast, one tenor's wife traveled with her husband everywhere while the musicians and stagehands snickered and belittled her: "You know when [tenor's name] is in the men's room because his wife is standing outside the door."

"Clinging to her meal ticket."

I never heard anyone suggest that her presence might have contributed to his success or his happiness.

Women who discouraged their husbands from playing around were mocked, and men who played around put pressure on other men to do the same. Groupies promoted the swinging atmosphere. In one city, one of the young women who drove Ray and me from the airport to the hotel announced: "Last summer I slept with all the leading tenors except one. This year, I plan to do them all." In another city, a voluptuous brunette in a low-cut red dress gushed to Ray about how talented he was, how sexy he was, and how hot the love scenes were. She glanced at me for a nanosecond and said, "Oh, you must be the wife," as she wrote down her telephone number and invited Ray to call. She was thrilled that Ray was based in New York because she lived in New Jersey and would love to show him all around New Jersey.

By the end of the Metropolitan Opera spring tour, I was looking forward to time alone with Ray when neither of us was preparing for a performance. Ray and I had traveled around the country to see each other work, but we hadn't had a real vacation since our honeymoon four years earlier at my aunt's beach house. At least one of us had always been working, so I planned a four-week trip to France that began in Paris and ended in Cannes.

We flew to Paris on Air France and during the flight, we were served *suprême de volaille au champagne* and *cœur de céleri étuvé au beurre*. I loved being surrounded by people speaking my beautiful second language. The next morning at the hotel, we had café au lait with warm, crispy croissants slathered with sweet butter and topped with dabs of jam. We visited Notre-Dame, the Eiffel Tower, Sainte-Chappelle, Montmartre, and the Arc de Triomphe. Ray took photos of everything from *Winged Victory* in the Louvre to men playing boules in the gardens. For dinner, we enjoyed *steak au poivre* and *pommes frites*, followed by *mousse au chocolat* or *crème caramel*. The taste of strong French coffee, thick vegetable soup, and celery root salad took me back in time. I showed Ray the Théâtre des Champs-Elysées where I had danced when I was seventeen, and we toured the Paris Opera House with its new Chagall ceiling. We attended a performance of *Le Bourgeois Gentilhomme* at the Comédie Française and saw a musical revue at the Casino de Paris that was choreographed by Roland Petit. I loved being back in the country where I had begun my career.

At the end of our week in Paris, we rented a car and set out to visit the châteaux of the Loire. As we drove toward Chartres, Ray took a photo of the cathedral, seemingly rising from a wheat field as we approached the city. In Blois, we watched a sound and light show at the wonderfully eclectic Château Royal de Blois with each wing in a different style. The oldest part of the castle is grey stone and dates from the 13th century. On one side is the red brick, Louis XII wing from the 15th century. On the other side is the ornate Renaissance wing with an exterior circular staircase, built by François I during the 16th century. Completing the hodge-podge effect is a Classical wing attributed to Mansart that was built in the 17th century. The Château Royal de Blois is the castle where Joan of Arc was blessed by the Archbishop of Reims before she led her army to Orléans.

The most beautiful castles were the Château de Chambord, an elegant, perfectly proportioned castle with lovely gardens, and the Château de Chenonceau, a castle that spans the Cher River and became famous for Catherine de Medici's nighttime parties that featured the first fireworks in France.

As we drove south to the Riviera, we stopped at the Roman Theatre of Orange that was built in the first century AD. The outdoor amphitheater seats nine thousand people, and the stage is more than two hundred feet wide. There were only a few other people in the theater that morning, and they gasped with delight when Ray stood center stage and sang a few bars from an aria while I listened from the back row of the theater. The acoustics were superb, and hearing Ray's voice in that setting was a thrill.

We drove along the coast of the Mediterranean Sea from Cannes to Monte Carlo. In Cannes, we strolled along the glamorous Promenade de la Croisette and ate ice cream cones with twin scoops of ice cream side by side—not one on top of the other, like in the U.S.

I was happy as a panda in a snowstorm—except for one thing: Ray was a fish out of water. By the time we reached the Riviera, Ray wanted to know how much it would cost to go home early.

A love of travel would not be the glue that would keep us together.

13

Back on the Boards (1973–1975)

The telephone rang. It was producer Gerry Roberts in Boston. He wanted me to play Liesl in *The Sound of Music* in three new Chateau de Ville theaters that fall. I had promised Ray I would take a year off, so I told Gerry I wasn't available. Ray called out from the other room, "TAKE THE JOB!"

I told Gerry I would call him back.

I reminded Ray that I still owed him three months, but he snapped, "You're going back to work eventually. You might as well do it now."

Ray had hoped that I would love being a full-time wife, but I wasn't that woman. I never had been. I never could be.

"Are you sure?" I asked.

"Yes. You like the role. You like the people. Take it."

I accepted the job without thinking about whether I really wanted to play Liesl again—or whether I wanted to perform in three small towns. Ray was throwing me a lifeline, and I grabbed it.

The first theater was in Randolph, Massachusetts, a short commute from the Copley Square Hotel in Boston. The other two were in Warwick, Rhode Island, and East Windsor, Connecticut.

I was glad to be back on stage, but this production was a pale imitation of previous productions, and there wasn't a lot to do after I left Boston. I was elected Equity deputy—the performer who functions as a liaison between the performers and the union. I filed weekly reports and solved problems. I convinced an 8-year-old that "I'm not going on stage until I get my overtime pay" was not a tenable position—that if she wanted a future in this business, she had to fulfill the terms of her contract. I assured her I would call the producer and report back the following day about why *none* of us got our overtime pay. (It had to do with checks being signed before the end of week, so that overtime pay lagged by one week.)

I also wrote to Equity on behalf of a cast member who was embarrassed that Equity had contacted Gerry Roberts and informed him that she had failed to pay her union dues and told him to take the dues out of her paycheck. If she had received a bill, she said, she would have paid it, and I believed her. I informed Equity that the union had embarrassed a talented and conscientious member and suggested that in the future, they contact delinquent members through the theater before contacting the producer.

Finally, a new stage manager scheduled "clean up" rehearsals so he could re-direct the show. Among other things, he wanted Liesl to be more aggressive and flirtatious—like the girl in the movie—and that was not what the director had staged and not what I wanted to play. I alerted Gerry Roberts, who put a stop to the meddling.

The Sound of Music closed just before Christmas, and during the following month, January 1974, someone told me I should check in with a group of dancers who were planning to get together after their evening performances to talk about their lives and figure out how to generate more work. I didn't follow up because I was scheduled to accompany Ray to Toledo and Dayton, Ohio, and I didn't think I could back out of the trip to sit up all night chatting with other dancers. But I thought: *If I weren't married, I'd be there—just out of curiosity, just to see what's going on.*

At the time, no one could have guessed that these talk sessions would lead to the juggernaut of *A Chorus Line.*

That summer, Ray was singing in Santa Fe, New Mexico, and after months of acting in commercials, playing a contestant in a pilot for a game show, and watching Ray work, I was back on stage at the Tibbits Opera House in Coldwater, Michigan. The Tibbits Opera House was a beautiful, 600-seat theater with no microphones. We performed a new show every week, and my roles included Hope in *Anything Goes,* Linda in *Play It Again, Sam,* and Nanette in *No, No, Nanette.*

The pace was hectic, and the temperature in the rehearsal room was stifling. We rehearsed one show during the day and played another show at night. For some of the musicals, I couldn't get complete scripts—only sides that contained my character's lines and the few words leading into them. I didn't know to whom I was speaking or what the scenes were about until the scenes were staged—only days before opening night. The weekly pay was the lowest of my career. I was living in the back bedroom of someone's home—a room and bath with its own entrance. I had to get permission to enter the living room to call Ray, and when I did, my landlady hovered in the doorway on the other side of the room. I wondered: *Is she a busybody, or is she afraid I'll steal the silver and take the next bus out of town?*

My career was going backwards. I watched my landlady appear and disappear in the doorway while Ray complained about my absence in Santa Fe. I asked myself: *What am I doing in Coldwater, Michigan?*

By the summer of 1975, it was clear that Ray and I had incompatible goals and expectations. Ray told me that before we were married, he had agreed to equal careers because "I would have agreed to anything—I didn't want to lose you." In fact, he said, he believed it was a wife's *duty* to adapt her lifestyle to that of her husband—and he didn't want me to continue my career because as long as I had a career, I might become more successful than he was. *That,* he said, would *crush* his male ego.

I had known since I was little girl that the patriarchy was bad for women. I was slower to learn that it was also bad for men.

Ray had an upcoming engagement in Glyndebourne, England, and although I had looked forward to seeing the English countryside, I suggested we use the time as a trial separation—to see how it felt.

I went back to ballet class. When I held my legs in the air for an extended period of time, they shook like a car engine with faulty spark plugs, but I knew that if I took class day after day, week after week, I would get stronger. And I did. The preceding year, I had averaged one voice lesson every two weeks, but now I went back to my pre-marital schedule of two per week. I began acting classes with Wynn Handman at the American Place Theatre. I signed with a new commercial agent, and within a month, I had booked three commercials and a small role in the feature film *Looking Up*, starring Marilyn Chris, Dick Shawn, and Harry Goz, and directed by Linda Yellen, a young, energetic blonde.

When I walked into the room to audition for the film, Linda laughed and said, "You're much too young!"

"I thought the role was a child bride," I said.

"Yes, she *was* a child bride, but now she has three kids and is streaking through the laundry room high on marijuana."

I agreed that probably wasn't a role for me.

"As long as you're here, you might as well read," she said.

Linda liked my reading, so she asked me to read for a spoiled, 19-year-old Jewish princess, and then for a super-polite, 14-year-old girl. Bingo. I had my first feature film as a girl of 14.

During that summer, I reveled in the solitude of our apartment. When I woke up in the morning and went into the kitchen to make coffee, I breathed in the rich aroma of ground coffee—not the pungent hot sauce or garlic salad dressing from Ray's midnight snack. I listened to records from start to finish without Ray jumping up and down to adjust the knobs on the tuner, the receiver, the equalizer, and the quadrophonic speakers. When I wanted peace and quiet to study or think, I no longer had to ask Ray to use the headphones, and when I was weary after a long day, I fell into bed and went right to sleep. The freedom was intoxicating.

In Glyndebourne, Ray was also enjoying the hiatus from marriage. When he returned to New York, we agreed that I would leave him the rent-controlled apartment close to the Met, and I would look for an apartment closer to the theater district for myself. However, I had a new show at the Framingham Chateau de Ville for the fall, and it didn't make sense to get an apartment before leaving town. Besides, Ray wanted to visit me in Boston, and we thought it would be awkward if people knew we were separating, so we confided only in Dan and Mara.

The show in Framingham was *Cabaret*. Producer Gerry Roberts had called me from Boston and said, "I know you're going to turn this down because it's just a dance role, but everyone on the creative team put you at the top of the list, so I had to call you and offer you the job." He told me that the company was performing the original choreography by Ron Field with one big change: the fruit shop dance in this production was a flashy pas de deux choreographed by Clint Hamblin (the choreographer of Chateau de Ville's *Carousel*). Gerry wanted me to replace the female dancer who was performing the pas de deux with Clint. I was delighted to get back to my roots as a dancer—back on solid ground—and to work with people I knew and liked. Boston was one of my favorite cities, and the production was well cast with Marty Ross as the MC, a role he had played on Broadway for two years.

Gerry taught me an important lesson: if you want an actor for a role—even if you're sure she'll turn it down—it doesn't hurt to make the offer because you might have just the right role at just the right time.

I remembered that lesson more than fifteen years later when I wrote the script for a holiday special that was designed to go direct to video: *The Elf Who Saved Christmas*. When I looked at the dialogue I had written for the villain, Mr. Buzzard, I kept hearing JoAnne Worley's voice. I had played Dainty June in *Gypsy* to JoAnne's brilliant Mama Rose at the Sacramento Music Circus, and I knew she was approachable. I called her and told her about the project.

"You wrote the script?" she asked.

"Yes."

"How wonderful! I'd love to read it!"

And that's how Mr. Buzzard became Mrs. Buzzard, and our direct-to-video show became a TV special that was licensed to USA Network, got great ratings and reviews, spawned a sequel, and later aired on every continent except Antarctica.

For *The Elf Who Saved Christmas*, I had access to my ideal actress, and Gerry had taught me: it never hurts to ask.

When Ray came to visit during the run of *Cabaret*, everybody told us what a perfect couple we were, and I was glad we had decided not to announce our upcoming separation. Ray and I had planned to spend Christmas in Delaware with my family, but when I told Mom that Ray and I were separating, my parents informed me that Ray was

At the Chateau de Ville Dinner Theatre in Framingham, Massachusetts, the Kit Kat Girls in *Cabaret* had swastikas hidden inside their armbands, which were revealed to chilling effect. My wig was a cheap grey one dyed yellow.

no longer welcome in their home. Dad urged me to move to Delaware immediately, establish residency, and file for divorce. I refused. I wanted to revive my career—not retreat to Delaware. Ray and I were working out a one-year legal separation that in New York, could be grounds for divorce. I was reluctant to abandon Ray for Christmas, but I needed to see my parents and make it clear to my father that although I appreciated his concern, I didn't need his help. Ray spent Christmas with Dan and Mara, and the four of us celebrated New Year's Eve together.

I had met Jack Gilford in 1967 when he was playing Herr Schultz in *Cabaret* and moonlighting as Frosch (the jailer) in *Die Fledermaus* at the Met. Eight years later, we were working together in *The Student Prince*.

In 1776, colonists in America signed the Declaration of Independence and declared themselves a new country, the United States of America, a sovereign nation no longer under the dominion of England. Two hundred years later, as the country celebrated the bicentennial, I began my new life as an independent woman. I found a terrific apartment in a building that spanned the block between 57th Street and 58th Street just west of 8th Avenue. The building had canopies and doormen on both streets and was much more convenient to the theater district than 72nd Street. I installed thick, Bigelow, cerulean blue carpeting and bought Danish modern furniture. I wanted a home very different from the home Ray and I had shared.

I immediately landed a job as a dancer in *The Student Prince,* a production that would play Miami and Fort Lauderdale for the rest of the winter. The cast was superb: Harry Danner, Allan Jones, Judith McCauley, and Jack Gilford.

The dancers in the show were first-rate, and the music was soaring and romantic. Best of all, by the time I left for Florida in late February, I had in my hands a contract for the biggest hit of the decade—a show that would change my life: *A Chorus Line.*

14

A Chorus Line: The Auditions (1975–1976)

A Chorus Line is a two-hour musical about Broadway dancers. The show takes place in real time as dancers audition for a new Broadway show. Every dancer wants the job, but the choreographer needs only four boys and four girls. *A Chorus Line* was conceived by Michael Bennett; the book is by James Kirkwood and Nicholas Dante, the music by Marvin Hamlisch, and the lyrics by Edward Kleban. The show was directed by Michael Bennett and choreographed by Michael Bennett and Bob Avian. Some people describe *A Chorus Line* as the show that revived Broadway after the slump of the late 1960s and early 1970s.

A Chorus Line originated with a group of dancers who assembled in early 1974 to talk about their lives and exchange ideas about how to create more work for themselves and for other dancers. During the workshops at the Public Theater in lower Manhattan, *A Chorus Line* was barely on my radar. I had worked with several people in the cast, including Carole (later Kelly) Bishop, Carolyn Kirsch, and Don Percassi, and I knew others from auditions or from seeing their work on stage, including Donna McKechnie and the dance captain Baayork Lee, but I didn't know any of the cast well.

A Chorus Line opened at the 229-seat Newman Theater in the spring of 1975, and everyone in the Broadway community was talking about this terrific show that had sold out downtown and was moving to Broadway. People told me it was a "dance show," but it is more precisely a show about dancers—and there is a difference. A dance show might be a revue with one dance number after another, like *Dancin'* or *Come Fly Away*, or it might be a story told through dance, like the Matthew Bourne ballets, but *A Chorus Line* is a show about Broadway dancers—who they are, what they do, and why they do it. It is to Broadway dancers what the film *The Turning Point* is to ballet—an inside look at the people and the pressure and the art. It is a peek into a highly trained, inclusive, multicultural community that works out of love.

In June of 1975, before *A Chorus Line* transferred to Broadway, there was an audition at the Newman Theater. I wondered why. *Are they replacing some of the Off Broadway cast? Are they looking for future replacements? Are the producers trying to scare the current cast as a negotiating tactic? Is Actors' Equity requiring the audition?*

Some people think that union-mandated auditions are a waste of time when a show is already cast, but I believe that no audition is a waste of time if the dancers are allowed to dance for people who can give them jobs.

At the Newman Theater, hordes of dancers waited to audition. The protocol was similar to the audition for *You're a Good Man, Charlie Brown*. A stage manager lined up the dancers by number and led each group into the theater. After an eternity of waiting, my group filed onto the stage. We stood with our toes at the upstage edge of a white line that stretched across the stage, parallel to the footlights. One at a time, we were asked to step forward, do a double pirouette to the right, a double pirouette to the left, and a time step. When it was my turn, a man seated next to Baayork Lee in one of the front rows said, "Okay, Lee, knock off the double."

Who is this man? How does he know I can spin?

More than a year later, Baayork answered those questions. She told me that when I walked onto the stage, Bob Avian, the co-choreographer, whispered to Baayork, "That's the little girl from *Henry, Sweet Henry*." Eight years earlier, I had auditioned for *Henry, Sweet Henry*, and Bob Avian had remembered me. Baayork told me that Michael Bennett had chosen his dancers for *Henry, Sweet Henry* prior to my audition, but the union had required the audition. Eight years later when I auditioned for *A Chorus Line*, it certainly didn't hurt that Bob Avian knew my work.

As I was leaving the audition, Baayork asked me if I had seen the show.

"I think it's sold out," I said. I had been told that everyone in New York was trying to get tickets.

"You *have* to see it," she said. "Come to the green room Sunday at three. I'll have a pair of tickets for you." At the time, I didn't know what a glorious gift that was.

On Sunday afternoon, July 6, as Ray and I took our seats, I could feel and hear the excitement in the theater. As the house lights dimmed, the chatter stopped, and there was complete silence. In the blackout, I heard dancers taking their places on stage. A rehearsal piano began to play, and the lights came up on three lines of dancers in colorful practice clothes facing away from the audience toward a line of mirrors (actually Mylar) on the back wall. Between the dancers and the mirrors, the choreographer, Zach, was teaching a jazz combination while the dancers marked the steps.

I struggled to see Zach—to see the choreography—but there were too many dancers between us. I caught glimpses of his reflection in the mirror. I looked at some of the downstage dancers, but they weren't all doing the same thing. Michael Bennett had placed me (and the entire audience) in the position of dancers stuck at the back of the room who are struggling to learn the steps that might mean the difference between dancing on Broadway and unemployment.

After teaching the final steps far upstage, Zach swept down to the footlights: "Let's do the whole combination facing away from the mirror. From the top. A FIVE, SIX, SEVEN, EIGHT!" The orchestra kicked in as all of the dancers, led by Zach, performed the jazz combination full out. Then Zach asked everyone to mark the ballet combination. The lighting changed as the dancers sang their thoughts, "God, I hope I get it," while Zach arranged them into groups of four. The lighting went back to reality as the dancers performed the ballet combination in their groups, and Zach made corrections. Then, while Zach demonstrated part of the jazz combination, the lighting changed again, and the dancers sang their fear: "God, I really blew it."

The lights switched back to reality for the jazz combination—group after group dancing as if their lives depended on each jump and each pirouette.

After everyone had danced, Zach asked a few questions, cut some of the dancers, and told those who remained to get their pictures and résumés. The lighting changed again as the dancers ran for their résumés and summed up the situation: "I've come this far, but even so / It could be yes, it could be no." Holding their résumés, the dancers marched downstage in unison as they sang their goal: "I've got to GET THIS SHOW!" At the end of the number, seventeen dancers stretched across the stage, toeing the white line, with their 8 × 10 photos in front of their faces. It was a brilliant opening sequence.

Zach explained that he wanted to know more about the dancers because he had some small parts to cast from the dancers he hired. One by one—sometimes joining together with mutual experiences—the dancers told their stories. The first stories were stories from childhood, and the dancers grew up before my eyes. Some of the stories were touching, some funny, and some heart-wrenching. I was in tears more than once. When Zach told Cassie that she didn't belong in the chorus because she was special, she said, "No, we're all special. He's special—she's special. And Sheila—and Richie, and Connie. They're all special. I'd be happy to be dancing in that line. Yes, I would."

Cassie was speaking for me.

The dancers seemed to range from about four feet ten inches to something over six feet. Their skin colors ranged from chocolate brown to lily white. They were blond, brunette, and strawberry blonde. As I watched the show, I tried to imagine which character I might play.

I could identify in some way with all of the girls. Maggie was born to save her parents' marriage, but failed. She is eager to please and longs to be loved. Connie is 32 years old and has mixed feelings about her recent casting as a 14-year-old brat. Cassie has had great success as a dancer on Broadway, but has been away for a while and wants to start over again in the chorus. Sheila, approaching 30, wonders how much time she has left—three years? Four? Judy is the ditz—similar to characters I had played in comedies. Bebe is afraid she isn't pretty enough, and Kristine is a basket case whenever she has to sing. Val is a pigtailed blonde with an outgoing personality—a taller version of me in *Hello, Dolly!*—and Diana is the dancer who wants to be taken seriously as an actress, but knows that dancing on Broadway is a gift—a gift all the more precious because it can't last forever.

I couldn't play the age of the older dancers, and I didn't look sexy, Jewish, or Puerto Rican. That eliminated Cassie, Sheila, Bebe, and Diana. Maggie was the best voice on stage, and Judy was the tallest girl—two more roles I thought unlikely. I was perfect for the role of Connie—except I wasn't Asian—I wasn't born in the year of the chicken. I wanted a shot at playing Kristine because I had a different take on the role from Renee Baughman, but Kristine was tall, a sight gag with a short husband, and was identified (along with Judy) as "tall" before the tap combination. For the first half of the show, I thought my best chance might be Val, the baby-faced blonde who wore her hair in pigtails, but Val's song, "Dance: Ten; Looks: Three" reveals the fact that plastic surgery has changed her life, and my body wasn't as good as Pam Blair's, nor was I as tall. I was usually the shortest girl in the cast, and the shortest girl in this show was Asian.

It's always a bad sign if you can't figure out which part you might play because it usually means you're not perfect casting for any of them. However, I had heard that Michael wasn't looking for carbon copies. If he liked me, who knows? A line change from "Why am I so tall?" to "Why am I so small?" would allow me to play Judy—except that Connie was the small one, and Judy was the contrast. As I tried to figure out which role I might play, I knew that the advertising for the show featured the logo of the original cast, and the audience would expect to see that logo replicated. I came closest to the logo as Maggie (the outstanding voice) or Connie (Asian), but the part I longed to play was Kristine, the wife who can't sing.

In July 1975, *A Chorus Line* moved to the Shubert Theatre on Broadway. *A Chorus Line* was blurring the lines between principal and chorus, so I thought it might be a good idea to get an agent for theater. I interviewed at a prestigious agency with Miss Agent, who asked me to keep in touch. That winter, I sent her my terrific review for *Cabaret* that read, "the brilliant duet performed by Clint Hamblin and Lee Wilson during act one is a showstopper. Those acrobatic lifts are astounding!"

In early January, back in New York, I auditioned for *A Chorus Line* again—this time at the Shubert Theatre on 44th Street. Michael asked each of us to step forward, give our real names, stage names if different, and state where we were born and when.

I said, "I'm Lee Wilson. That's my real name, and I was born in Wilmington, Delaware." I stepped back into line and looked at the dancer to my left.

A girl further down the line called out, "How old are you, Lee?"

I wanted to clobber her. Instead, I stepped forward again and said to Michael, "I've been twenty-two for so long I'm seriously thinking of turning twenty-three."

"Don't do anything rash," said Michael. "Next."

We spent hours learning and dancing the ballet and jazz combinations, and some of us were asked to sing an up-tempo song. By this time, I knew that Michael Bennett was looking for two new casts. He wanted the original cast to open in California as the National Company, so he needed a new cast for New York and an International Company that would open in Toronto, play London, and then return to the U.S. to tour. The two new casts would rehearse together.

I asked Miss Agent why she hadn't submitted me for the January audition. "Darling," she said, "I didn't know you could dance."

"Didn't you get my review of *Cabaret*?"

"Oh. Yes. It's somewhere on my desk."

That was a sign I needed to move on, but I didn't see it.

In February, I was called back for another audition. At this audition, Michael asked me to sing Tricia's lines in the opening number. Then he asked me to go over to the piano and sight-read Maggie's part in "At the Ballet." I concluded that I was auditioning for the role of Tricia, who is cut after the opening number, but understudies Maggie, Connie, and Kristine and sings group numbers in an off-stage sound booth. Tricia is my favorite role among the understudies. She shows off her Maggie-like voice in the opening number, has a spoken line, and dances both the ballet and the jazz combinations full out in the appropriate styles.

At the end of the afternoon, Michael asked some of us to come back the following day at 10:00 a.m. I explained that I had rehearsal for *The Student Prince* from 10:00 a.m. to 6:00 p.m.

"Come during your lunch hour," he said. "As soon as you get here, come directly to me. I'll clear the stage so you can sing."

The following day on my lunch break, I ran from Showcase Studios to the Shubert Theatre, caught my breath, and told Michael I was ready to sing. After I sang, Michael told me, "If you haven't heard from us within twenty-four hours, come to the theater at half hour and tell the stage manager I asked you come."

I was pretty sure I had the show, and I did.

Peter Neufeld, the company manager, called to tell me that Michael wanted me to play Tricia in the National Company and understudy the original cast members Kay Cole, Baayork Lee, and Renee Baughman in the roles of Maggie, Connie, and Kristine. I told Peter that I needed to have a contract before I left New York that Sunday because I would have to give notice to *The Student Prince* on opening night in Florida and wouldn't want to do that without a signed contract. Peter said he would have the contract for me Saturday afternoon.

I called Miss Agent, told her I had the job, and asked if she could pick up the contract and look it over while I was rehearsing. I had heard there were some controversial provisions, so I needed her help.

"Darling," she said, "I'm much too busy to pick up a contract. There's nothing to negotiate anyway—everybody is offered the same contract—but I'll go over every word of it with you Saturday evening."

I asked when and where I should meet her, and she said she'd be at a party and didn't know the telephone number of the host. She gave me her home number and told me to call her home Saturday night and her mother would give me the host's telephone number. Miss Agent said she would find a quiet place where we would go over every detail of the contract on the telephone.

I arranged with Peter Neufeld to pick up the contract myself early Saturday evening and saw that it had 24 provisions added to the Standard Minimum Production Contract. The first six were the most important. Provisions one and two stated that the Manager had the right to convert the Standard Minimum Contract into an 18-month Run-of-the-Play Contract. If the Manager chose to convert, it would be by written notice prior to the fifth consecutive performance and would bind me to the show for 18 months. Provisions three and four guaranteed me five weeks' work, instead of the standard five days. Provisions five and six stated that I would serve in the New York Company, the National Company, or the International Company, and that I could be transferred to another company "on two weeks notice except for an extraordinary emergency when the Actor may be required to move to another company immediately. It will be completely the decision of the Manager and the Director as to what constitutes an extraordinary emergency." *Yikes*! I had told the stage manager that I was interested in the New York Company or the National Company—not the International Company—and now they wanted to send me *anywhere* at a moment's notice. I needed an agent to fix this.

Saturday evening, I called the number Miss Agent had given me. Her mother didn't know anything about me or where her daughter might be. I asked her to have Miss Agent call me whenever she got home—no matter the hour.

I spent the evening in my new, semi-furnished apartment, packing for Florida, with a contract in my hands that would take me far from friends and family and commit me to one show for 18 months—a contract with at least one provision I couldn't accept. I didn't sleep a wink. The next morning, I called Miss Agent and left a message. No response. I called again that afternoon just before the bus left for the airport. No response. I was frantic, but as the bus rolled toward the airport, a funny thing happened. I realized that Miss Agent had done absolutely nothing to get me this job—or any other job—and ten percent of everything I would earn during the next 18 months would amount to a lot more than the cost of a telephone call from my hotel in Miami to Peter Neufeld in New York. I knew Peter from *Here's Where I Belong* and believed I could trust him. That trust was not misplaced.

When I called Peter, my main concern was the paragraph about moving from company to company. "Don't worry about that," he said. "Equity will never let that happen. They've already told us, 'This isn't the Army. These dancers will have leases on apartments. Some have children. You can't just pick them up and move them.'" Peter told me that if Michael Bennett wanted me to perform with another company, I would have to agree. I asked Peter what would happen if the show didn't have a long run in Los Angeles, and he said that everyone would tell me that *no* show could play the Shubert in Los Angeles for a year, but he was confident that the show would still be playing L.A. in 18 months.

In addition to not allowing dancers to be moved from company to company without their consent, Equity made another beneficial (and lucrative) decision for the dancers. Management wanted all dancers to sign principal (white color) contracts—including the dancers who are cut after the opening number—because every dancer has a name. Equity ruled that giving dancers names doesn't mean that they aren't chorus performers (who had pink contracts). Some dancers thought white contracts were more prestigious than pink ones, so they didn't want Equity to intervene, but Equity was right. The names of the dancers who are cut after the opening sequence are never mentioned. No one without additional information could know that Lois is the ballerina, or that Tricia is the one who sings the solo lines, and the jobs that the understudies perform on a nightly basis (dancing, singing, saying a few lines, and singing in the off-stage booth) are chorus jobs—not principal roles. This is important because when a chorus dancer plays a principal role, she gets additional pay: one-eighth of her own salary for each performance. The contract I signed was on white paper, but Equity insisted that the dancers who were cut after the opening number be classified as chorus and get additional pay when performing the roles they covered. For me, this would mean additional pay for almost two hundred performances in 16 months.

I signed all five copies of the contract, wrote a cover letter, and mailed everything back to Peter. I finally had a hit show. I would once again be working with the best of the best in musical theater. I would have six weeks of rehearsal with Michael Bennett and Marvin Hamlisch, and I would be joining the original cast of the hottest show in New York.

My joy was tempered. I was leaving my beautiful new apartment before it was completely furnished. I was leaving my new commercial agent, Cynthia Raglan, who was already becoming a friend. I was leaving New York, my home for the past twelve years, and I was leaving Ray. I would be an understudy for the first time, and I would be performing with a cast that had helped develop the material and had a strong identification with their roles. I didn't know it yet, but I would also be working with the most difficult stage manager of my career.

15

A Chorus Line: Rehearsals and San Francisco (1976)

On March 15, 1976, I walked into the rehearsal studio at City Center for my first rehearsal of *A Chorus Line*. The atmosphere was electric. Many of us had auditioned over a period of nine months to get our jobs, and we knew we were part of something special.

There were two complete casts. One cast was the International Company, which had some of the youngest dancers; the other cast was a combination of the *new* New York Company and the National Company. Five principals in the Original Broadway Company (the roles of Mike, Sheila, Bobby, Mark, and Larry) and all of the original understudies were staying in New York, so 14 new dancers were joining them to create the *new* New York Company. The Original Broadway Company with five new principals and all new understudies was going to California as the National Company. During rehearsals, the five new dancers for the National Company and the 14 new dancers for the New York Company formed one complete cast (17 on the line plus Zach and Larry, Zach's assistant). This meant that I would learn the show along with the Maggie, Connie, and Kristine who were taking over in New York, but I would actually understudy the Originals: Kay Cole, Baayork Lee, and Renee Baughman.

Every morning, when we arrived at the theater, there were platters of Danish pastries and urns of hot coffee. To ease us into the workday, Baayork Lee gave a warm-up that began with the dancers sitting on the floor and got progressively more demanding. It was a luxury to warm up on company time, and Baayork Lee is the Energizer Bunny who energizes everyone around her. When Michael Bennett arrived, the energy went up another notch. Although we had learned the ballet and jazz combinations at the auditions, we went over every detail of every step again and again and again. We performed the combinations in groups of four, one group after another—over and over again. We applauded each group and cheered on the dancers who had trouble with the pirouettes. We learned the number "One" in which we had to be as precise as the Rockettes, and the boys quickly learned that the position and timing of their elbows is crucial, or they hit the girls in the boobs.

Michael Bennett sat on the floor with each company and explained the relationships among the characters while we all took notes. I had learned at the audition that Michael didn't want us to smile during the opening number, and now, he reminded us that he wanted to see competition and desperation—not a performance. No matter how good friends we might be off stage, *A Chorus Line* is not a tea party. It is a tension-filled audition. He asked each of us to identify why this job is so important and how we feel about the competition.

The three roles I understudied had different backgrounds and different needs. Based on what Michael told us and what was in the script, I fleshed out their biographies for myself:

Maggie learned when she was a child that she couldn't depend on her parents to give her a loving home, so the dance studio became her home. At the time of the audition for Zach, Maggie's only family is the dance community, and she needs this job to remain part of that family.

Connie has previously been a dance captain for Zach. She has been around long enough to know that no audition is a slam dunk, but she is fairly confident she has the job—right up to the moment she doesn't get it.

Kristine, a newlywed with no Broadway credits, is hoping to prove herself to her husband, Al, and to the Broadway community. Al has worked with Zach in the past, and Kristine is terrified that her inability to sing will condemn her to sitting home alone at night while her husband dances on Broadway. At this final callback, she is one step short of a panic attack.

Michael and Theoni Aldredge, the costume designer, decided that when I played Connie, I would wear a hot pink leotard instead of black jumper/pants over a muted turtleneck like Baayork. (The new Connie in New York also wore hot pink, but she had a scoop neck leotard, and I had a turtleneck.) I was also assigned nude tights and beige shoes for all three roles I understudied—even though the original Maggie, Connie, and Kristine all wore black. I liked the costume changes because the hot pink leotard and nude tights would stand out against the black background. Michael also liked the shoes I was wearing for rehearsals—flat Capezio folk dance shoes with a strap across the arch, so those became my shoes for Connie.

We began rehearsals without a Cassie/Sheila understudy in the National Company, but shortly after the understudy was hired, Michael put an arm around me, led me away from the other dancers, and said, "I need a favor."

I stopped breathing.

"I need you to play Lois instead of Tricia," he said.

Oh, no. "Tricia sings. And she has lines. I don't want to give that up."

"I know. But I can't put Renata in pink tights."

I looked at the new understudy. Renata Vaselle was a zaftig German woman who looked like a voluptuous Sheila and a powerful Cassie. She *didn't* look like someone who would try to impersonate a ballerina at a Broadway audition.

Michael continued, "You're the *only* one I can put in pink tights."

I looked at the other two understudies: Mary Ann O'Reilly, the understudy for Val and Judy, exuded sex appeal. She wouldn't be caught dead in pink tights. Rebecca York, the understudy for Diana and Bebe, had a good body, but she had put on ten pounds waiting to hear if she had the job and was wearing baggy sweatpants and a sweatshirt.

"I need your ballet technique," said Michael. "I'll return the favor."

I agreed to play Lois.

On the fourth day of rehearsal, Miss Agent contacted me. "Darling," she said. "We don't have your contract on file at the office. You must bring it in as soon as possible."

Was she serious?!

She was. She wanted a commission for the next 18 months. When I declined to pay it, she accused me of being dishonorable and followed up with a letter addressed to me, with copies to Peter Neufeld and Actors' Equity. The letter was filled with inaccurate statements and claimed that I was morally, though not legally, obligated to pay commission on the contract "with all the terms I negotiated." She wanted me to sign a Special Management Contract so her agency could assist and protect me (and collect commissions) during the next 18 months.

I wrote a two-page rebuttal and never heard from Miss Agent again.

More than a year later when I returned to New York on vacation, I told Terry Marone at Equity about my experience with Miss Agent. Terry said that Miss Agent wasn't the only agent who lurked in the wings waiting to see which dancers would be offered contracts before swooping in to sign them to get 18 months of commissions. She found it disheartening that some dancers were so pleased that an agent wanted to represent them that they signed with an agent at precisely the time they didn't need an agent.

During rehearsals, Lauree Berger, the new Maggie in the New York Company, was filming a series of commercials, so I played Maggie for several days and ended up in many of the rehearsal photographs. I was playing Maggie in a two-page photo in *The New York Times Magazine* on May 2, and was singing "At the Ballet" (as Michael cued my entrance) in a photo that was published in *After Dark* magazine and also appeared in the film *Every Little Step*.

Maggie was a much better role for my voice than the higher soprano roles of Luisa in *The Fantasticks* and Hope in *Anything Goes*, and I sang the music exactly as written—without the vocal embellishments that gave Kay Cole's performance a contemporary, rock feel, but neither Michael nor Marvin suggested I do anything differently, and I loved performing Maggie's dialogue.

Michael Bennett is cueing me, as Maggie, in "At the Ballet" during rehearsals for *A Chorus Line* at City Center. The other dancers (left to right) are: Don Correia, Lauren Kayahara, Justin Ross, Charlene Ryan (on her knees, her head hidden behind my arm), Scott Pearson, Gillian Scalici (standing), Sandahl Bergman, Bill Nabel, Paul Charles, and George Pesaturo. Photo: Ken Regan/Camera 5

My nervous, tripping-over-her-words Kristine was also quite different from the original frozen-in-terror-quivering-leg Kristine of Renee Baughman, but the first time I rehearsed Kristine and Al's number "Sing!," Michael's face was a big smile as he said, "Do exactly that." It seemed to me that Michael was encouraging the new dancers to bring their own personalities to their roles, and some of the new dancers were very different from the Originals. Cookie Vasquez, the new Kristine in New York, was an irreverent, outgoing dancer who used her lisp for comedic effect—very different from Renee's serious, terrified Kristine. Donna McKechnie, the original Cassie, had short curly hair, a long, flexible torso, a soprano voice, and her heart on her sleeve. Ann Reinking, who replaced her, had long straight hair, a short torso with very long legs, a much lower vocal range, and was a woman fighting to maintain her dignity as she begged for a job. The dance created for Donna featured upper body movements that showed off the flexibility of her torso while Annie performed additional jumps that showed off her long legs.

Whenever one actor replaces another, people compare the two, and it seemed to me that Michael had chosen distinct and contrasting personalities so that when people made comparisons, they were often comparing apples to oranges, or at least golden apples to red.

On the evening of April 18, 1976, I watched *A Chorus Line* sweep the Tony Awards: Best Musical (Joseph Papp and the New York Shakespeare Festival, producer Joseph Papp), Best Book of a Musical (James Kirkwood and Nicholas Dante), Best Original Score (music by Marvin Hamlisch, lyrics by Ed Kleban), Best Direction of a Musical (Michael Bennett), Best Choreography (Michael Bennett and Bob Avian), Best Actress in a Musical (Donna McKechnie), Best Featured Actress in a Musical (Carole Bishop), Best Featured Actor in a Musical (Sammy Williams), and Best Lighting Design (Tharon Musser). The triumph was somewhat muted because in the categories of Featured Actress and Featured Actor, *A Chorus Line* had two nominees, and only one could win. My heart went out to Bob LuPone, who played Zach so well, and to Priscilla Lopez, who had captured my heart as Diana. (In her next Broadway show, *A Day in Hollywood/A Night in the Ukraine*, Priscilla would win *her* Tony Award.)

Two weeks later, the National Company of *A Chorus Line* flew to San Francisco, where we were treated like conquering heroes. The show was almost completely sold out two days before we opened, and people showered us with invitations, good luck talismans, and plants for our apartments. The company took out an ad in the newspapers thanking the city for its warm welcome and promising to return soon.

A couple of days before the first preview at the Curran Theatre, I learned that Baayork Lee's father had died and that Baayork would miss all five previews. I knew all three roles that I covered, and I was ready for the challenge. The following day, I played Connie in the stage rehearsal and was pleased with how well it had gone, but I had no sooner finished the rehearsal when I overheard that the company was flying in Donna Drake, the original Connie understudy. I was crushed. After five years of working in regional theater, I desperately wanted to be accepted back into the Broadway community and now I was being shoved aside. I didn't know anyone in the company well enough to confide my disappointment, so I went to the San Francisco offices of Actors' Equity to confirm what I already knew: The job of an understudy is to be ready to do the part, but there is no requirement that the producer allow the understudy to go on. A producer can bring in anyone he wants. Often, when a star takes a leave of absence, producers replace her with another star. (When Gwen Verdon took a short leave of absence from *Chicago*, Liza Minnelli, not the understudy, performed the star role of Roxie Hart and gave a brilliant performance.)

However, Connie was not a star role—not even one of the larger roles in an ensemble show—and Donna Drake was not a big name. No one was going to ask for a refund because I was performing rather than Donna Drake, and flying a dancer from New York to San Francisco would cost far more than paying me one-eighth of my salary per performance. I wondered if my job were at risk. Before leaving Actors' Equity, I confirmed that although *A Chorus Line* had the right to convert my contract to an 18-month Run-of-the-Play Contract prior to my fifth consecutive performance, it had no obligation to do so. The producers could leave me on my current contract, which allowed either party to give the other two weeks' notice at any time. I wouldn't know the intentions of the management for a few more days. If the contracts of the other understudies were converted, and mine wasn't, I could guess that the company was planning to replace me. I held my breath.

During the first rehearsals at City Center, we had seemed like one big happy family because we were nearly all new to the show, but now, there was a distinct hierarchy—the Originals were at the top; the new people "on the line" were in the middle, and the understudies were on the bottom. The second-class status of the understudies was underscored in Los Angeles where people referred to the principals, whose dressing rooms were on stage level, as "the upstairs people" and the understudies, who dressed one level down, as "the downstairs people." (At that time, "Upstairs, Downstairs" was a hit TV series about the aristocratic Bellamy family upstairs and their servants, downstairs.) Even though the understudies performed in the opening number and sang in an off-stage booth to augment the voices onstage, they were always called "the understudies."

When I arrived at the Curran Theatre for the first preview on Thursday night, my Lois costume was in my dressing room, but not my costumes for Maggie, Connie, and Kristine. I went to wardrobe and asked Kathe, the wardrobe mistress, for my understudy costumes.

"I'm not giving them to the understudies," she said. "If you're going on, I'll be the first to know."

"What if someone is injured, and I have to go on immediately?"

"I'll bring the costume to your dressing room."

That didn't make sense, but after being bumped from playing Connie, I didn't want to make waves.

The first preview was a great success. Everyone seemed pleased to see Donna Drake, and notwithstanding my disappointment that I wasn't playing Connie, I enjoyed performing in the opening number and singing in the booth.

At the second preview, I danced the opening number and was listening to the beginning of "At the Ballet" when Michael Bennett rushed into the dressing room and said, "You're on!"

"For whom?"

"Connie."

I would later learn that during Bobby's monologue, Donna Drake had started to sway. The two male dancers on either side of Donna each put an arm around her and managed to keep her on her feet, but during the beginning of the next song, "At the Ballet," while most of the cast backed up into the dark and faced the back wall, the two men walked Donna into the wings, left her with the stage manager, walked to the upstage wing, and inched their way into the line facing upstage in the dark.

Michael Bennett, in the audience, saw the problem, ran into the understudy dressing room, and was now standing inches away from me.

I grabbed my electric blue rehearsal leotard. "Wardrobe wouldn't give me my costumes. May I wear this?"

"You can wear anything you want," he said.

I jumped into my nude rehearsal tights, my blue leotard, and my folk-dance shoes, and ran upstairs with Michael. I slithered into the line that was facing upstage in the dark. As "At the Ballet" came to a close, Don Correia, who was playing Mike, took my hand, squeezed it, and whispered, "Here we go."

With the rest of the line, I turned around, walked downstage, and took Connie's pose in the logo.

It was exhilarating to be on the line, and I knew that what I did in the next hour and a half would probably determine my future with the show. I had to prove that I belonged on stage with the Originals. The time went by in a flash. At the end of the performance, some of the principals stopped in the wings to congratulate me, and the girls in the dressing room said I had made the understudies proud.

That night as I exited the stage door, a woman in the crowd pointed at me and said, "Look! That's the little girl who came late!" I was delighted that she had noticed that the electric blue leotard hadn't danced the opening number and had justified my absence. I signed autographs and then walked across the street to David's Deli to get a Monte Cristo sandwich. Nicholas Dante and James Kirkwood, the book writers of *A Chorus Line*, were sharing a booth and invited me to join them. They told me that I was "absolutely perfect"—that I looked as if I'd been doing the show for years—and regaled me with stories about the creation of the show. Nick told me that after he wrote the Paul monologue, which is based on his own experience, he called a friend and told him he wanted an honest opinion. When Nick finished reading, there was total silence. Then the friend asked, "Where will you put the Tony Award?"

I would have paid for an evening with these friendly, funny, talented men, but on the contrary, they insisted on picking up my check.

The following day when I arrived at the Curran Theatre for the Saturday matinee, all of the understudies had all of their costumes in their dressing rooms. Donna Drake did both Saturday performances, but on Sunday, I was back on the line as Connie for the final preview, and my contract was converted to an 18-month Run-of-the-Play

Contract with a bump up in salary. Within three weeks, I had performed all three roles I covered.

Nevertheless, I was bruised from being pushed aside, and Baayork, who was back in the show for the press opening on Tuesday, May 11, quickly noticed that my usually sunny disposition was a bit cloudy. She invited me to Lehr's Greenhouse for dinner between shows and asked what was wrong. I explained that I was hurt that the company hadn't trusted me to play Connie at the first preview.

"That had nothing to do with you," she said. "Michael had promised Donna Drake that when Kay Cole left the show, she could play Maggie—but he didn't give Donna the role. He felt he owed her something special, so he gave her the trip to San Francisco."

If only someone had explained that to me at the time!

A wound can heal, but it leaves a scar.

At the end of May, I flew from San Francisco to Los Angeles to meet the tenants of a two-bedroom apartment only a mile from the Shubert Theatre in Century City. A friend of a friend lived in the building and told the tenants I was the perfect person to water the plants, bring in the mail, and contribute toward the rent while they were on vacation. I liked the roomy, light-filled apartment; the location was perfect, and the two-month sublet gave me plenty of time to find a more permanent home. During that weekend, I asked everyone I met, "Who are the best commercial agents in L.A.?" and I compiled a list of six agencies. A month later, when the company traveled to Los Angeles, I wanted to hit the deck running.

16

A Chorus Line: Los Angeles (1976–1977)

I was a stranger in the strange new world of Los Angeles. From the age of 15, I had lived in cities where I could walk or take public transportation, but in Los Angeles, everybody drove. Nobody walked. People drove to the 7–11 even when it was only half a mile away. At theaters, restaurants, and shopping malls, some people didn't even park their own cars—to avoid walking half a block. Instead, they gave their car keys to total strangers—valets. Later, the drivers stood in line, waited for the valets to find their cars, and paid exorbitant fees to get them back.

In Los Angeles, the streets were filled with Mercedes Benzes, Rolls-Royces, Bentleys, and cars that looked as if they belonged on a racetrack. There were white limousines and black limousines and stretch limousines.

A year and a half earlier, I had acquired a driver's license while I was performing in a play in Jacksonville, Florida. I had taken two lessons at a driving school, and when the instructor arrived for my third lesson, I informed him that I had an appointment to take my driver's test.

"No, no, no, no, no," he said. "Not after two lessons!"

"We can't miss my appointment," I said cheerfully, and off we went to the DMV.

I aced the written test and parallel parked as if I had been doing it for decades. Within an hour I was the proud owner of a Florida driver's license.

A year and a half later, with no other driving experience, I was at the wheel of a lethal weapon on the streets of Los Angeles. My vehicle of choice was a dented blue Gremlin from Rent-a-Wreck. Driving is stressful—especially when the cars that are cutting in front of you are worth a small fortune. I also hated wasting time driving from place to place. When I rode a bus or a subway, I could learn lines or read a book, but I accomplished nothing while I was driving.

In Los Angeles, people routinely underestimated distances. When someone in Beverly Hills said, "You're only five minutes away," what she meant was, "If you have a driver who knows that Olympic Blvd. is faster than Santa Monica Blvd., and if he knows all of the one-way streets, and if you hit all green lights, the driver can drop you off in about ten minutes, but if you *don't* have a driver, and you need to find a parking place, allow thirty minutes."

One day, I had two auditions on Sunset Blvd. After the first audition, I asked the casting director how far it was to the next audition.

"Only a few blocks," she said.

"Great," I said, "I'll walk."

Before the casting director could recover from her shock, I was out the door.

I was late for the second audition, so the casting director called my agent. "Where is Lee?"

My agent called the first casting director. Unable to contain her laughter, the casting director chortled, "She's walking!"

In Los Angeles, "Only a few blocks" means only a few major intersections, which in this case was about a mile and a half.

The other thing that struck me about L.A. was that most of the buildings were new. I kept expecting someone to say, "That's a wrap. Strike the sets," and then the entire town would disappear. When *A Chorus Line* opened, the Shubert Theatre was less than four years old, but in true Los Angeles style, the beautiful theater was demolished thirty years later. For contrast, the Broadway theaters in which I had performed during the 1960s and early 1970s were built before 1930 and are still hosting Broadway shows in 2024. Some of the European opera houses in which I performed, like the Bordeaux Opera House and the Teatro di San Carlo in Naples, were built in the 18th century and are still cultural centers in their communities.

In 1962, when I moved to France, I had to learn French idioms and theater terms. In Los Angeles, I had to learn idioms and film terms. In Los Angeles, when people say, "Let's do lunch" ("do," not "have"), it is not an invitation to pull out your appointment book and say, "When?" The sentence "Let's do lunch" is interchangeable with "It's nice to see you." ("See you," not "meet you" because "see you" eliminates the possibility that the other person might be offended that you've met half a dozen times, but don't remember her.) I also learned that the gaffer is the head of the lighting department and that a screening is the showing of a film that is not open to the general public—usually *not* an event that requires cocktail attire, but an event that does require shirts and shoes.

A Chorus Line had two opening nights: a benefit performance on July 6 and the press opening on July 7. The benefit performance honored Helen Hayes and was followed by an outdoor dinner party at the Century Plaza Hotel across the street from the theater. I was one of the few cast members who stood in the wings after the performance and watched Helen Hayes give her speech. The others presumably heard her speak over the intercom, but I wanted to see the great actress live. At the party, people talked about film grosses and TV ratings and ogled TV stars I didn't recognize. I couldn't have felt more like an outsider if everyone had been speaking Chinese.

The party after the press opening was at the Backlot, which people told me was a famous gay nightclub with loud disco music and illegal drugs. I skipped the party. I also skipped a party that Saturday night at the home of producer Allan Carr. People told me I was making a big mistake—that Hollywood did business at parties—that actresses were discovered at parties—but I preferred to meet people in their offices in the morning, so that's what I did.

The company arrived in Los Angeles on Sunday, June 27. The next day, I called all six commercial agencies on my list, and the words "A Chorus Line" were the "open sesame" of 1976. Four days later, I had interviewed with five of the six agencies. The sixth, the Jack Wormser Agency, left a message with my answering service informing me that their agents would see the show in three weeks, and I shouldn't sign with anyone before then. I went to the Jack Wormser Agency and explained that I had met with the other agencies on my list and had told them I would get back to them within a week. Could anyone see me today? Minutes later, I was meeting with senior agent Roger Heldfond. I liked Roger immediately, and we chatted for almost an hour. When I asked him what age range he thought I could play, he said he would submit me for high school, college, and young wife—everything from 16 to 24.

This was exactly what I wanted to hear. Some agents wanted me specifically because I was over 18, but could play younger—a valuable commodity because minors require teachers or welfare workers on the set—so the agents wanted to establish me in that narrow age range, but I knew that my time in that range was limited. Other agents thought my résumé precluded me from playing teenagers and didn't want to submit me for younger than early twenties. As my conversation with Roger drew to a close, he asked if he could submit me for an audition the following day—with no obligation to sign with the agency. I liked his approach. It was a nice change from the agent who at the end of my interview, held out his hand and said, "Congratulations, you have the best agents in Hollywood."

The week after my interview with Roger Heldfond, I signed with the Jack Wormser Agency, and within three months, I had filmed commercials for Hang Ten Shirts, KFC, Era detergent (with Mary Wickes), Winston Tires, Folgers coffee (with Mrs. Olson), and Fox Photo (with George Gobel). I had played a preppy college girl, a high school student, a French exchange student, a kook who talks to plants, a suburban housewife with glasses, and a career girl.

In New York, I acted in commercials for additional income. I never saw my commercials on TV, and my residual checks were the only evidence I had that they were on the air. In Los Angeles, commercials had more prestige. They were part of the city's big business of film and television. Production companies invited me to see my commercials on a large screen at their offices. They gave me still photographs and copies of the film. One company sent me roses. Ushers at the theater, cast members of *A Chorus Line*, and friends of my parents in Delaware all saw my commercials.

I loved the speed of commercials. I auditioned one week, shot the next, and within a month, it was on the air. In just 30 or 60 seconds, we would tell a story that would move people or inform people or make them laugh. My commercial work was very satisfying. My stage life was more complex.

As the summer progressed, I became less and less confident of my ability to sing Maggie. Part of this was my basic insecurity about singing, and part of it was the negative attitude of our stage manager, Pat Drylie. If you've seen cartoons in which a character walks around with a black cloud over her head, you can visualize Pat Drylie. During understudy rehearsals, Pat tried to mold me into a carbon copy of Kay Cole, whose voice I heard every night over the monitors. Soon, Kay's interpretation began to sound "right" to me. I asked Kay about her voice teachers, the Sweetlands, and Kay invited me to observe one of her lessons. I quickly learned that Kay's performance in "At the Ballet" was only the tip of the iceberg. Her voice went up and up and up. I thought that if I tried to do what Kay was doing, I'd be hoarse for days. Since I was standing by for Maggie six days a week, I didn't think I could take that risk. In retrospect, I wish I had taken at least one lesson from the Sweetlands. They might have taken a different approach with me. I'll never know.

Pat Drylie was a confidence-crusher. Whenever the understudies went on, Pat let us know how unhappy she was—how bad it was for the show. She hated making replacement announcements. "At this performance, the role of Maggie, usually played by Kay Cole, will be played by Lee Wilson. The role of Lois, usually played by Lee Wilson..." etc. Since the understudies in the opening number all had names, Pat had to make *two* announcements every time someone on the line was out, and audiences, who didn't know that half of those roles were chorus roles, were groaning by the third announcement. At the end of August, after doing ten performances as Maggie in less than a month, I began hinting that I didn't want to cover the role.

What I needed was for someone to sit me down, look me in the eye, and say, "Michael Bennett saw hundreds of girls and he chose *you*. He directed you, and he knows your performance. Do you think *you* know better than Michael Bennett?"

Well no. Of course not.

But that wasn't what I heard. I heard Pat Drylie complaining about the understudies, implying that we were all inferior, and *why can't you sing like Kay Cole*?

Finally, I asked Pat Drylie to hire someone else to cover Maggie. My request wasn't a big risk. The company couldn't fire me because I was on an 18-month contract. All they could do was say "no." Besides, the company needed another understudy. To my delight, Lisa Donaldson was hired to cover Maggie. I felt as if I already knew Lisa because when we were in San Francisco, I had read an article about San Francisco dancers who had auditioned for *A Chorus Line*, and Lisa was one of the dancers profiled in the article. As soon as Lisa knew the role, I asked for and received a rider to my contract stating that I was no longer responsible for the role of Maggie. What a relief!

The cast of *A Chorus Line* was constantly changing. Of the four female understudies who rehearsed in New York, only Renata Vaselle and I remained with the National Company the entire 18 months. Rebecca York, the understudy for Diana and Bebe, quickly lost the weight she had gained and took over the role of Diana in New York. Mary Ann O'Reilly, the understudy for Val and Judy, clashed with Pat Drylie over her performance as Val, and Mary Ann left the company along with her husband, Andy Bew, who covered Zach.

Near the end of September, less than three months after the Los Angeles premiere, some of the Originals, including Donna McKechnie (Cassie), Robert LuPone (Zach), Renee Baughman (Kristine), and Priscilla Lopez (Diana), left the company as scheduled. Ann Reinking (Cassie), Joe Bennett (Zach), and Cookie Vazquez (Kristine), who had replaced the Originals on Broadway, came out west, and Chris Bocchino, who had replaced Rebecca York as the Diana and Bebe understudy, moved up to play Diana. Linda Dangcil was hired to be the new Diana and Bebe understudy and an alternate understudy for Maggie.

Linda was one of the warmest, most generous people I've ever met, and she quickly became my best friend. She was in the original

Broadway production of *Peter Pan* and had numerous TV credits including *The Flying Nun* and the bi-lingual children's show *Villa Allegre*. In November, I was asked to do a screen test for the role of Chrissy in a new TV series, *Three's Company*, and it was Linda who partially allayed my fears about the daunting contract that gave the producers an option for seven years if I were cast. *Seven years! What if I hated the job?* Linda assured me that even if I got the show, the odds were slim that the series would run that long. Even if it did, the producers would want to keep me happy and would renegotiate my salary—even though I had a signed contract with my salary laid out for seven years.

This made no sense to me, but Linda explained that this was how the television business worked. Unhappy actors called in sick and disrupted production, so producers took preventive action by offering them more money. Linda also explained that "merchandizing" gave the company the right to make Lee Wilson dolls and Lee Wilson lunch boxes—although they wouldn't actually be Lee Wilson products, they would have my likeness as the character I was playing. I thought it would be terribly embarrassing to see my face on a lunchbox, but Linda assured me that merchandizing rights were standard in a TV series contract.

However, before I could test for the role, the producers of *Three's Company* wanted a letter from Michael Bennett stating that he would release me from my contract with *A Chorus Line* if I were cast. Michael wrote the letter and returned the favor as he had promised when he asked me to play Lois instead of Tricia.

However, I didn't get the role of Chrissy. Suzanne Somers did, and *Three's Company* was on the air for eight years. During negotiations for the fifth season, after Suzanne Somers had won a People's Choice Award and had received a Golden Globe nomination, she was fired for demanding equal pay with the male lead, John Ritter, who was making five times her salary. According to the *Hollywood Reporter*, the studio's best offer would have given Somers a raise from 20 percent of Ritter's salary to 23 percent.

Linda Dangcil was also the unflappable person who knew what was going on upstairs. There was always tension backstage, but one week the tension seemed particularly high. I asked Linda if she knew why, and she did. She told me, "Coke was stolen from one of the upstairs dressing rooms, and the dancer is pretty upset."

"I don't blame her," I said. "I was more than a little peeved when that happened to me."

"To *you*?!" Linda looked surprised.

"Yes. Last week. I put my soda in the fridge at half hour, and when—"

"Lee! Coke. Powder."

"Ooooooooh. Cocaine."

I associated drugs with Sherlock Holmes, Coleridge, and Hollywood producers—not Broadway dancers—although I now understood why one of the girls on the line would sometimes careen three feet to her right during an attempted pirouette.

Pat Drylie was elusive during performances, and I heard a rumor that she went to Harry's Bar during the show. Years later, a friend told me he had met our stage manager while having a drink at Harry's Bar. As he chatted with her, he asked, "What do you do?"

"I'm the stage manager for *A Chorus Line*."

He looked at his watch. "Isn't that playing right now?"

"It runs itself," she said with a dismissive wave of her hand.

She was wrong. The cast wasn't always performing to the best of its ability. In fact, when Michael Bennett came back to see the show, he told the company, "The understudies are the only people dancing. The rest of you look as if you're hanging around waiting for your songs. If I see that again, I'll tell Zach to choose the understudies. I don't care what costumes they're wearing, if they dance better, they go on." That didn't happen, of course, but it put some nervous energy back into the opening number and lifted the spirits of the understudies, who sometimes felt underappreciated.

The dancers on the line weren't the only ones slacking off. Sometimes the understudies didn't bother to go upstairs to sing in the booth. One day, Pat peered into the booth and saw only two or three of us. I knew that heads would roll. Pat couldn't fire an understudy on an 18-month contract for missing one cue, but she could fire a new understudy recently hired to cover Cassie and Sheila—a dancer who really needed the job and was supporting a child. That dancer was the only understudy with what I thought was a legitimate reason not to be in the booth: she was still learning her roles and was building up stamina for the role of Cassie by performing the show full out in the studio where monitors relayed the sound of the show upstairs. When Pat fired the hard-working, well-liked dancer, the other understudies were appalled, and their distrust of Pat Drylie increased.

Tim Cassidy, who understudied Bobby and later played the role in New York, got the last laugh. One day as Pat was auditioning dancers for replacements, Tim walked out of the wings onto the stage wearing absolutely nothing except his eight-by-ten headshot that he held in front of his face. After that revealing moment, Tim disappeared for a while, and there were rumors of "a nervous breakdown," but when Tim returned to the show, he gleefully imitated Pat's shocked expression and fluttering hands as she had tried to shoo him back into the wings. Tim was a brilliant comic whose lack of inhibitions and outrageous behavior kept us laughing, even though some of us worried about the risks he was taking.

There were rare weeks when I played Lois at all eight performances, and there were two-month stretches when I played Kristine and/or Connie forty or fifty times. By the fall of 1977, I was playing Kristine eight performances a week.

One night, while I was playing Kristine with Ben Lokey as my husband, Lidell Jackson, the understudy for Richie, was on the line as Richie. While dancing the jazz combination in his group of four, Lidell went into the deep knee bend, fell to the floor, clutched his knee, and writhed in pain for what seemed like an eternity before two of the other dancers dragged him into the wings.

The rule for the understudies was: if the character has *not* been established with his or her song or monologue, the understudy goes on. If the character *has* been established, the other dancers cover the lines as assigned in a supplement to the script. The character of Richie had *not* been established with his song, but there was no one to replace Lidell. The only other understudy who knew Richie's song and dance was Danny Taylor, and Danny was on the line that night playing Mike. At the end of the opening number, as we stood on the line with our photos in front of our faces, Ben and I shifted slightly right of our marks to fill the gap left by Richie. During the song "And…" Ben leaned into Richie's light and sang Richie's lines. The show progressed: "At the Ballet," then "Sing!," then "Hello Twelve, Hello Thirteen, Hello Love." Ben covered Richie's lines, but Richie's song was getting closer, and it's not a self-contained song that can be cut. It's the exuberant finale to the fourth montage.

Connie did her bit as "four foot ten," and we went into another ensemble section, "Goodbye Twelve." Just before Richie's line "You show me yours," Ron Dennis, the original Richie, came shooting out of the wings, sang the line, and the house erupted into applause. The last montage culminated with Richie's "Gimme the Ball," and at the end of the song, the house went wild.

Ron Dennis was on vacation, but he was still in L.A., and the company had tracked him down at the home of a friend. In the days before cell phones, that was a feat.

Nine and a half months after my last performance as Maggie, Pat called me a few hours before the matinee. Lisa Donaldson (then playing Maggie) and Linda Dangcil (the Maggie understudy) were both unable to sing. Pat needed me to play Maggie. She said the only alternative was to cut the role. I was terrified during the matinee, but during the evening performance, I actually enjoyed playing Maggie again. I had always loved the character, and in the previous nine months, I had been listening to Maggies who sounded a lot more like me than like Kay, and I was no longer judging my performance by Kay's unique style and voice.

I was also happy to be back on the line so soon after my two-week vacation. During the first two weeks of June, I had gone back to New York to visit my home only to realize that home might be L.A.

17

Leaving *A Chorus Line* (1977)

During my vacation, I saw New York through different eyes. New York was congested, dirty, and noisy. In midtown Manhattan, pedestrians crossed the streets against the stoplights and pushed me along with them. Trash littered the streets. Bags of garbage, piled high on street corners, stank in the hot night air. Screeching subways assaulted my ears, and skyscrapers blocked the sun.

A year earlier, when *A Chorus Line* arrived in Los Angeles, I asked people why they lived in Southern California. Some answered, "for work," which was certainly the reason *I* was in L.A., but most people said, "the weather." *How shallow*, I thought. *What about great theater and opera and art*? Los Angeles had nothing to compare with Broadway or the Metropolitan Opera or the Metropolitan Museum of Art.

However, I soon realized that "the weather" was not only sunshine and moderate temperatures, but also access to the wonders of nature. In Los Angeles, I lived only fifteen minutes from the vast, sparsely populated beach in Santa Monica. When I drove into the San Fernando Valley, I traveled through mountains. In winter, when I drove east on Santa Monica Blvd., I saw mountains covered with snow in the distance. My new apartment after I left *A Chorus Line* had expansive views of oak trees, palm trees, cypress trees, and blue sky from every room.

Today, new construction has defiled many of the views I treasured, but I still enjoy walking on the wide sidewalks from the Santa Monica Pier to Venice Beach—past the chess players and the beach volleyball courts to the shops and cafes and fortunetellers. In

Palisades Park, I walk along the bluffs overlooking the ocean. I take the footbridge across the highway to the beach and let my toes sink into the wet sand at the edge of the surf. I watch the waves roll in and the sun set behind the mountains. I watch the clouds turn pink and orange and gold. I gaze in wonder at the full moon—white, yellow, or orange—as it reflects the light of the sun and reminds me that the sun behind me shines as brightly at night as it does during the day, and I find that awesome.

I love the rows of purple jacaranda trees and the tall palm trees that line the streets. I love the scent of jasmine when I walk to the 7–11. Nature is rejuvenating, and I missed it when I returned to New York.

My 58th Street apartment was even less furnished and less homey than when I had left because I had lent Ray my Baldwin piano and my answering machine while I was in California. Ray and I had dinner together, and he said he was unhappy in New York and wished he could live in the West.

I also had dinner with Cynthia Raglan, my New York commercial agent. I loved seeing her again, but I felt as if I had been away from New York for a lifetime. If I returned to the Big Apple, would the casting directors still remember me?

During the seven years I was married, Ray and I had socialized with other couples, but most of our friends, including Dan and Mara, were Ray's friends first. If I had stayed in New York, invitations would have gone to Ray and his latest girlfriend, not to me. In Los Angeles, I had my own friends—friends who had never met Ray. I took regular ballet classes with Stanley Holden (formerly a principal with the Royal Ballet), and the Stanley Holden Dance Center was a welcoming community for local and visiting dancers, which have included Mikhail Baryshnikov, Juliet Prowse, Mary Tyler Moore, Meg Tilly, Toni Basil, and Bebe Neuwirth.

While on vacation in New York, I saw three Broadway shows: *A Chorus Line* to see new interpretations and to remind myself how great the show really is (something you can forget when night after night you look through the anxious eyes of the characters you play); *Annie*, which was delightful and gave Dorothy Loudon (*Lolita, My*

Love) the star role she deserved; and Lily Tomlin's *Appearing Nitely*, a one-woman tour de force. It occurred to me that if I flew to New York twice a year, I could see most of the important shows. I had only five months left on my contract with *A Chorus Line*, and I was seriously considering a move to Los Angeles.

After my vacation, I began working with Bobby Gorman to learn new music for the inevitable auditions ahead. Bobby and I had performed together in *How Now, Dow Jones*, and he had relocated to L.A. Throughout the summer and fall, I continued to shoot television commercials, including Bank of America, Chevrolet, Continental Airlines, MFA Insurance, and Jack-in-the-Box. I also guest-starred on a sitcom, *The San Pedro Beach Bums*, which conveniently shot on a Monday, my day off from *A Chorus Line*. I could definitely make a living in L.A., and since *A Chorus Line* was moving on to Chicago in January, I had to choose between New York and Los Angeles. I had more friends on the West Coast than in New York, and I wanted to see more of the West—something I hadn't been able to do with eight shows a week.

In late September, I auditioned for a new TV series, *The Tony DeFranco Show*. Tony DeFranco was the youngest member and star singer of The DeFranco Family, who had had a gold record ("Heartbeat—It's a Lovebeat") when Tony was 13. On August 31, 1977, Tony had turned 18, and producers Sid and Marty Krofft were looking for a girl to play opposite him in a new variety show. The Krofft brothers had narrowed it down to two girls and wanted both of us to test opposite Tony on October 1. The test was on a Saturday afternoon.

When a performer is under contract to a stage show, her first obligation is to that show, but performers routinely call in sick when they have more lucrative or more rewarding work. I didn't want to call in sick when I wasn't, so I had told my agents that I couldn't work after noon on Wednesdays, Saturdays, and Sundays, or after 6:00 p.m. the other days of the week, except Monday. This schedule had cost me quite a few commercials, and, as I discovered when I arrived at my screen test for *Three's Company*, I had also missed an on-set rehearsal that the other actresses had attended the day before the test. However, on October 1, I had only five more weeks with *A*

Chorus Line. The date of the screen test couldn't be changed, and I didn't want to give up the chance to star in a variety series when it was down to two girls. I decided to call in sick to *A Chorus Line*.

With the exception of my scheduled two-week vacation, I had never missed a performance, so I wanted to make sure my understudy wasn't caught by surprise. I told her I was going to be very ill for the matinee on Saturday, but would recover for the evening performance.

"No!" she said. "You can't be out. I'm going on for Chrissy [Bocchino]."

"Why is she going to be out?"

"Her voice. She said it won't hold up for two shows."

"If Chrissy can do the matinee, can you play Kristine at the matinee and Diana at night?"

Sure she could.

Up I went up to Chrissy's dressing room and explained that I would be very ill for the Saturday matinee. She wanted to know why.

I swore her to secrecy and told her about the screen test. Of course, she'd do the matinee. Chrissy was a sweetheart.

After the screen test, when I arrived at the Shubert for the evening performance, one of the male understudies told me that throughout the matinee, Pat had been pacing the corridor (visualize the black cloud), muttering, "Lee is out. Lee is out. Lee is out," as if Pat were Chicken Little and the sky were falling. With so many dancers missing performances, I would have preferred to tell Pat in advance that I'd be back for the evening performance, but that was a risk I wasn't willing to take.

In the following years, I missed two more performances for television work—one in 1980 and one in 1985, but I was able to handle both situations with more transparency. In 1980, I was performing in the world premiere of *Jane Heights*, a musical spoof of *Jane Eyre* and *Wuthering Heights* written by James Prideaux (book and lyrics) and Arthur B. Rubinstein (music). The cast was headed by Rosanna Huffman (*Half a Sixpence* on Broadway) as Jane, and the dashing, young Howard McGillin played Heathcliff. Our director, Roy Christopher, predicted Howard's future when he whispered to me during rehearsals, "If that boy doesn't become a star, there is no justice in the world." Today, Howard's many Broadway credits include the Phantom in *The Phantom of the Opera*, Steven Kodaly in *She Loves Me*, and Honoré Lachaille in *Gigi*. *Jane Heights* was a wonderful company—some of us met regularly for lunch for years afterwards—and I loved playing Adele, Mr. Rochester's ward, who dances on pointe and speaks fractured French.

During the first ten weeks I was under contract to *Jane Heights*, I shot commercials as an office worker for Hallmark cards, a flight attendant for Continental Airlines, a reporter for the American Dairy Association, and a nun for the *Phoenix Gazette*. I worked as far away as Long Beach and Palm Springs, but I always made half hour in plenty of time. However, the promo for the hit TV series *The Incredible Hulk* was different. As the Hulk, Lou Ferrigno wore special contact lenses that could only be in his eyes for fifteen or twenty minutes at a time. On the set, a nurse with a stopwatch made sure the Hulk's lenses came out on time and didn't go back in too soon. The instant the Hulk was ready to shoot, everyone else was already in position. However, by early afternoon, I realized I might miss the evening performance. (*Jane Heights* was on an Equity Hollywood Area Theatre contract, a low-salary contract that allowed actors to miss performances for more lucrative film and television work.)

At 3:00 p.m., I asked the director of the commercial, Stan Dragoti (*Love at First Bite*), if he thought I would be finished in time to do the show. He said he would be able to answer that question at 6:00 p.m. I called my understudy, Tina Paradiso, and told her that I was calling her off the record to give her a heads up. The commercial looked as if it might shoot into the evening hours. If I couldn't do the show, I would call the stage manager at 6:00 p.m., and he would call her. I didn't know for sure, but my gut feeling was that she would be on that night. In fact, Tina did go on, and I heard that she was well prepared and cute as a button.

The other performance I missed for television work was in 1985. I was playing Kristine in *A Chorus Line* at the Grand Dinner Theatre in Anaheim. I had a good relationship with the producer, Frank Wyka, so I told him the truth—that I had been offered a guest-starring role on *The Facts of Life*, a role I really wanted to play, which taped on a Tuesday evening. I told him I would earn more money for three days' work on *The Facts of Life* than I earned in many weeks at the Grand. If Frank could give me that Tuesday evening off, I would be very grateful, and my understudy would have plenty of time to invite her agents, family, and friends. Frank agreed, and that's what we did. Director John Bowab and the wonderful cast of *The Facts of Life* welcomed me with open arms. The girls had been told that I was performing in *A Chorus Line* and wanted to know all about the show. George Clooney, who would later become the superstar actor and producer, was charming and easy-going, and the taping before a live audience was as exciting as an opening night.

More than a decade later, when I went to get a smog check for my car, the mechanic said, "I know you."

"I haven't been here before."

"From television."

"I've done some TV commercials."

"Not commercials. I'll think of it. I recognized your voice before I even saw you."

When he returned with the smog certificate, he said, "*The Facts of Life*. The 'Doo-Wah' episode with El DeBarge. I love that show!"

Syndication (and now streaming) keeps shows alive indefinitely. I still get residuals for *The Facts of Life*. The amounts are small, like the residuals from *Pennies from Heaven*, in which I was one of more than a hundred dancers, and *Short Circuit*, which used part of my 1980 Pepsi "Skywriter" commercial. Even the Pepsi commercial, sometimes called "Marry Me, Sue," has continuing life because it has been posted on YouTube.

As for *The Tony DeFranco Show*—the show for which I called in sick to *A Chorus Line*: Sid and Marty Krofft decided not to go forward with the show.

On November 6, 1977, I gave my last performance with the National Company of *A Chorus Line*. People often asked me, "Do you wish you had been a part of the original cast?" The answer is "no." I joined the show at the perfect time for me—when it was already a smash hit, and the people on the creative team knew exactly what they wanted. I loved working with the creators of the show when they were the toast of the town; I loved the experience of arriving in Hollywood with most of the original cast of the hottest show on Broadway, and when I left the show after 18 months, I was more than ready for something new, including an imminent screen test for another TV series that never went into production.

During the month of December, I found a large one-bedroom apartment near the Stanley Holden Dance Center. I ordered a new yellow Subaru to be delivered in January, spent Christmas in Delaware with my family, packed up my New York apartment, and was back in Los Angeles for New Year's Eve. I was sorry I hadn't had time to live in my 58th Street apartment, but I couldn't do everything. In real life, as on stage, I had to make choices. In 1976, I chose the brilliance of *A Chorus Line* in Los Angeles over potluck in New York City. Eighteen months later, I chose nature over cultural institutions. I chose to see the West, rather than more of the East, and I chose the city I hoped would prolong my career.

In New York, I was the divorced woman who had been performing on Broadway for ten years with a ballet career before that. In Los Angeles, I was the young girl from *A Chorus Line* who still had to reassure employers and social workers that she was, in fact, over the age of 18. To tip the scales further in the direction of Los Angeles, where film and television work was more plentiful, the Screen Actors' Guild had a health care plan for pensioners, and Actors' Equity did not. I was almost 32 years old, and although stage was my first love and the arena where I planned to spend most of my time, I wanted to make sure that I had at least 20 qualifying years in the SAG pension plan before my age caught up with me.

As I settled into my new apartment in L.A., I never imagined that six years later I would be back on Broadway—for one night only—in a performance of *A Chorus Line* that has never been equaled.

18

A Chorus Line: The Record-Breaking Show (1983)

Tom Porter, a stage manager for *A Chorus Line*, called me from New York in the fall of 1983. He told me that on September 29, *A Chorus Line* would become the longest-running show in Broadway history, and there was going to be a celebration in New York. My first instinct was to skip the celebration. I had been away from home all summer performing in musicals, and I wanted to shoot a few commercials to plump up my bank account and keep my commercial agents happy.

I had begun the summer playing Dainty June in *Gypsy* at the Sacramento Music Circus, a theater in the round in a huge canvas tent. JoAnne Worley (*Laugh-In*) was the warm, funny, brassy Mama Rose; her then-husband Roger Perry (*The Facts of Life*) played Herbie, and Marcia Wallace (*The Bob Newhart Show*) played Tessie Tura. Leland Ball, with calm self-assurance, directed the talented, fun-loving cast. William Glackin in *The Sacramento Bee* gave the show a rave review: "This is a powerhouse of a production with Jo Anne Worley its impressive central dynamo. At first her Rose is almost pure, humorous ebullience, a showbizzy figure that is doubly convincing: It shows us the charm that the kids and Herbie love, and it also shows us the performer in the mother that is trying to perform through the children."

"But Rose the manipulator, Rose the insistent, self-deluding dreamer is there, too, along with the Rose who is blind to how terrible the kiddie act is. And in Act II when times get tougher the truth gets uglier and plainer, and Worley's performance deepens

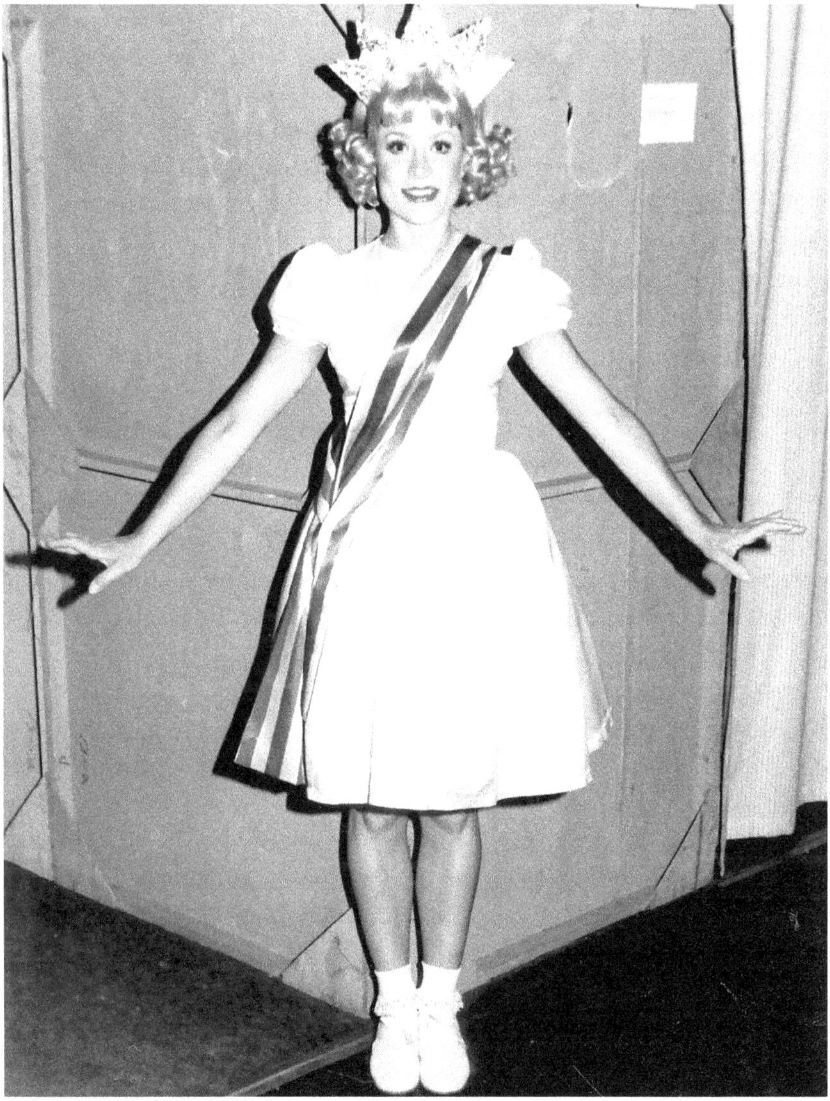

In the summer of 1983, I played Dainty June in *Gypsy* at the Sacramento Music Circus, a theater in the round, where pirouettes were not merely single, double, or triple, but one and a half—or two and a quarter.

with it, until, in 'Rose's Turn,' the monster becomes pitiful, and her ruin, something we can all recognize: somebody who wanted to be noticed. Not so far from Louise after all."

After the last performance of *Gypsy,* I caught an early morning flight to San Diego where rehearsals for *Hello, Dolly!* had already begun. Sixteen years earlier, when I had joined the Broadway cast of *Hello, Dolly!,* I had known that Minnie Fay was a perfect role for me, and it was. I was a bit worried when I heard that my Barnaby, Fred DeBerg, was only 16, but he was so mature, so talented, and so professional that we all forgot about his age until we talked about going somewhere after the show and he reminded us that he was still a minor and his mother would have to drive.

The open-air Starlight Bowl was unique. The theater was in the flight path for the San Diego International Airport, so the stage was equipped with traffic lights for the performers. When the green lights turned yellow, they signaled that a plane was approaching, and when the lights turned red, everyone on stage froze in position until the plane had passed and the lights turned green. If the lights turned yellow during a song, we took our cues from the conductor who would conduct the stop and the start. This took getting used to, but I loved playing Minnie Fay.

I ended the summer back in Sacramento playing Frenchy in *Grease* starring Eddie Mekka, the actor who had played Carmine on *Laverne and Shirley.* When I first saw *Grease,* shortly after it opened on Broadway, the audience was younger than the average Broadway audience, and it was wildly enthusiastic about the transformation of Sandy Dumbrowski from an innocent schoolgirl into a greaser's dream, but in spite of the energetic production, period-perfect choreography, and terrific performances, my feelings were mixed. It seemed to me that Sandy's future was brighter at the beginning of the show than at the end. The character I loved was Frenchy, who, unlike the other girls in her clique, dreams of having a career. Frenchy wants to become a beautician. She practices on her friends and drops out of high school to attend beauty school. Unfortunately, she flunks out. Undaunted, she returns to high school with a beautician-adjacent job—demonstrating makeup at Woolworth's. Frenchy isn't bright, but she is imaginative, self-reliant, and has a good heart. I enjoyed seeing the world through her eyes.

Grease was followed by a season retrospective performance in

As Minnie Fay in *Hello, Dolly!*, I sang "Elegance" with Jan Lacey (Mrs. Molloy), Roger Michelson (Cornelius), and Fred DeBerg (Barnaby). Photo: Cindy Lubke Romero/San Diego Union Tribune/ZUMA Press Wire.

which I sang and danced "Dainty June & Her Farmboys" ("I Have a Moo Cow") from *Gypsy*. I flew home on Labor Day, and one week later, booked a Dial commercial to shoot on September 22. Now, Tom Porter was on the telephone urging me to fly to New York on September 24.

The more Tom described the event, the more I realized: *This isn't an ordinary celebration. This is a BIG DEAL.* Michael Bennett was inviting dancers from companies in Spain, Germany, Australia, Sweden, Japan, and England. Hundreds of dancers would take part in the show, and Michael and the New York Shakespeare Festival would pay our airfares, hotels, and per diem. Tom asked me to bring any costumes, hats, or shoes I might have. All I had were my shoes: tan character shoes for Kristine and tan folk dance shoes for Connie. Tom told me to bring the character shoes and my latest 8 × 10 headshot.

I flew to New York on Saturday, September 24. The following evening, Michael gave a party at his building at 890 Broadway. I caught up with people I hadn't seen in years, but I still had no idea of the scope of the event.

Monday morning at 10:00 a.m., more than 300 dancers, numerous stage managers, and other people connected with the production, filled the Shubert Theatre. We had only three days of rehearsal before the show on Thursday night—a show preceded by the afternoon "dress rehearsal" that would also have an invited, black-tie audience. We checked in and began accumulating the goodies we would bring home, including oval buttons with "A Chorus Line" across the top, our names in the middle, and "3389" at the bottom because the record-breaking performance was the 3,389th performance on Broadway. We sat in the house as Michael explained how the show would unfold and identified the dancers who would perform each section of the show.

The current New York company that performed every night would dance the opening number. In a lightning-quick move before lights come up on the 17 dancers toeing the line with their photos in front of their faces, that company would be replaced by the original Broadway company, which would perform the next section when the dancers step forward and give their names. There would be eight sequential casts, ending with a company that was comprised of dancers from companies all over the world, speaking many different languages, including German, Spanish, Swedish, and Japanese. This company would perform the "Alternatives Scene," which begins with Zach's line, "What do you do when you can't dance anymore?" There was no Kristine from any of the foreign companies, so Michael asked all Kristines who could play the role in a foreign language to raise their hands. He asked each of us to stand, give our name, the company in which we had performed, and the language in which we could perform the role. Michael chose me.

I translated Kristine's dialogue into French, and on Tuesday morning, confirmed with native French speakers at the Alliance Française that my translation was accurate and colloquial.

Rehearsals for the "Alternatives Scene" were a jumble of different languages. We had grown up in different countries with different cultures, but we had common experience as dancers, and, as alumni of *A Chorus Line*, we knew the intention of every line in the scene. This "Alternatives Scene" underscored the universality of our experience. The scene ends when Zach, the choreographer, asks, "If today were the day you had to stop dancing. How would you feel?" Diana answers with the song "What I Did for Love." In rehearsal, during the introduction to the song, Michael Bennett led Priscilla Lopez, the original Diana, to stand directly in front of Susanne Nordin, the Swedish Diana, but Priscilla was too choked up to sing. After a moment, she began to talk/sing her way through the song, and as she said, "Look, my eyes are dry," tears were streaming down her cheeks, and she laughed—a wonderful moment featured in the film *Broadway: Beyond the Golden Age*.

Whenever I left the theater, everyone seemed to be talking about the coveted invitations to the performance and the rehearsal. I overheard a man claim he was so offended that he had been invited to the afternoon dress rehearsal instead of the evening performance that he had refused the ticket. *Really*?!

Tuesday night, I went to see the current cast of *A Chorus Line* at the Shubert before returning to the Milford Plaza Hotel a few steps away. Throughout the week, in a loop, the illuminated names of all the dancers participating in the show rolled across the marquee of the Shubert Theatre in alphabetical order. It was thrilling to see the names of the dancers I knew, and Linda Dangcil waited patiently after taking a photograph of her own name to take a photo of mine.

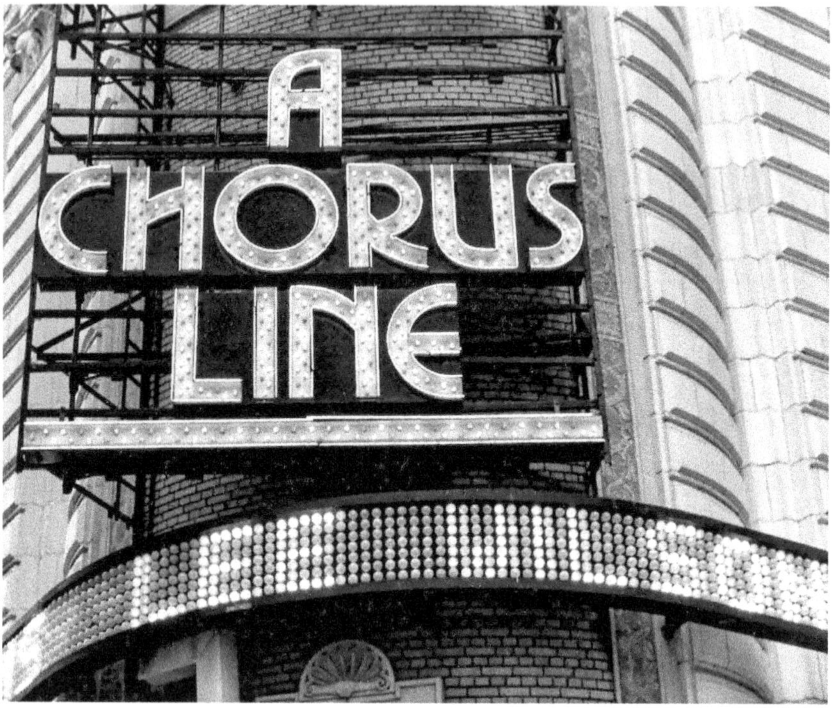

On September 29, 1983, *A Chorus Line* became the longest-running show in Broadway history, and Michael Bennett created a gala to remember. More than 330 dancers participated in the performance, and during the week prior to the black-tie event, our names scrolled across the marquee of the Shubert Theatre. Photo by Linda Dangcil; courtesy of Dick Hamilton.

Wednesday morning, the warm and wonderful Alyce Gilbert, the wardrobe mistress, fitted me for my Kristine costume. We all had large, white *A Chorus Line* shopping bags to hold our costumes. The show was coming together, and I knew Michael's innovations would surprise and delight the audience because they surprised and delighted me.

Thursday morning was the tech rehearsal. Every single person involved in the production had to sign a release so the performance could be filmed for the Lincoln Center Library archives. The Booth Theatre, next door to the Shubert, served as a huge dressing room to supplement the dressing rooms at the Shubert. That afternoon at 2:00 p.m., the dress rehearsal was a full performance for the invited, black-tie audience. Between shows, we had a choice of restaurants for a complimentary dinner, and I chose Sardi's, the restaurant with Continental cuisine and caricatures of Broadway notables on the walls.

At 8:00 p.m. that evening, the star-studded audience enjoyed hors d'oeuvres and champagne under tents in Shubert Alley. A ceremony followed the champagne, and long past the 10:00 p.m. curtain time, the music began for the 3,389th performance of *A Chorus Line* on Broadway.

There was a movie screen set up on the stage of the Booth Theatre so all of the dancers could watch the show before and after their cues, and we were all bristling with nervous energy and excitement. After the opening number when the Originals magically replaced the current New York company, a banner flew in above the dancers' heads that read: "The Original Broadway Company." The audience gasped and broke into applause. Watching the Originals give their names was a step back in time.

The next big surprise was Chikae Ishikawa as Diana, who sang "Nothing" in Japanese. I could hear the audience's confusion as they tried to decipher the first few words, followed by their understanding and delight.

Later, a trio of girls sang Val's song, "Dance: Ten; Looks: Three," aka "Tits and Ass." Karen Jablons sang "tits," Mitzi Hamilton sang "and," and Delyse (DeLee) Lively sang "ass."

Donna McKechnie, the original Cassie, was even better than she was in her Tony Award–winning performance when the show first opened on Broadway, and the scene between her and Zach discussing their break-up was even more poignant now that Donna and Michael had married and divorced. Donna began the Cassie dance alone, but was soon joined by seven additional Cassies—a sea of red leotards and swirling skirts. The additional girls underscored the universality of Cassie's experience. Just like Cassie, at least three of the eight girls had weathered well-publicized relationships with star choreographers—Donna McKechnie with Michael Bennett, Ann Reinking with Bob Fosse, and Wanda Richert with Gower Champion.

Sammy Williams, the original Paul, began the monologue that

was the centerpiece of his Tony-winning performance, but tonight, Sammy was joined by a chorus of Pauls—boy after boy who knew he was gay, but didn't know where he belonged until he discovered the world of dance.

The seventh cast performed the tap combination, during which Paul is injured. Dancers from "The Foreign Companies," including me, were standing offstage right. As Paul was carried off stage left, the seventh cast followed him, and our cast entered stage right in the same formation to take their places—just as each generation of dancers replaces the previous generation. A banner dropped in above us: "The Foreign Companies."

The "Alternatives Scene" is a discussion about what options dancers have when they can't dance any more, but there are comedic moments, and David Atkins, the Australian dancer playing Mike, got a big laugh with his line, "Nothin' runs forever, right?"

Zach, from his omniscient spot in the rear of the house, posed his final question: "If today were the day you had to stop dancing. How would you feel?" The luminous Priscilla Lopez walked out of an upstage wing, took her place in front of the Swedish Diana, and began to sing, "Kiss today goodbye / The sweetness and the sorrow." Midway through the song, the rest of us joined in, and our counterparts from earlier in the evening came out of the wings and sang with us: "Won't forget, can't regret / What I did for love."

At the end of the song, most of us backed away into the wings while 16 dancers from the Original Broadway Company, walked to the line. From those 16, Zach chose eight—four boys and four girls. Zach's final line, "And I'm very glad we are going to be working together," launched the finale with more than 330 dancers who filled the recently reinforced stage, the balcony, and the aisles. As I watched the cheering audience, I remembered a matinee performance of *Vanities* at the Mark Taper Forum that I had seen when I was performing in *A Chorus Line* in Los Angeles. I was seated next to a white-haired woman, and at intermission I asked her if she liked the play. "Oh, yes," she said. "It's so much better than the show I saw last week."

"What show was that?" I asked.

"*A Chorus Line*," she said. "They didn't even put on costumes until the final number."

"*A Chorus Line* takes place at a dance audition," I said.

"I know," she said. "But all of that should take place *before* I get to the theater."

I didn't argue. We all have our preferences, but on Thursday, September 29, 1983, it seemed as if *everyone* loved *A Chorus Line*. There were, of course, dancers who were disappointed that they didn't get to do their numbers or that they had to share them with

In the record-breaking performance of *A Chorus Line*, Priscilla Lopez, the original Diana, sang "What I Did for Love," surrounded by dancers from companies all over the world. Behind Priscilla is the Swedish Diana, Susanne Nordin, who played the "Alternatives Scene" in Swedish. I played Kristine in French because there was no Kristine from a foreign company. (I am standing at left.) Sitting beside me is the dancer playing Al; in front of us with her legs stretched out and her face in darkness is Melinda Buckley as Val. At right, seated, is Ilona Papp as Judy. Maiza Tempesta is the voluptuous Sheila, and standing behind Maiza, is David Atkins as Mike. Photo by Martha Swope © New York Public Library

other dancers, and there were several Originals who didn't participate: Nancy Lane (the original Bebe), Pam Blair (the original Val), and Robert LuPone (the original Zach). Those dancers were missed, but the show was generally a love fest.

The party continued throughout the night in Shubert Alley. The celebration reportedly cost close to half a million dollars, but *A Chorus Line* was on the front pages of all the newspapers, and the boost to the box office far exceeded the cost of the event. On October 1, Frank Rich summed up the experience for *The New York Times*: "It is perhaps impossible to explain or understand all the factors that transformed a promotional event into a theatrical experience that was even more poignant than it was thrilling ... in a feat of artistry and logistics that boggles the mind, [Michael Bennett] gave us a new show that accomplished the seemingly impossible: he made us look at now overfamiliar material through fresh eyes."

Performing the "Alternatives Scene" with the Foreign Companies in the record-breaking show is one of the highlights of my life. If *A Chorus Line* had been my last performance on Broadway, it would have been a fitting finale, but, in fact, my longest run and first cast album were still in the future.

19

Las Vegas and the West (1978–1986)

After I left *A Chorus Line* in November 1977, gave up the lease on my New York apartment, and officially moved to L.A., my first stage job was playing the French maid Claudine in *Pajama Tops* at the Union Plaza Hotel in downtown Las Vegas. *Pajama Tops* is a French farce, and June Wilkinson, a former Playboy phenomenon, played the lead role of Babette, a role she had played on Broadway. Offstage, June wore white t-shirts that showed off her considerable assets, and whenever she walked through the casino, men stopped in their tracks and stared. *Pajama Tops* was scheduled to run for three months, but was extended to six.

In 1978, Las Vegas was a small town with a glamorous Strip (Las Vegas Boulevard) and a busy, brightly lit, but less glamorous, downtown. Traffic on the Strip moved slowly, but steadily, and I often chose this route to go downtown so I could admire the hotels, which had acres of land surrounding them and were separated from downtown by a landscape that could have been Anywhere, USA. Las Vegas had planned for rapid expansion with wide streets and dedicated left turn lanes, but that expansion was still in the future. From my apartment near the Strip, I could drive to the Union Plaza Hotel downtown, all of the hotels on the Strip, the University of Nevada, Las Vegas, or McCarran Airport in less than fifteen minutes. What a change from the traffic on the freeways of Los Angeles! How different from Las Vegas today!

I loved the fact that some restaurants, drugstores, dry cleaners, and supermarkets were open 24 hours a day. Food was cheap, and the entertainment was superb. I reveled in the spectacle of

Caesars Palace with its Greco-Roman design. I felt like royalty in the restrained luxury of the Desert Inn. On my day off, I usually saw two shows—one at 8:00 p.m. and the other at midnight. I saw dozens of headliners, including Frank Sinatra, Tony Bennett, Paul Anka, Shirley MacLaine, Helen Reddy, Juliet Prowse, and Sammy Davis, Jr., who used only his first name on the marquee: SAMMY! Some nights, after performing in my second show, I enjoyed an early morning lounge act, including George Carlin, whose "Seven Dirty Words" comedy routine was still controversial. Today it seems quaint that one of the seven dirty words—words you could not say on television—was "tits." Las Vegas also had some classical entertainment, and I attended performances by Andrés Segovia, Ballet West, and Nevada Dance Theatre.

The shows in Las Vegas hotels fulfilled two functions. The first was to lure people into the casinos so they would gamble. Therefore, the showrooms were located so that people had to walk through the casino to get to the theaters, and performances were generally limited to 90 minutes to get people back to the gambling tables. The second purpose was to break the momentum of gamblers on a winning streak. The pit bosses were in contact with the head of food and beverage to strategize about the high-stakes gamblers. When gamblers were winning, the hotel would offer them free food and drinks or a free show.

Las Vegas had its own language and traditions: A person with juice (clout) could comp a whale (a high-stakes gambler) to dinner, a show, or the best suite in the hotel. A surveillance system, the "eye in the sky," saw everything that happened within the casino—but not what happened in the hotel corridors or the parking lots. A "working girl" was not *any* young woman with a job, but a woman who catered to men's sexual desires. A maître d' in a showroom, unlike a hostess at Denny's, could earn huge amounts of money. In 1978, the minimum wage in Nevada was $2.30 an hour, but people pouring into the showrooms regularly greased the palms of showroom maître d's with 20, 50, and sometimes even 100 dollar bills to get good seats. Popular shows at the Hilton attracted more than a thousand people per show, 12 shows a week. Even the servers could make $1800 a week in tips. However, in 1978, times were changing. The feds were investigating the mob, and what locals referred to as the Golden Age of Vegas was coming to an end. Ticketron, a company that issued theater tickets for reserved seats, was replacing maître d's. Marketing for the city changed from the Sin City of the Rat Pack, where "boys will be boys" and prostitutes abound, to a fun-filled destination for the entire family.

I was having a grand time in Las Vegas, so I signed on for the next show, *Anything Goes*, in which I played one of Reno Sweeney's angels, a role that had more dancing and was much more fun than the ingénue role of Hope I had played in Michigan. We performed two shows a night, six days a week. At the Union Plaza, *Anything Goes* was cut down to a brisk 90 minutes, but Charles Supin in the *Las Vegas Review-Journal* chose the show as one of the five best shows in Vegas. The hotel passed out free aces to people who attended the show to encourage them to play blackjack, and after the last performance of *Anything Goes*, I was given one of those aces. I sat down at the blackjack table with another member of the cast, exchanged twenty dollars for chips, and played my ace. I whispered to my cast mate that I was going to double my money and leave. That whisper got the attention of a pit boss who watched me bet one dollar a hand and chuckled as he concluded that I was no threat to the house. I doubled my money and left the table.

Shortly after my long run in Las Vegas, I went to San Antonio, Texas, to play Chava in *Fiddler on the Roof* with Fyvush Finkel as Tevye. Fyvush Finkel is probably best known for his Emmy-winning performance as Douglas Wambaugh in the television series *Picket Fences*, but he began his career in Yiddish theater. I have seen *Fiddler on the Roof* many times, including twice on Broadway, and I haven't seen a better Tevye. Bess Meisler was a perfect Golde and a fountain of information about Jewish traditions.

Our director was Pat Baldauff, who had directed me in *The Fantasticks* in New Orleans, and I was glad to work with him on a role that was much more comfortable for me than Luisa. *Fiddler* was the rare show in which I had no fear of singing solo. The song "Matchmaker" was perfect for my voice.

The actor playing Fyedka, my love interest, was an excellent actor and dancer, but a bit of a prima donna. In one scene, we were directed to stand in profile to the audience. However, when Fyedka entered, he stopped upstage of me. I would have had to turn away from the audience to see his face, so I moved upstage to put us both in profile. The following night he stopped further upstage. I moved further upstage. After a few performances, we were as far upstage as we could go without moving out of the light. The stage manager had given Fyedka notes to come downstage to no avail. Finally, the stage manager told me. "You have to find a way to bring the scene downstage."

"Anyway I want?"

"Anyway you can."

I asked Claire Haney, the actress playing Tzeitel, to help me find a solution. I had an idea. Would it play? She said it would.

That night I stayed downstage where the scene had been blocked. Fyedka stopped far upstage of me. I gave a shy glance at him over my shoulder and played the scene out front—as if I were too shy to look him in the eyes. When he realized that he was getting lost in the background, he came running downstage. Claire told me that the stage manager laughed out loud. The problem was solved.

San Antonio had a beautiful River Walk with open-air restaurants overlooking the boats on the San Antonio River. It was a lovely place to stroll on a sunny afternoon. I also enjoyed the armadillo races in the nearby town of New Braunfels—a town that now holds the Armadillo Alympics.

Armadillos in the Alympics earn their spots by winning in lower-level competitions. There are many rules and regulations for the Alympics, two of which are related: First, there is no discrimination on the basis of sex. Male and female armadillos compete side by side. Second, "If love at first sight develops" between two armadillos during the race, those armadillos are disqualified and removed from the tracks.

In 1979, there was a fair-like atmosphere. People seated in the bleachers cheered, yelled, and banged beer cans together to encourage their favorites. Armadillos can reach a running speed of thirty miles per hour, but despite the enthusiasm of the crowd, the majority of the armadillos moseyed down the track stopping and starting like indecisive shoppers at Costco.

When I performed in stage shows, I had time to explore a city from one end to the other and sometimes a nearby town as well. When I shot commercials, I saw the hotel and the shooting locations, but when I was hired as the hostess of *Journey*, a travel show for young, active couples, I went on a whirlwind tour of New Mexico. In Taos, I went rock climbing and whitewater rafting. In Santa Fe, I toured the Shidoni Gallery, where I watched the pouring of red-hot metal and took a golf cart ride through the outdoor sculpture garden. I interviewed Spanish dancer María Benítez and watched her perform at La Fonda. I modeled clothes from local boutiques and interviewed painter Harry Fonseca, known for his paintings of Coyote, a trickster in Native American culture. In Albuquerque, I went ballooning and rode the Sandia Peak Tram, the longest aerial tram in the U.S., which rises to an elevation of more than 10,000 feet. I got very little sleep, but I loved every minute of the shoot. Unfortunately, the producer later told me that there was a disagreement between him and the financier, and *Journey* ended in limbo.

As usual, when a job ended, I filed for unemployment insurance. As usual, I filled in the month and day of my birth and scribbled in the space for the year. For the first time, the official at the unemployment office confronted me. "I can't read the year," she said.

"That's the way I always write it," I said. "This form goes to my employer, and I don't want him to know my age."

"If I can't read it, you don't get unemployment insurance."

I argued. She refused to budge, so I wrote in the date.

Shortly thereafter, the producer, who had worked side by side with me for ten days on location, told me he was shocked when he learned how old I was. "I would never have hired you if I had known your age," he said. "I'm glad I did, but you should *never* tell people your age."

The California requirement that I give my birthdate when I filed for unemployment benefits worked against me, but one California law gave me jobs that should have gone to children.

Shortly after filming *Journey*, I auditioned for the lead role of Esther in *Meet Me in St. Louis* at the Harlequin Dinner Playhouse. Esther is 17. In the movie, she was played by Judy Garland, who was 21 at the time. I put on my curly pigtails and period dress and sang. I got a callback and sang and read. Shortly thereafter, the director, Tom White, called and offered me the role of Tootie.

Tootie?! Tootie is five.

"Even on a good day, I don't look five," I said.

"We know that," he said, "but we're combining the roles of Tootie [6-year-old Margaret O'Brien in the film] and Agnes [13-year-old Joan Carroll]. We think you can play Tootie as twelve."

To play Tootie, I had to look younger than Esther. Tom assured me that I did. I had to be too young to be interested in boys, which could easily mean 13 or even 14. I told Tom I would play Tootie provided there was no mention of her age, and he agreed. My Tootie would be a tomboy who relished the freedom of being a kid and resisted growing into a proper young lady in a corset. However, when I received my copy of the script, I realized there was one scene that betrayed the fact that the role was written for a small child—the scene in which Tootie expresses her fear that if the family moves to New York, Santa Claus won't be able to find her house. When I reread the script years later, I saw that if we had cut a few lines, there would have been no indication that Tootie wasn't 12 or 13. However, at the time, I simply hoped the audience would go along with us. Only one review, the one in *Drama-Logue*, mentioned that I was too old for the role: "Lee Wilson is obviously too old for Esther's little sister Tootie but she overcomes the handicap with a winning performance." It went on to say, "The ridiculous requirement of having to hire a tutor (at $900 per week) for child actors has caused dinner and other Equity theatres to stop using youngsters."

I suspect the California law was drafted with the film business in mind because performances in most dinner theaters take place in the evening and on weekends and don't conflict with school. In other states, I worked with children who managed to perform eight shows a week and excel in school and other activities.

I had actually become aware of the tutor requirement

earlier in the year when I played Dainty June in the Grand Dinner Theatre production of *Gypsy*, a show I almost lost because of an agent.

When the casting notice for *Gypsy* appeared, I had no theater agent, but one of the better-known agents had been pursuing me. I couldn't attend the regular Equity call, so I asked him to submit me for Dainty June at the agents' call.

"You don't want to work at the Grand," he said.

"Why not?"

"There's no money."

"I don't care about the money," I said. "I want to play Dainty June, and I want to play the role *now* because in fifteen minutes, I'll be too old."

"What about me?! Equity won't allow me to invade minimum." (Agents can only take a full 10 percent of an actor's salary if they negotiate at least 10 percent above minimum, which I was sure he could do—but his commission of 10 percent at the Grand would not be a big commission.) "I can get you a lot more money at St. Louis Muny," he said.

"Are they doing *Gypsy*?"

They weren't. The agent agreed to submit me for Dainty June at the Grand.

During the dance audition, I saw my competition and expected to be offered the role, but I heard nothing. Two weeks later, my agent called with another audition.

"What happened with Dainty June at the Grand?" I asked.

"We turned it down. There wasn't any money."

"Wait! They offered me the role of Dainty June?"

"Yes, but they didn't have enough money."

I fired the agent and called the theater.

"I'm so glad you called," said the voice on the phone. "Every day, Frank [producer Frank Wyka] tells me he *needs* Lee Wilson, but he can't afford her."

"I'm sure we can work it out," I said.

As I talked with Frank, I learned that I would be playing Baby June as well as Dainty June because the theater couldn't afford to hire a tutor for children. (If the reviewer for *Meet Me in St. Louis* was correct about the cost of a tutor, it was almost three times the cost of an Equity actor.)

I had had problems with theater agents, but my commercial agents had been terrific. The Jack Wormser Agency had become Joseph, Heldfond & Rix, and the two agents submitting me in the early 1980s were Diane and Joel. When I told Joel I had been desperate to play Dainty June at the Grand because in fifteen minutes I would be too old, he laughed and said, "You'll be playing Dainty June when you're forty-five." I thought it highly unlikely that I'd play teenagers when I was in my mid-forties, but Joel was right.

At the end of 1984, Diane and Joel left Joseph, Heldfond & Rix for Cunningham, Escott, Dipene. Successive agents at Joseph, Heldfond & Rix had performed well for me in the past, so I decided to stay with the agency. However, the following year, 1985, I didn't book as often as I had in the past. *Was I in a slump? Was I old news? Was it because the new agents were submitting me in an older age range—late twenties and early thirties?* I was almost 40, but in real life, people usually assumed I was in my early to mid-twenties. That October, when I picked up the script for a guest star role in *The Facts of Life*, I asked the person who handed me the script, "How old is the character of Stacey?"

"About your age. Twenty. Twenty-one," she said.

As soon as I had a tape of *The Facts of Life*, I made an appointment with Sandy Joseph and asked her to watch some of my recent commercials and two scenes from *The Facts of Life*.

"What do you want me to say?" she said. "We can't submit you for eighteen because the casting directors know you."

I told her I wasn't asking to be submitted for 18, but for 25, and she agreed that was the appropriate age range. Shortly after our meeting, I booked a Motts commercial, and Sandy sent me a note: "25!" However, both of the new agents told me that notwithstanding this one commercial, they didn't think I could play 25.

I appreciated their honesty, but I disagreed. It was time to change agents. I moved to CED with Diane and Joel and booked roles in Jack-in-the-Box and McDonalds training films, both age 25, and a

Totes umbrella commercial as an undergraduate student. I thought I had solved my age problem, but I was wrong. Age would be a factor in my next job in Las Vegas, and after a weird experience in Arizona, new legislation in California would threaten my career.

20

The Ticking Clock (1986–1988)

In the spring of 1986, I auditioned for the role of Dainty June at the Union Plaza Hotel in Las Vegas and didn't get the job. I was surprised. The director, Ernie Sarracino, had been in the cast of *Pajama Tops*, in which I had played the saucy teen-age maid, and we got along well. Ernie also knew that my reviews in previous productions of *Gypsy* had been terrific. The girl he hired, Cathy Fries, was younger than I, but I didn't think she would look younger on stage.

At every union audition, there is a monitor from Actors' Equity. At this audition—and at most Los Angeles auditions in the late 1970s and early 1980s—the monitor was Lucy Jordan. Several weeks later, Lucy told me that she had been astonished that Ernie hadn't hired me for Dainty June, so she had asked Ernie, "Why didn't you hire Lee?"

"I know how old she is," he said.

"She doesn't look it," said Lucy. "I saw her play Dainty June in Sacramento, and she was wonderful."

"I'm sure she was," said Ernie, "But I can't get past her age."

I don't know how Ernie knew my age, but in Las Vegas, all prospective employees of casinos must be fingerprinted and undergo a background check. When I was hired for *Pajama Tops*, my age was on the paperwork for the background check, and I suspect that someone who saw the paperwork leaked my birthdate to Ernie.

To my delight, during the run of *Gypsy* in Las Vegas, Cathy called me and asked me to replace her. She had been offered the Los Angeles Company of *Cats* as understudy to the lead role of Grizabella, and *Cats* was her dream job. However, *Cats* wanted her in one week—less than the standard two weeks' notice. The producer at the Union Plaza, who knew me from *Pajama Tops* and *Anything Goes*, had agreed to release Cathy *if* I could replace her and *if* she could teach me the role in three days with no other cast or crew involved. Could I do it? Of course I could. I already knew the lead actresses: Charlene Kase, Mama Rose at the Grand Dinner Theatre, was playing Mama Rose, and Charlene's daughter, Lauren Hathaway, a lovely actress and an equally lovely person, was playing Louise. I knew the music and dialogue for the show. All I had to learn was the staging, the choreography, and the cuts that brought the running time down to 90 minutes.

As I watched the show the night before my first rehearsal, I watched Lauren grow from a shy young girl into the sexy stripper—and I was in awe of the way Charlene sang Mama Rose two performances a night six nights a week. I also saw that Cathy's wig made her look older than she looked in real life. I certainly didn't want an aging hairstyle. I asked the producer for permission to have the wig re-styled at my own expense.

"What do you want to do?" he asked with a frown.

I told him I wanted bangs and a pageboy with curls.

He looked confused.

"Exactly like Dainty June in the movie," I said.

Bingo! I had permission.

After my first performance, Baby June came into my dressing room and announced, "My mom says you're older than Cathy. But you look *a lot younger.* Are you *really* older?"

Yes, the wig made a big difference.

I loved being back in Las Vegas. I loved working with Charlene and Lauren, and I was pleased and thankful that Cathy had landed the hottest show in L.A. and had given me one more Dainty June.

When I returned to L.A., the Arizona Theatre Company hired me to play the Little Nun in John Guare's Pulitzer Prize–winning play *The House of Blue Leaves.* The role was small, but the experience was unforgettable.

The House of Blue Leaves is set in 1965, and the play is often billed as a black comedy, or a zany comedy, but although it has laughs, it is a serious play about unrealistic expectations, fear of humiliation, and obsession with fame in a chaotic world.

I met the director, John Clark Donahue, at the audition. With his round face, bald pate, and rim of white hair, he seemed perfect casting for an Irish priest, but he had an unsettling gaze. However, I liked the producer, so I took the job.

When I arrived at the first rehearsal, Mr. Donahue had covered the walls of the rehearsal room with a timeline of important events during the early 1960s, and he asked us to share our memories of that time—a time I remembered well. In 1962, new liturgy allowed priests to celebrate mass in English, a controversial decision; in November 1963, the first Roman Catholic President of the United States, John F. Kennedy, was assassinated; in 1964, the Civil Rights Act outlawed discrimination based on race, color, religion, sex, or national origin; and throughout the early 1960s, increasing millions of women were taking birth control pills despite the fact that the pills were illegal in many states and condemned by the Catholic Church. In 1965, the year in which the play is set, Malcolm X was assassinated; riots in Watts killed 34 people, and the Vietnam War was escalating. *The House of Blue Leaves* is firmly rooted in its time, and Mr. Donahue wanted us to be familiar with the history of the early 1960s.

Three of the four lead actors—the actors in the roles of Bunny, Bananas, and Ronnie—had worked with Mr. Donahue at the Children's Theatre Company (CTC) in Minneapolis and were fans of his improvisatory style.

Mr. Donahue arranged for the three of us who played nuns to go to a convent, talk with the nuns about their lives, and learn how to put on a habit. He also insisted on a working telephone on the set so that a character onstage could make a telephone call and have a real conversation with the character he called.

What he *didn't* do was block the show. He also didn't require the actors to learn their lines. I was astounded when he said that the script is "merely a blueprint" for the kind of behavior the playwright wants to see on stage and that the actors have no obligation to use the words in the script.

What?!

The House of Blue Leaves is under copyright protection. No one can legally change or delete a single word without permission. Well-known playwrights, including Neil Simon and Edward Albee, have withheld their plays from theaters where the directors wanted to remove swear words, change the race or gender of a character, or set the play in a different location.

The penalties for willful infringement of copyright can be as high as $150,000 and can extend to everyone involved: producers, directors, actors, etc. This wasn't the first time I had been involved in a show that had changed and/or deleted some of the playwright's words. In the past, I had assumed that the theaters had permission for any changes they made, but now I wondered: Did the Harlequin have permission to combine Agnes and Tootie? Did the Union Plaza have permission to cut their plays and musicals to ninety minutes? I didn't know. However, I was willing to bet that John Guare had not told Mr. Donahue or the Arizona Theatre Company that the actors could improvise the dialogue in his Obie Award–winning play. I hoped that anyone in the audience who was familiar with the play would think, "They muffed a lot of lines," not "How do I contact John Guare?"

Improvisation on stage meant that I never knew what might happen or how long I had between entrances. One day, Ronnie's monologue ran six minutes; the next day it ran two. One evening, I was told that Ronnie had walked into the audience and handed out cough drops.

One bit of business needed to be set: Ronnie, who was over six feet tall and wore combat boots, bounded over the back of a sofa where I was stretched out. To avoid injuring my legs, we agreed that I would keep my legs together, and he would straddle me—except he sometimes landed on my shins. At the dress rehearsal, when he landed hard on my aching shins, I realized that if I let this go on, he might break my legs. I called out to Mr. Donahue, who was sitting in the audience, and told him that this action had to be consistent because it was too dangerous for Ronnie to land on my shins. Mr. Donahue spoke with the patient tone of an adult talking to a very dense child: "Lee. He's not going to feel it the same way every night."

I gave him my sweetest smile and said in dulcet tones, "Then I might feel like playing this scene from the wings."

He stared at me for a long moment. I stood my ground. Finally, he said, "Do what you have to do," as if granting me a huge favor.

Ronnie never again landed on my shins. However, during one performance, he broke a water glass just before Bananas played a scene barefoot. When Mr. Donohue gave us notes after the show, he was still thrilled by the danger. "The audience was on the edge of their seats! I wish you could have seen their faces! *This* is why people come to live theater!"

No, no, no!

No one contradicted him. His disciples nodded in agreement. But when Mr. Donohue looked at me, I looked away.

One of the actresses who had worked with Mr. Donohue at the Children's Theatre told me, "I don't understand you. You're so talented—but you *limit* yourself by using *only* the words in the script!"

I told her it was illegal to change the words because of copyright law, and she rolled her eyes.

The disciples treated Mr. Donohue as if he were a genius, but it seemed to me that the emperor had no clothes.

After I was back in Los Angeles, I told someone about working with Mr. Donohue, and he said, "John Clark Donahue! I wondered where he'd surface."

"Surface?"

"He was artistic director of a prestigious children's theater in Minneapolis until he pled guilty to molesting some of the boys. He was sentenced to ten months in prison [the Hennepin County workhouse]."

What was astonishing to me when I read the news reports is that the woman who hired John Clark Donahue at CTC knew Donahue had been fired from a previous job for molesting a minor. Also, throughout Donahue's two-decade tenure at CTC, some of the staff, donors, parents, and students knew that Donahue and other people employed by the theater were having sex with students, but they kept quiet. The theater was growing in stature, and they thought Donahue was their golden ticket to fame. At Donahue's sentencing, Judge

Charles Porter concluded: "collectively this community knew what was going on at Children's Theatre."

How ironic that John Clark Donahue, a man whose fame in the Minneapolis theatrical community had warped the ethical and moral codes of the people around him, was hired to direct a play about people planning to blow up the Pope and put a spouse in the "looney bin" to get one step closer to fame.

In Tucson, my life outside the theater was no better than my life on stage. My assigned and partly subsidized apartment reeked of cigarette smoke. Cigarette burns dotted the sofa, the armchair, the kitchen floor, and the bathroom linoleum. I asked to move to another apartment in the complex, but there were no other apartments available. Construction on a building next door woke me up every weekday morning, and I got food poisoning after eating a tuna fish salad sandwich at an outdoor restaurant.

I considered giving my notice, but we were playing Tucson for only two and a half weeks before going to Phoenix for another two and a half weeks. I had never been to Phoenix and wanted to see the city. Besides, if I gave my notice, I wouldn't be eligible for unemployment insurance until I found another job. There were good ballet schools in both cities, so I went to ballet class, and while I was in Phoenix, I shot two commercials, including my first commercial as a mom.

At the end of the run, when I booked a bank commercial in Los Angeles, I discovered that a new law had been passed that limited my ability to hide my age—the Immigration Reform and Control Act of 1986 (IRCA).

This act was signed into law by Ronald Reagan on November 6, 1986. Its stated purpose, according to the official website for the Department of Homeland Security, is "to control and deter illegal immigration to the United States." A side effect of this law was that all of my employers, beginning in 1987, learned my age no later than the first day of my employment. The IRCA required me to put my birthdate on an I-9 form and to show my employers either my U.S. passport or my driver's license and my Social Security card. The IRCA form contained the ominous words, "I am aware that federal law provides for imprisonment and/or fines for false statements, or use of false documents, in connection with the completion of this form" and "I attest, under penalty of perjury...."

The ten years I had dropped when I moved to California came roaring back.

For the next year, I performed in commercials and industrial films and did a few small parts on TV. I played the wife of Chazz Palminteri (*A Bronx Tale*) on *Divorce Court*. I played a teacher in a TV movie with Marion Ross (*Happy Days*), and I danced on pointe as a member of a classical ballet company on *The Tracey Ullman Show*. I performed in star-studded benefit performances at the Dorothy Chandler Pavilion and at the Hollywood Bowl, but I didn't get auditions for TV pilots as I had when I was younger, and I knew that television work would become scarce as people learned my age.

Two deaths reminded me that life is short. The first was Richard Levinson, the husband of Rosanna Huffman, who had played Jane in *Jane Heights*. Richard and his writing partner William Link had created many TV series, including *Mannix*, *Columbo*, and *Murder She Wrote*. Their award-winning TV movies included *That Certain Summer* and *The Execution of Private Slovik*. Richard died of a heart attack at age 52.

The second death was Michael Bennett, who was only 44. Three years older than I. Michael died on July 2, 1987. On the day he died, I was in Vancouver, and I didn't learn about his death until July 6. I was driving north on La Brea Avenue when I heard the news on the radio. I could feel myself shaking inside, so I pulled over to the side of the road and listened to the report. Michael had died of AIDS in Arizona. He was a shining light of my generation, the future of Broadway, and now he was gone.

How much time did *I* have?

21

Meet Me in St. Louis Auditions and *Annie Get Your Gun* (1988–1989)

I saw the open casting call for a Broadway production of *Meet Me in St. Louis* and knew that I wanted one more dance on Broadway. I had enjoyed performing in the show at the Harlequin, and I loved the score that included "Meet Me in St. Louis," "The Boy Next Door," "The Trolley Song," and "Have Yourself a Merry Little Christmas." *Meet Me in St. Louis* is a reminder that a happy life is not synonymous with a life lived on a big stage, and that people should savor the everyday joys of life. This heartwarming show would be a perfect bookend to my Broadway career that had begun with the life-affirming *Hello, Dolly!*

The song "Meet Me in St. Louis, Louis" was first published in 1904 and celebrated the Louisiana Purchase Exposition, better known as the St. Louis World's Fair. In 1941 and 1942, *The New Yorker* published eight stories by Sally Benson (née Smith) about the Smith family who lived at 5135 Kensington Avenue, Benson's childhood home. Benson added four new stories to the original eight, and Random House published them as the novel *Meet Me in St. Louis,* the same title as the MGM movie that was already in development.

The Smith family consists of Mr. and Mrs. Smith, their five children (Lon, Rose, Esther, Agnes, and Tootie), Grandpa Prophater (Mrs. Smith's father), and Katie the cook. The movie also features the character of John Truett, the boy next door, as a love interest for Esther. The Smiths in the film are an idealized family in an idealized past with beautifully lit sets, gorgeous costumes, a great score, and a superb cast headed by Judy Garland as Esther, and Margaret O'Brien as Tootie.

In the late 1940s, Christopher Sergel dramatized the book as a straight play and moved an event that occurs late in the film—Mr. Smith's announcement that the family is moving to New York—to the opening minutes of the play to give the play more narrative drive. In the straight play, Mr. Smith and his boss are the antagonists as the girls try to sabotage the move—a completely different plot from the film and the subsequent musicals.

In 1960, Sally Benson wrote the book for a stage musical based on the film. This was the version (with numerous cuts and changes) in which I performed at the Harlequin Dinner Playhouse.

In the Benson version, the curtain rises as the Smith family and other townspeople watch the groundbreaking ceremony at the site where the Louisiana World's Fair will take place in one year. The first person to speak is Tootie. "I can't hear! I can't see! I might as well be in my grave!" Grandpa Prophater swings Tootie onto his shoulder so she can see—action we omitted because I was too big to be lifted onto Grandpa's shoulder. Mr. Smith, looking through binoculars, tells Tootie that Governor Francis has left the podium and picked up a shovel to break first ground. "A silver shovel," says Mrs. Smith. One by one, every member of the family, including Katie, weighs in on the upcoming fair. When the groundbreaking is over, Tootie is disappointed that all she's seen is "one sterling silver shovel," so Grandpa Prophater tells her about the wonders to come: "airships that fly to the moon" and "a gondola on the lagoon." When he finishes the verse of "Meet Me in St. Louis" and begins the chorus, Tootie joins in, and finally everyone on stage is singing "Meet Me in St. Louis, Louis." With charm and humor, the opening scene sets up the importance of the fair, the characters in the Smith family, and the love that binds them together.

As the crowd leaves the groundbreaking, Rose meets Douglas, and Lon meets Lucille. Soon afterwards, Esther sings of her longing for the boy next door, and the three love stories are set in motion. Just past the halfway point, Mr. Smith proudly announces that the family is moving to New York where he will be head of the New York office.

This upsets the plans of everyone else in the family, and Esther tells her father that they simply can't leave just when St. Louis is about to become "the center of attraction of the entire universe." Eventually, Mr. Smith realizes that the move is making his family unhappy, so he calls everyone together and announces, "We're not moving to New York! And I don't want to hear another word about it! We'll stay right here until we rot!"

Mrs. Smith assures him: "We haven't rotted yet, Lonnie." Unlike the real Smith family that relocated to New York and missed the World's Fair, this fictional family stays home in St. Louis, and the musical ends with the Smith family enraptured by the glamorous World's Fair.

Now, in 1988, producer/director Louis Burke and choreographer Joan Brickhill were casting a Broadway musical with a new book by Hugh Wheeler (*Sweeney Todd, A Little Night Music*) and additional songs by the original composer and lyricist, Hugh Martin and Ralph Blane. At the age of 42, I knew that no show is a guaranteed hit, but *Meet Me in St. Louis* certainly had the potential to outrun any of my previous Broadway shows.

The casting call for principal performers had specific age and height requirements, and I was the right height for Esther (between five feet one and five feet four). I knew my voice wasn't good enough to play the role on Broadway, but I went to the principal call so the director could see me in period dress and hear me sing before I went to the chorus audition as a dancer.

I put on a high-necked, white cotton blouse with short, puffed sleeves and a white cotton full skirt. To make the ensemble look like a dress, I folded an oblong, turquoise cotton scarf around my waist and tied it in the back in a big bow. I attached long, curly pigtails around my own shorter pigtails and tied white grosgrain bows around each pigtail—the hairstyle I had chosen for Minnie Fay when I played opposite a 16-year-old boy. I slashed my résumé so that the credits were reasonable for a girl in her late teens or early twenties. The roles included Dainty June in *Gypsy* (three productions), Minnie Fay in *Hello, Dolly!*, Frenchy in *Grease*, Claudine in *Pajama Tops*, and the Little Nun in *The House of Blue Leaves*.

When I arrived at the Debbie Reynolds Dance Studio, the parking lot was overflowing with actresses who had come to audition for the role of Esther. Because it was an open call, anyone could audition—professional and non-professional. There were news cameras everywhere, and a reporter I recognized from the evening news interviewed me as a starry-eyed girl hoping for the chance to sing and dance on Broadway.

The first person to look at my picture and résumé was Jay Binder, the casting director from New York. He looked at me carefully, looked back at my résumé, and asked, "Lee, how old are you now?"

I used the same line I had used 13 years earlier for Michael Bennett: "I've been twenty-two for so long, I'm seriously thinking of turning twenty-three."

"You're twenty-two," he said. "The director will ask. *And he cares.*"

Jay Binder was right. One of the first things Louis Burke wanted to know was my age. He also asked me to stand up straight against the back wall so that someone with a tape measure could verify my height.

Louis Burke had white hair, a white beard, an accent I couldn't place (South African with Shakespearean overtones), and an air of flamboyant theatricality. After I sang, he asked me if I could dance, play the piano, or ice skate. I told him I was an excellent dancer, could play the piano, but had never tried to ice skate. We chatted for several minutes, and he asked me to come back the following day and sing for him again. The following day, after I sang, he asked me to read two scenes: the scene after Lon's going-away party when Esther asks John to accompany her throughout the house as she turns out the lights, and a later scene in which Esther apologizes to John for beating him up. Mr. Burke asked again if I could ice skate, and I told him I could learn.

I went directly to the Culver City Skating School and signed up for lessons with Cathy Machado, a bronze medalist at the U.S. Skating Championships and a former Olympian. The class met only one day a week, so I decided to skate three or four times a week during public sessions. My third day on the ice, the manager of the rink introduced me to Gene Nelson—the former movie star who had played Will Parker in the 1955 movie of *Oklahoma!* and Buddy in the Broadway show *Follies*. Gene told me that he had begun his career as an ice skater with Sonja Henie and had first performed on Broadway in an ice show. The manager of the rink had pointed me out and told Gene that I was learning to skate for a Broadway show, and Gene made it his mission to whip me into shape in record time. "Take the ice! Take the ice!" he yelled from the sidelines. "Make them get out of your way!" To his frustration, I always deferred to skaters who were better than I was—which was almost everyone over the age of five.

Skating was a new challenge. I loved the fact that each day I was better than the day before. I had grace and style in my upper body, but my feet were another matter. As a ballet dancer, whenever I stood in attitude or arabesque, my supporting foot was turned out, but I quickly learned that when I leaned into a spiral (an arabesque penché) and my supporting foot inadvertently turned out, I would come to a screeching halt and tumble face first onto the ice. Some skaters wore knitted gloves to keep their hands warm and protect them when they fell, but I wore fur-lined leather gloves that gave me more protection and didn't get soggy when I fell into puddles.

After a few weeks of renting skates at the rink, I bought my own white Riedell skates, and to supplement my beginner's class with Cathy, I began private coaching sessions with Gary Visconti, twice a gold medalist at the U.S. Skating Championships. Cathy taught me basic technique. Gary showed me how to capitalize on my grace and flexibility, and during the public sessions, Gene yelled at me to skate faster and be more aggressive. I skated for four months, but heard nothing more about *Meet Me in St. Louis*. In addition to daily bumps and falls, I had one jarring collision with another skater whose working leg slammed into my thigh, slashed through my tights, and left an angry red line the length of my thigh. For the next few weeks, my entire thigh was black and blue and yellow with a red slash.

I didn't enjoy skating as much as dance, and dance was cleaner, safer, warmer, and a reliable source of income. I heard nothing from Louis Burke, so I stopped skating. I told myself that *Meet Me in St. Louis* wouldn't be the first or the last show to announce a Broadway production that didn't materialize.

I was ready for fun, and in early 1989, fun appeared: a three-city, Florida tour of *Annie Get Your Gun* starring Donna McKechnie. Donna was a terrific Annie. On the outside, she was a strong, outspoken woman with a powerhouse voice who could outshoot any man, but when she sang "They Say It's Wonderful," she showed Annie's vulnerability and her yearning for love. Donna got rave reviews everywhere we went.

Playing opposite Donna was Nolan Van Way. Nolan was tall, dark, and handsome with a macho quality that was perfect for Frank Butler. Nolan worked in both musical theater and opera, and he had a terrific voice, but some of the reviewers thought his acting was stiff.

In Palm Beach, I window-shopped in front of the elegant stores on Worth Avenue and explored the lobby of The Breakers Resort. In Fort Lauderdale, Donna rented a yacht and invited the company to spend the evening cruising the inland waterways. We floated past the home of Burt Reynolds and Loni Anderson, and later in the run, after seeing the show, Loni came backstage to visit with Donna. Harvey Evans (our Barnaby in *Hello, Dolly!* on Broadway) was playing Charlie Davenport, and he was still a fun-loving prankster. He gave the entire cast brightly colored, plastic water pistols and dropped water balloons from the roof of the theater.

In Orlando, the last city in the three-city tour, I visited Disney World, including EPCOT. Donna's mother flew in to see our final performance, and I could only imagine how proud she must have been as she watched her Tony Award–winning daughter in a role that seemed tailor-made for her talent. The final song of the show (prior to the curtain call) is "Anything You Can Do." During the song, Annie and Frank both claim they can do anything better than the other. Frank sings, "Any note you can hold, I can hold longer." Annie sings, "I can hold any note longer than you." Frank says she can't. Annie says she can. Finally, both hit a note and hold it and hold it and hold it and hold it. Finally, Frank runs out of breath and concedes, "Yes, you can." During the contest, Donna was left of center stage with the people rooting for her (including me) further left. Nolan was right of center with people rooting for him further right. It is the responsibility of the actor playing Frank to appear to run out of breath before

Annie does, but Nolan didn't have to pretend. Donna could outlast him—but at this final performance, when Donna ran out of breath after holding the note longer than usual, Nolan was still singing. I was shocked.

I saw Donna running out of air. Why didn't he? How did he hold the note so long?

After the show, one of the dancers on Nolan's side of the stage told me that Nolan had cheated. During the cheering, he had taken a quick breath. The dancer said that Donna was in her dressing room in tears.

During the flight home, I walked up to Nolan's seat and asked, "Did you take a breath to outlast Donna?"

"Yes."

"Why?"

"I thought it was funny," he said.

It wasn't. And he knew it. It hurt the show. It hurt Donna, and Nolan's status shriveled in the eyes of the cast.

It is difficult to lose a competition night after night. When I was performing in *A Chorus Line*, it didn't matter which role I played—Maggie, Connie, Kristine, or Lois—Zach never chose me to be in his show, and I felt rejected eight times a week. It is even more difficult to know that even if the competition were fair—even if it weren't scripted for you to lose—you still couldn't win. And if you are a man raised in a patriarchal society, it must be even more difficult to be beaten by a woman—especially a woman getting rave reviews.

Early in *Annie Get Your Gun*, Annie sings the "I want" song that tells the audience what she longs for. Annie is a great shooter, she tells us, but "You Can't Get a Man with a Gun." At the end of the show, after the song "Anything You Can Do," there is a final contest between Annie and Frank: a shooting contest. Annie's friend Sitting Bull knows that if Annie wins, she will lose the man she loves, so he has sabotaged Annie's gun. Annie realizes that someone has tampered with her gun and grabs another one. She is confident she can still win, but Sitting Bull reminds her: "You can't get a man with a gun." Annie gets the point. She fires wildly, loses the contest, and proclaims Frank Butler "the greatest sharpshooter in the world."

Annie Get Your Gun opened on Broadway in 1946, but it acknowledges a fact that is still true today: the better a woman is at her job and the higher she rises in the hierarchy, the more likely people are to say that she is too aggressive, out for herself, not feminine, not trustworthy, and someone they wouldn't like.

To be desirable, Annie has to lose.

When I returned to L.A., two things happened in quick succession: the new Broadway production of *Meet Me in St. Louis* scheduled a chorus call for dancers at DR Studios, and Bruce Pomahac, the conductor for *Annie Get Your Gun*, left a message for me to call him. When I returned the call, Bruce told me that *Meet Me in St. Louis* was opening on Broadway in the fall, and that he was the musical director. My hope for a last dance on Broadway was now a real possibility.

22

Meet Me in St. Louis (1989–1990)

I had met Bruce the first day of rehearsal for *Annie Get Your Gun* when he told me that his last name was spelled like "Omaha" with a "p" at the beginning and a "c" at the end. Bruce had the cherubic face of a choirboy and an optimistic outlook. I knew that Bruce liked my voice, which gave me confidence and increased the odds that I could return to Broadway in *Meet Me in St. Louis.*

For the dance audition, I wore the same high-necked, white cotton blouse with short, puffed sleeves that I had worn to the principal audition the previous summer, but instead of the white skirt and a turquoise waistband, I wore white cotton shorts with narrow red and white striped suspenders that attached to my shorts with little red hearts.

The choreographer was Joan Brickhill, a trim, blond woman of 65 who had been a big star in South Africa and was married to Louis Burke. Joan wore gradient dark glasses indoors and out. Louis and Joan sat at the front of the room while Joan's assistant, Herman-Jay Muller, demonstrated the choreography. At the end of the dance audition, some of us were asked to do 16 fouettés on pointe. When we broke for lunch, I noticed that my blouse had shredded down the back. I didn't have time to go home and change, so in the afternoon, I danced in my shredded blouse.

That night, someone assisting the producers called me at home to relay information he thought I might appreciate: At the end of the day, Louis and Joan had spread out the photos of the dancers they liked. Louis pointed to my photo, and said, "She's very *poised* for twenty-two. I'll bet she's twenty-*five*."

I was delighted. Louis couldn't deny that I had passed the age test, so the following day, at my singing audition, I gave him my full résumé. This was a risk, but I didn't want to blindside the director in New York where I would not be able to hide my age. Louis didn't comment. I sang the ballad "I Got Lost in His Arms" from *Annie Get Your Gun*, and Louis asked me if I knew "The Boy Next Door." My heart sank. I didn't want to be an understudy—especially not for the leading role of Esther. Fortunately, as I sang, I saw Louis look at Bruce and shake his head, and when I finished the song, Louis asked me to come to the skating audition the following day.

I went to the rink early and warmed up. Fifteen minutes before the audition, I got off the ice, put on my skate guards, and Louis introduced me to Michael Tokar, the ice choreographer who had starred in *Ice Capades*.

A few minutes later, when I stepped back onto the ice, my feet skidded out from under me. I grabbed the side of the rink, but couldn't get my balance.

Was I so nervous I couldn't stand up?

Michael Tokar pointed to my feet and said, "Skate guards."

Oops! This was not the assured impression I had hoped to make. Fortunately, Louis Burke and Joan Brickhill hadn't seen my faux pas.

I assessed the other skaters and managed to get myself paired with Brian Jay, the shortest, youngest-looking boy who was cute as a button, secure on the ice, and a strong, considerate partner. With Brian, I skated quite well (considering my short history on ice), and after 13 years in Los Angeles, I was headed back to Broadway.

In mid–August, I flew to New York to find an apartment. During the first three days, I looked at small, dark, expensive apartments. At night, I saw three wonderful shows: *Black and Blue* (a revue celebrating Black culture that had won Tony Awards for Best Choreography and Best Actress); *M. Butterfly* (a stunning drama by David Henry Hwang that had made BD Wong a star and brought Tony Awards to the actor and the playwright); and *Rumors* (the latest comedy by Neil Simon).

On the fourth day, I found a perfect apartment only two blocks from the Gershwin Theatre. It was a third-floor walkup with a large living room/bedroom, a separate kitchen with enough space to do a ballet barre, and a bathroom with a good strong shower. At one end of the main room were two large windows overlooking a garden—a luxury in the city of New York.

On September 4, 1989, the cast of *Meet Me in St. Louis* gathered for a reading of the script at 890 Broadway. The principals had been rehearsing for a week, so they had already formed the nucleus of the family, which now expanded to include the chorus. Louis Burke proudly introduced the lead actors: George Hearn, Tony Award winner as Best Actor in a Musical for *La Cage aux Folles*, was playing Mr. Smith. Charlotte Moore, with at least eight Broadway plays on her résumé, was Mrs. Smith. Dublin-born Milo O'Shea (two Tony nominations and numerous films) was Grandpa Prophater, and 70-year-old Betty Garrett, star of stage, screen, and television, was Katie the cook. I knew Betty as the comedic taxi driver in the musical film *On the Town*, but the younger members of the cast knew her as the Irish-American neighbor Irene Lorenzo in *All in the Family*. These actors provided the star power.

The younger roles were played by relative unknowns. Donna Kane, who had made a splash Off Broadway in *Dames at Sea*, was making her Broadway debut in the role of Esther. Michael O'Steen (Lon) had one previous Broadway credit in *Starlight Express*. Juliet Lambert (Rose), Rachael Graham (Agnes), Courtney Peldon (Tootie), and Jason Workman (the boy next door), were all making their Broadway debuts.

As Louis described the opening number and the movement of the sets, I could see that the opulent Broadway production would be very different from the Harlequin production. At the Harlequin, *Meet Me in St. Louis* was an intimate show about a family; the Broadway production was designed to wow. It had twice as many songs, big production numbers, spectacular costumes, elaborate sets, a full-size trolley, a five-ton ice-skating rink, a two-story Smith house, and real water in the fountains at the Louisiana Purchase Exposition.

The first dress I saw at my costume fitting was my dress for Lon's going away party. It was off-white with turquoise trim—an expensive and more durable version of the outfit I had worn to my first audition. Robert-Charles Vallance, assistant costume designer, told me that the neck would be cut down, but he wanted to mark the neckline while I was wearing the dress.

"Could we leave it high?" I asked. "Would that still be period?"

"It would," he said, "But it would be younger."

"Younger is good," I said. "I'm twice the age of the other girls. I need all the help I can get."

Robert-Charles laughed. "I've seen your résumé. It's been all over town."

The dress had short, puffed sleeves that Robert-Charles said would become mutton sleeves.

"Could we possibly leave them short?" I asked.

He nodded. "That would be younger."

During the five-minute breaks that the union required every hour, some of the dancers performed their specialties to show the choreographer what they could do, but unlike my younger self who would "warm up" with five or six pirouettes and was always looking for a bigger, better role, I just wanted to be part of the show and enjoy the talent that surrounded me.

I overheard a couple of dancers trying to guess who might receive the Gypsy Robe—an honor given to the chorus member who has the most Broadway shows and personifies the dedication and professionalism of the Broadway gypsy. (Broadway gypsy: a singer and/or dancer who goes from one Broadway show to the next.)

The tradition of the Gypsy Robe began as a joke. Bill Bradley, who was in the chorus of *Gentlemen Prefer Blondes*, convinced Florence Baum, another member of the chorus, to give him her old dressing gown. Bradley sent the robe to his friend Arthur Partington on opening night of *Call Me Madam* and claimed that the tattered robe had been worn by glamorous Ziegfeld girls and would bring luck to his new show. *Call Me Madam* was a hit, so Arthur Partington added a rose from one of Ethel Merman's costumes and sent it to a friend as a good-luck charm on opening night of *Guys and Dolls*. It was a hit, and a tradition was born. At first, friends sent the robe to friends, but at some point, the tradition seemed to be dying out, so Actors' Equity took charge and formalized the presentation: An hour before curtain time on opening night of all musicals that have a chorus, everyone in the company gathers on stage, and the robe is presented to the member of the chorus who has the most Broadway shows. The recipient circles the stage three times while everyone touches the robe for luck; then the recipient visits every dressing room to spread the luck. Each recipient, with the help of the costume department, adds a memento to the robe, and on opening night of the next Broadway musical, presents the robe to the next singer or dancer. In 2018, the Gypsy Robe was rebranded as the Legacy Robe.

As I listened to the dancers in *Meet Me in St. Louis* compare the credits of the two performers that they thought were frontrunners for the robe, I realized that I might have more Broadway credits than either of them. Was it possible that I might receive the Gypsy Robe? I wouldn't know until opening night.

One evening after rehearsal, we gave a presentation for the people who book theater parties. The cast sat on stage behind Louis Burke while he told the "theater ladies" that he had scoured the country to find the 32 most talented teenagers in America, and here they were! Behind me, one of the older boys whispered, "God, I can barely *remember* my teens," and I stifled my laugh.

Prior to the dress rehearsal, we had a costume parade for the creative team. We had different costumes in every scene, and each costume had multiple parts: Over our underwear, we wore tights, bloomers, and footwear that included pointe shoes, custom-made, custom-dyed dress shoes, custom-made boots, and ice skates. Under our corsets, we wore undershirts because the corsets had to be dry cleaned, and wardrobe wanted something washable between our corsets and our skin. Then we added our bustles (pads that sat on our butts and tied around our waists that gave us the profile of the women in the Seurat painting *A Sunday on La Grande Jatte*). Then came the voluminous petticoats and dresses. We had wigs in every scene with hats and/or hair bows and sometimes jewelry. All of my costumes and wigs fit perfectly.

After the costume parade, Robert-Charles Vallance told me Louis had asked him, "Why does Lee look so much better than the other girls?" Robert-Charles had answered, "Lee has been playing teenagers for twenty years. She knows what she needs. The others *are* teenagers. They will *all* look good by the time we open." And they did.

The ensemble earned its pay. The opening number was a choreographed street scene with lots of action that included a boy on a bicycle, a boy on roller skates, and three fashionable girls on pointe (including me) who danced a pas de six with three delivery boys. This ballet culminated in the dramatic entrance of the giant yellow trolley on which everyone was singing "Meet Me in St. Louis." In the second big number, Lon's going away party, we sang and danced "Skip to My Lou," a jolly social dance, followed by the even more exuberant "Banjos" that ended with high kicks and acrobatics. The dimly lit Halloween Ballet brought Tootie's fears to life as her dolls, on pointe, rose from the dead and danced attitude turns with aerial and back walkovers. Some of the lifts were difficult, and some of the men had the thankless and backache-inducing job of wearing heavy house costumes to stalk Tootie. "The Trolley Song," was a dream sequence with lots of fog that on humid days settled into oily puddles that were a hazard for the dancers who were racing around the swirling trolley and skidding in the oil.

The second act began with the ice-skating number, "Ice," which featured Rachelle Ottley, who was not only an excellent dancer and skater, but also a soprano who understudied the role of Rose. The costume department was caught by surprise when I (a dancer) was chosen to be one of the small group of singers who sang "The First Noel," but I had my own blouse and shoes to fill in until wardrobe had time to catch up. The Christmas Ball contained a traditional waltz and an Irish dance featuring Joanne McHugh, a trained Irish dancer who looked as if she had defected from Riverdance.

The ball ended with more aerial acrobatics. "Paging Mr. Sousa" was a marching number that began in the aisles and progressed onto the stage, and our final scene took place at the St. Louis Exposition with a reprise of "Meet Me in St. Louis." Fountains gushed real water, and an LED light display wowed many of my friends. Although some of the dancers mocked the exuberant choreography by singing "Theme park, plenty of theme park" to the tune of "Banjos," there was no question that the singers and dancers were outstanding.

On opening night, November 2, 1989, the girls' dressing room was filled with gifts: coffee mugs, music boxes, flowers, chocolates, telegrams, good-luck cards, and sterling silver keychains with sterling silver trolleys from Louis and Joan. I was surprised and delighted to receive a welcome-back-to-Broadway card from Alyce Gilbert, the wardrobe mistress of the New York Company of *A Chorus Line,* which was still running at the Shubert Theatre.

An hour before curtain time, we all went on stage for the presentation of the Gypsy Robe, and I was thrilled when I heard my name. The muslin robe was already decorated with panels from previous shows, including *Les Misérables, Chess,* and *Legs Diamond,* but there was a nice space on the lower back for *Meet Me in St. Louis.* After putting on the robe, I walked around the stage three times while everyone touched the robe and took photographs.

I visited all of the dressing rooms to spread the luck of the robe, and finally, I put on my costume, wig, and pointe shoes for the opening ballet and went upstairs into the wings.

The audience was enthusiastic. The opening night party at the Puck Building was festive, and the reviews were all over the map.

Some critics were enchanted. Howard Kissel in the *Daily News* began his review by writing that he usually hates to see performers in the aisles, but by the time the chorus of *Meet Me in St. Louis* came strutting down the aisles near the end of the show, "I had been utterly disarmed. Here were enormously talented kids who had been singing and dancing their hearts out all evening long. They had a Middle American innocence I thought had been banished from the musical theater by its grandiose pretensions in recent years. It was all I could do to keep from crying ... everything about the show seems to strike

On opening night of *Meet Me in St. Louis,* director Louis Burke congratulated me for receiving the Gypsy Robe (now rebranded as the Legacy Robe).

just the right note." Doug Watt in the *Daily News* (Sunday edition) wrote, "Broadway hasn't seen as splendiferous a musical comedy as 'Meet Me in St. Louis' in a long, long time."

However, Frank Rich in *The New York Times* didn't see the point of the show since the film is available on videocassette. He guessed

The diamond pattern on the collar of the robe was from *Legs Diamond*; *Chess* decorated the right sleeve; *Phantom of the Opera*, the left sleeve; and *Les Miz* covered the upper back. Rachelle Ottley is at left reaching out to touch the robe for luck, and Christina Pawl is the blonde at right.

that its purpose was "to spread the goodwill earned by the overture," which he said it did "despite such obstacles as insipid acting, an inane book and a complete lack of originality." Nevertheless, he did say that

Meet Me in St. Louis "is superior to the other latter-day Broadway adaptations of M-G-M musicals, *Seven Brides for Seven Brothers* and *Singin' in the Rain*."

Meet Me in St. Louis was selling well enough to run, and I planned to enjoy every minute of the show and to participate in every show-related event. Some events, such as the TV commercial, were mandatory; others were optional. Sometimes there were sign-up lists, and the producers chose the participants from the people who signed up. I signed up for everything.

The Sunday night after we opened, I presented the Gypsy Robe to Jan Horvath of *3 Penny Opera*, and met Sting, who starred in the show and is every bit as charismatic up close as he is on stage. The following day, our "day off" on our Equity contracts, we filmed a TV commercial for *Meet Me in St. Louis*.

In mid–November, we signed contracts for the Macy's Thanksgiving Day Parade, recorded the vocals, and rehearsed in Herald Square. On Thanksgiving morning, my alarm went off at 4:30 a.m. I looked out the window and saw snow covering the garden and decorating the trees. As I walked along 50th Street to the theater, I made the first crunchy footprints in the blanket of pure, white snow. At the Gershwin, all of us in the ensemble put on our makeup and changed into our costumes and wigs for "Paging Mr. Sousa." Then a trailer drove us downtown where the streets were jammed with trailers filled with marching bands and performers from other Broadway shows. While we waited to perform, we ate hot biscuits from Popeyes. The street in front of Macy's was wet and dirty, and we were wearing white skirts and white pants, so the wardrobe department supplied us with clear plastic raincoats, which everyone referred to as "condoms." Wardrobe insisted we had to perform in the raincoats because there wouldn't be time to have the skirts and pants cleaned before our performance later that day. The network executive said we had to take the raincoats off or he wouldn't allow us to perform. After some heated dialogue between the executive and wardrobe, we performed *without* raincoats in light snow flurries.

During the month of December, Gloria Rosenthal interviewed

The ensemble of *Meet Me in St. Louis* is lined up waiting to perform "Paging Mr. Sousa" with George Hearn in the 1989 Macy's Thanksgiving Day Parade. (The line facing photograph left is led by Brian Jay, and I am the dancer behind him.) I was more than a little surprised to hear the number introduced as "the show's absolute number one hit, 'Stopping [sic] Mr. Sousa.'" Yikes! The score for the show included songs that were already classics: "Have Yourself a Merry Little Christmas," "The Boy Next Door," "The Trolley Song," and "Meet Me in St. Louis"—but "Stopping [sic] Mr. Sousa" is the number one hit? I think not. Photo by Robert Woods.

me for an article she was writing about the Gypsy Robe, and the cast of *Meet Me in St. Louis* presented a sing-along "Messiah" at the Gershwin to raise money for Equity Fights AIDS. Milton Rosenstock conducted the *Meet Me in St. Louis* orchestra, and all of the people involved—from the Nederlander Organization to the orchestra, cast, and crew—donated their time and talent. We also had a Christmas party with a gift exchange, and Louis Burke played Santa.

In January, we performed for the patients and staff at St. Vincent's Hospital and celebrated our 100th performance with a party at the Hard Rock Cafe. Throughout the run, we had put-in rehearsals for additional swing dancers and replacements. In March, we recorded the original cast album—my first and only cast album.

On Easter Sunday, I was one of the cast members, along with Betty Garrett and Charlotte Moore, who paraded in costume through the Plaza Hotel dining room and met Ivana Trump (who was running the hotel) before enjoying Easter dinner at the Plaza. Courtney Peldon, our Tootie, had two birthday parties—one in the green room with the company, and another in the lobby for the press. At the first party, I asked Courtney how old she was, and she answered promptly, "I'm really nine, but to my fans, I'm eight." (A girl is never too young to lie about her age if she wants a career in show business.) At the press party, Courtney's sister Ashley, who was acting in the soap opera *Guiding Light* shared the spotlight. *Aha*! That's why there were two parties—one where Courtney was the center of attention and a second for maximum publicity. Even at the age of nine, Courtney seemed to understand that the press favored Ashley because TV credits are more marketable than stage credits.

We performed in the Manhattan Theatre Club Spring Gala and participated in the annual Easter Bonnet Competition, a fundraising competition and performance to benefit Broadway Cares/Equity Fights Aids. (In 1990, the fourth year of the competition, we raised $245,000, but that amount has grown steadily. In 2019, the Easter Bonnet competition raised almost $6,600,000.) With many other cast members, I went to see Betty Garrett in her nightclub act, *Betty Garrett & Friends*, in which she spoke about the blacklist and how it had affected her life and that of her husband, Larry Parks. Betty's special guest was Victoria Lynn Burton, the young girl who understudied the roles of Agnes and Tootie and finally had the opportunity to show off her powerhouse voice.

On Sunday and Monday nights, I went to see shows on and off Broadway. My favorites were *Grand Hotel, City of Angels, A Few Good Men, Lettice and Lovage, Closer Than Ever, Tru,* and *Cat on a Hot Tin Roof.* On April 28, 1990, *A Chorus Line* closed after fifteen years on Broadway, but new powerhouse musicals were poised to run for decades—*Cats, Les Misérables,* and *The Phantom of the Opera.* Broadway was booming, and spirits were high.

I went up to the top of the Empire State Building for the first time. I toured Wall Street and visited the World Trade Center. I went to Tavern on the Green for New Year's dinner and to Sam's and Joe Allen for hamburgers and French fries. I wanted to store up a lifetime of memories.

On Sunday, June 3, 1990, the cast of *Meet Me in St. Louis* performed live on the Tony Awards, which were televised from the Lunt-Fontanne Theatre (the theater where I had performed in *How Now, Dow Jones*). *Meet Me in St. Louis* was nominated for Best Musical, Best Book of a Musical, Best Original Score, and Best Choreography. I had heard that the closing notice might be posted if we didn't win at least one Tony, and people seemed to think that Best Original Score was our best chance. As we waited to perform, we listened to the show in our trailer. I held my breath as Sandy Duncan announced, "The nominees for Best Original Score Written for the Theatre are: Andrew Lloyd Webber, Don Black, Charles Hart, *Aspects of Love*; Cy Coleman, David Zippel, *City of Angels*; Robert Wright, George Forrest, Maury Yeston, *Grand Hotel: The Musical*." A long pause. "The winner is...."—everyone in our trailer jumped up and wailed, "No! Stop! She forgot *us*!"

Then we heard Linda Lavin's low-pitched voice, "One more nominee." Sandy Duncan gasped and quickly added, "Hugh Martin, Ralph Blane, *Meet Me in St. Louis*."

Forgetting our show seemed an ominous sign, and it was. The Tony Award for Best Score went to *City of Angels*. One week later, on June 10, 1990, we gave our last performance.

It had been almost 23 years since I had stood in the wings of the St. James Theatre in my blue sailor dress, straw hat, black ankle boots, and newly blonde pigtails eager to make my Broadway debut. During those years, I had performed in hits and flops and one-night stands. I had reveled in the genius of choreographers Agnes de Mille, Alvin Ailey, Danny Daniels, and Michael Bennett. I had performed from Boston to San Francisco, from San Antonio to Detroit. Now it was time to move on.

Before the end of the year, I had written the teleplay for *The Elf Who Saved Christmas*, a half-hour holiday special that starred JoAnne Worley, premiered on USA Network, and eventually aired

Baayork Lee (left), the original Connie in *A Chorus Line* and a recipient of the Isabelle Stevenson Tony Award, helped me prepare for my *Rebel on Pointe* book signing at Barnes & Noble in New York. Photo courtesy of Baayork Lee.

on every continent except Antarctica. After the premiere, USA Network commissioned a sequel, *The Elf and the Magic Key*, which I also wrote and produced. In 2001, my TV movie *The Miracle of the Cards* starred Catherine Oxenberg, Peter Wingfield, Richard Thomas, and Kirk Cameron, and introduced Thomas Sangster (now Thomas Brodie-Sangster) as 8-year-old Craig Shergold, the English boy who developed a brain tumor and broke the Guinness Record for receiving the most get-well cards. *The Miracle of the Cards* won two *Movieguide* Awards—one for the film and the other for the lead actress.

At St. Mary's College of California, I finished the BA that I had begun at the age of 18 at Columbia University, and in 2014, the University Press of Florida published my ballet memoir *Rebel on Pointe*, the story of how I danced my way out of the stifling suburbs of 1950s

I'm well into my 70s, but I'm still kicking! Photo by Lesley Bohm.

Delaware, into the opera houses of Europe and onto the Broadway stage.

As I write this new memoir, it has been more than three decades since I danced for a living, but I still dance for the joy of dance, and I give thanks every day that I had the good fortune to dance on Broadway.

Bibliography

"Agnes de Mille Describes Her Choreography for RODEO." YouTube video, 1:56. Posted by Rodgers & Hammerstein, September 18, 2020. Accessed November 20, 2023. https://www.youtube.com/watch?v=vJPuk9dPJFI.

Bart, Lionel, Charles K. Peck, Jr. *La Strada.* Working draft. 1969.

Benson, Sally. *Meet Me in St. Louis.* New York: Random House, 1942.

Benson, Sally, Hugh Martin, and Ralph Blane. *Meet Me in St. Louis.* New York: Tams-Witmark, 1960.

"A Chorus Line, Michael Bennett cueing a dancer at second company rehearsal." Yale University Library. Accessed December 22, 2023. https://collections.library.yale.edu/catalog/2027743

DePaolo, Bella. "The Secret Lives of Single People." *Psychology Today.* May 17, 2019. Accessed November 20, 2023. https://www.psychologytoday.com/us/blog/living-single/201905/the-social-lives-single-people.

"Easter Bonnet Competition Sets All-time Fundraising Record." Posted by Broadway Cares/Equity Fights Aids. Accessed November 29, 2023. https://broadwaycares.org/easter-bonnet-competition-sets-all-time-fundraising-record/#:~:text=Records%20were%20shattered%20and%20inspiring,Cares/Equity%20Fights%20AIDS%20event.

"Erik Cigars TV Commercial." YouTube video, 0:30. Posted by Enrique Vásquez. August 16, 2006. Accessed January 15, 2024. https://www.youtube.com/watch?v=InMXhrgmnoE.

Estrada, Ric. "American as Apple Strudel Close Up: Hanya Holm." *Dance Magazine.* February 1968, 50–53.

"Every Little Step." YouTube Movies & TV. Sony Pictures. Accessed January 10, 2024. https://www.youtube.com/watch?v=SZi3jknFwqE. 22:12–22:21.

Farrell, Suzanne, with Toni Bentley. *Holding On to the Air.* Gainesville, Florida: University Press of Florida, 2002. 187.

Fields, Herbert, Dorothy Fields, and Irving Berlin. *Annie Get Your Gun.* Rehearsal script, 1988.

Furth, George, and Stephen Sondheim. *Company.* New York: Music Theatre International. Date unknown.

Gesner, Clark. *You're a Good Man, Charlie Brown.* New York: Fawcett, 1970.

Gussow, Mel. "Alan Schneider, Pioneering Director, is Dead." *New York Times.* May 4, 1984. Accessed November 29, 2023. https://www.nytimes.com/1984/05/04/obituaries/alan-schneider-pioneeringdirector-is-dead.html.

"Hello Dolly! Pearl Bailey 1968 Tony Awards." YouTube video, 9:34. Posted by MrPoochs-mooch, April 13, 2012. Accessed November 20, 2023. https://www.youtube.com/watch?v=d4eS0x16v1k.

"History of the Robe." Posted by Actors' Equity Association. Accessed November 29, 2023. https://actorsequity.org/aboutequity/awards/Robe/RobeHistory/.

Jones, Tom, and Harvey Schmidt. *The Fantasticks.* New York: The Drama Book Shop, Inc. 1964.

Kirkwood, James, Nicholas Dante, Marvin Hamlisch, and Edward Kleban. *A Chorus Line.* New York: New York Shakespeare Festival. Rehearsal script, revised March, 1976.

Lake, Veronica, with Donald Bain. *Veronica.* New York: Bantam, 1972. 213–214.

Laurents, Arthur. *Original Story By: A Memoir of Broadway and Hollywood.* New York: Applause Theatre Books, 2000.

"Macy's Thanksgiving Day Parade 1989 full." YouTube Video, 2:57:33. Posted by Macy's parades recovery, December 5, 2020. Accessed January 13, 2024. https://www.google.com/search?q=macy%27s+thanksgiving+day+parade+1989&oq=macy%27s+&gs_lcrp=EgZjaHJvbWUqBggAEEUYOzIGCAAQRRg7MgYIARBFGDkyDQgCEAAYgwEYsQMYgAQyDQgDEAAYgwEYsQMYgAQyBwgEEAAYgAQyDQgFEAAYgwEYsQMYgAQyDQgGEAAYsQMYyQMYgAQyDQgHEAAYkgMYgAQYigUyDQgIEAAYkgMYgAQYigUyCggJEAAYsQMYgATSAQg0MjEzajBqN6gCALACAA&sourceid=chrome&ie=UTF-8. 44:45–49:10.

McKay, Rick. *Broadway: Beyond the Golden Age.* PBS Great Performances, S48 Ep 29. August 14, 2021.

McNally, Terrence, Robert Waldman, and Alfred Uhry. *Here's Where I Belong.* Rehearsal script, 1968.

Miller, Kay. "May 19, 1991: Sex-abuse case was a long time in the making; the kids raised the curtain." *StarTribune.* May 19, 1991. Accessed November 28, 2023. https://www.startribune.com/may-19-1991-sex-abuse-case-was-a-long-time-in-the-making-the-kids-raised-the-curtain/359549381/?refresh=true.

Nabokov, Vladimir. *Lolita.* New York: Putnam. 1966.

"1990 Tony Awards—Complete." YouTube video, 1:56:27. Posted by MissPoochsmooch, August 14, 2014. Accessed November 19, 2023. https://www.google.com/search?q=tony+awards+1990&oq=tony+awards+1990&gs_lcrp=EgZjaHJvbWUyCQgAEEUYORiABDIICAEQABgWGB4yCAgCEAAYFhgeMggIAxAAGBYYHjIICAQQABgWGB4yDQgFEAAYhgMYgAQYigUyDQgGEAAYhgMYgAQYigUyDQgHEAAYhgMYgAQYigWoAgCwAgA&sourceid=chrome&ie=UTF-8#fpstate=ive&vld=cid:9d2436e6,vid:Rf1dPwufHqo,st:0. 24:40–25:24, 46:36–51:38.

"Pepsi 1980 Marry Me Sue Skywriting Commercial." YouTube Video, 0:59. Posted by Memory Museum. Date unknown. Accessed November 28, 2023. https://www.youtube.com/watch?v=fhAgifo4GTI.

Prince, Harold. *Sense of Occasion.* Milwaukee: Applause Books. 2017.

Purdum, Todd S. *Something Wonderful: Rodgers and Hammerstein's Broadway Revolution.* New York: Holt, 2018. 66–67, 80–85, 104–107.

"'Put on a Happy Face'—Bye Bye Birdie on Ed Sullivan." YouTube video, 6:31. LPL musicals. Posted April 9, 2019. Accessed Nov. 20, 2023. https://www.youtube.com/watch?v=PdXUNViOj0Y.

Riedel, Michael. *Razzle Dazzle: The Battle for Broadway.* Simon & Schuster, 2015.

"Robes and Their Recipients." Posted by Actors' Equity Association. Accessed November 29, 2023. https://actorsequity.org/aboutequity/awards/Robe/RobeRecipients/.

Rodgers, Richard, and Oscar Hammerstein, II. *Six Plays by Rodgers and Hammerstein.* New York: Modern Library, 1959.

Rodgers, Richard, Oscar Hammerstein II, Howard Lindsay, and Russel Crouse. *The Sound of Music.* New York: Random House, 1960.

Rutchick, Joel. "Children's theater founder sentenced for sex abuse." UPI. November 8, 1984. Accessed November 29, 2023. https://www.upi.com/Archives/1984/11/08/Childrens-theater-founder-sentenced-for-sex-abuse/6960468738000/.

Secrest, Meryle. *Stephen Sondheim: A Life*. New York: Vintage, 2011.

Sergel, Christopher. *Meet Me in St. Louis.* Chicago: Dramatic Pub. Co., 1948.

Shulman, Max, Carolyn Leigh, and Elmer Bernstein. *How Now, Dow Jones.* Rehearsal script, 1968.

Stevens, Gary, and Alan George. *The Longest Line.* New York: Applause Books, 1995.

Stewart, Michael, and Jerry Herman. *Hello, Dolly!*. New York: Signet Books, 1968.

Bibliography

"3389 A CHORUS LINE Gala Rehearsals @ 890 Broadway." YouTube video, 57:43. Posted by zahifito, February 10, 2023. Accessed January 10, 2024. https://www.youtube.com/watch?v=7NxXDJL18Y4. 19:50–42:23.

Viertel, Jack. *The Secret Life of the American Musical: How Broadway Shows Are Built.* New York: Sarah Crichton Books, 2017.

Wheeler, Hugh, Hugh Martin, and Ralph Blane. *Meet Me in St. Louis.* New York: "Playing Version," 1989.

Wilson, Chris. "This Chart Shows Hollywood's Glaring Gender Gap." *Time.* October 6, 2015. Accessed November 25, 2023. https://time.com/4062700/hollywood-gender-gap/.

Wilson, Lee. *Rebel on Pointe: A Memoir of Ballet and Broadway.* Gainesville, Florida: University Press of Florida, 2014.

Zadan, Craig. *Sondheim & Co.* New York: Macmillan, 1974. 59, 140.

Index

Numbers in ***bold italics*** indicate pages with illustrations

Index

www.ingramcontent.com/pod-product-compliance
Ingram Content Group UK Ltd.
Pitfield, Milton Keynes, MK11 3LW, UK
UKHW041944140426
5217IPUK00014B/641

9 781476 696362